BRIMFUL OF ASIA

'Read this book as a smartly conceived and adroitly completed rescue mission. Of all Britain's musical artists, Asian bands are the most ensnared and assaulted by journalistic, academic and political clichés. Rehan Hyder cuts his way through all this verbiage to get to the musicians themselves. In *Brimful of Asia* music is used to make sense of complicated lives and lives are examined to make sense of complicated music. An essential book for cultural and popular music studies alike.'

Simon Frith, University of Stirling, UK

'*Brimful of Asia* is filled to the brim with insight, analysis, and interpretation of some of the most important music being made in the world today. With deft mastery over a broad range of ideas and issues, Rehan Hyder locates the emergence of artists of Asian ancestry on the popular music charts in Britain as part of the global shake-up that is dramatically altering relationships between culture and place in many different ways all around the world. *Brimful of Asia* has much to say about artists, audiences, and artistry in a tumultuous time of transformation and change.'

George Lipsitz, University of California, San Diego, USA;
author of *Dangerous Crossroads*

Brimful of Asia

Negotiating Ethnicity on the UK Music Scene

REHAN HYDER
University of the West of England, Bristol, UK

ASHGATE

Published by

Ashgate Publishing Limited
Gower House
Croft Road
Aldershot
Hants GU11 3HR
England

Ashgate Publishing Company
Suite 420
101 Cherry Street
Burlington
VT 05401-4405
USA

Ashgate website: http://www.ashgate.com

British Library Cataloguing in Publication Data

Hyder, Rehan

Brimful of Asia : negotiating ethnicity on the UK music scene. – (Ashgate popular and folk music series)

1.Popular music – Great Britain – History and criticism 2.Popular music – Great Britain – Asian influences 3.Rock groups – Great Britain 4.Popular music – Great Britain – 1991–2000 5.Popular music – Great Britain – 2001–2010 6.South Asians – Cultural assimilation – Great Britain 7.South Asians – Great Britain – Ethnic identity

I.Title

781.6'4'0941

Library of Congress Cataloging-in-Publication Data

Hyder, Rehan, 1968–

Brimful of Asia : negotiating ethnicity on the UK music scene / Rehan Hyder.

p. cm.— (Ashgate popular and folk music series)

Includes bibliographical references.

ISBN 0-7546-0677-5 (alk. paper) – ISBN 0-7546-4064-7 (pbk. : alk. paper)

1. Popular music—Great Britain—Asian influences. 2. Popular music—Social aspects—Great Britain. 3. Asians—Great Britain—Ethnic identity. I. Title. II. Series.

ML3492.H93 2003
781.64'089'95041—dc22

2003065056

ISBN 0 7546 0677 5 (Hbk)
0 7546 4064 7 (Pbk)

Note: Some of the quotes within this book contain strong language, which readers might find offensive.

Typeset by Bournemouth Colour Press, Parkstone, Poole.
Printed and bound in Great Britain by MPG Books Ltd., Bodmin.

Contents

List of Figures

General Editor's Preface

The upheaval that occurred in musicology during the last two decades of the twentieth century has created a new urgency for the study of popular music alongside the development of new critical and theoretical models. A relativistic outlook has replaced the universal perspective of modernism (the international ambitions of the 12-note style); the grand narrative of the evolution and dissolution of tonality has been challenged, and emphasis has shifted to cultural context, reception and subject position. Together, these have conspired to eat away at the status of canonical composers and categories of high and low in music. A need has arisen, also, to recognize and address the emergence of crossovers, mixed and new genres, to engage in debates concerning the vexed problem of what constitutes authenticity in music and to offer a critique of musical practice as the product of free, individual expression.

Popular musicology is now a vital and exciting area of scholarship, and the Ashgate Popular and Folk Music series aims to present the best research in the field. Authors will be concerned with locating musical practices, values and meanings in cultural context, and may draw upon methodologies and theories developed in cultural studies, semiotics, poststructuralism, psychology and sociology. The series will focus on popular musics of the twentieth and twenty-first centuries. It is designed to embrace the world's popular musics from Acid Jazz to Zydeco, whether high tech or low tech, commercial or non-commercial, contemporary or traditional.

Professor Derek B. Scott
Chair of Music
University of Salford

Acknowledgements

This is a project that has spanned nearly a decade and during this period I have been deeply indebted to a number of people without whom this book would not have been possible. I would like to begin by thanking Charles Husband at the University of Bradford for first encouraging me to develop my ideas in this area, and Paul Rixon for supporting throughout the research of the original thesis. As for the actual writing of the book, I would like to thank both my department at the University of the West of England and the Arts and Humanities Research Board for generously funding the 12-month sabbatical which finally gave me the space to complete this project and, in particular, Martin Barker and Jon Dovey for their support in achieving this. At Ashgate I would like to thank Derek Scott for giving the green light for this project, the constructive comments of the anonymous reader whose report has helped shape the finished book, and a special mention to Rachel Lynch for her patience and guidance over the last few years.

As for the support of friends and family, this book simply would have never happened without them. The camaraderie of my fellow researchers Aidan Arrowsmith and Ian Toon during the dark days of my PhD in Stoke-on-Trent is gratefully acknowledged, as is the pastoral support provided by my old mate Andrew Pike and the always generous hospitality of Terry Banks and Yut-Mei. The unstinting support of my Mum, Dad and brother Shaun simply cannot be measured and I thank them as ever for always being there for me and putting up with my many moods. I would also like to give a special mention to Carolyn Hair who with grace and good humour has stood by me and kept me going through the last few years, and whose help and support have seen me through to the completion of this project.

Finally I would like to express my gratitude to the people who have allowed themselves to be interviewed and become the central subjects of this book. The generosity they have extended to me in terms of their time and support has both surprised and inspired me, and without this the work simply would never have happened. I would like to mention Rich at Nation Records, Mark at Tandoori Space and Chris Sharp at Wiiija for their help in getting hold of people and for providing me with illustrative materials, but most of all to my interviewees I extend my sincere thanks and wish them well in their future endeavours and look forward to hearing, reading and seeing what they will come up with next.

Chapter 1

Introduction

During the spring of 1992 a new cultural phenomenon began to emerge on the UK music scene as a number of Asian bands and musicians started to attract attention on a national scale. Suddenly, where before there had seemingly only been silence, Asian voices and sounds began to demand to be heard and spoke with a stridency and tenacity that confounded all expectations. Disparate voices in Yorkshire, the Midlands and London began to make themselves heard and, by the time summer had come around, the music press was full of reports of this new wave of Asian bands. At the time this was happening I was studying for my Masters degree in race relations in Bradford and, as someone who was not only a fledgling musician but also part-Asian – my father was born in Pakistan and my mother in England – I followed these developments with a keen interest. In the years that followed I began to realize that the experiences of these individuals provided a unique opportunity to investigate notions of ethnicity and identity in the context of a developing multi-ethnic society. The fact that Asians were entering the mainstream of the music industry for the first time meant that their sense of 'Asianness' was put under constant scrutiny and interrogation in public: what did it mean to be Asian? How did this affect their music? What did this say about Asians in Britain? The expectations and frequent stereotypes traded by a wide range of inquisitors was such that the individuals in question had to be both reflexive and challenging in their responses, ensuring that their sense of self was as much public as it was private. This is extremely significant since it reflects the very nature of identity in the contemporary world; it comes not only from within an individual, from memories and history, but is worked out and negotiated in the big wide world outside; that which is happening now and embodies a myriad array of people, opinions and influences. Who we think we are is only part of the story, since what others think of us is a contingent part of the process of self, and this is no more true than in a contemporary setting like multi-ethnic Britain at the turn of the 21st century.

So, in a sense, this is a book as much about Britain in the 1990s as it is about the experiences of the individuals focused upon. The decade has proved to be pivotal in the growing influence and acceptance of South Asian culture on the mainstream and it is important to recognize the significance of this for the nation as a whole, rather than focus on what it means for a particular 'ethnic minority' group. How then does one tackle such complex and sometimes contradictory issues as ethnicity and cultural identity? The realm of the creative arts is an obvious place to look, but how does one make sense of something as hard to define as music and performance? To seek an absolute understanding of both of these issues seems somewhat misguided and impractical and I have attempted to reflect the ongoing process of musical and ethnic identity formation by first considering the problems associated with such research.

Writing ethnicity

The first question I asked myself was how to write about issues of ethnicity without perpetuating notions of fixed identities and static communities. Indeed one of the common irritations experienced by members of Asian bands is the expectation that they somehow speak for all Asians; that their experiences and artistic endeavours somehow represent the authentic voice of 'Asian Britain'. It is important to state at the outset that my detailed focus on the experiences of a number of specific bands and musicians is not intended to be a definitive account of British Asian identity, but to qualitatively examine the complexities at play in terms of ethnicity and identity in multi-ethnic Britain. This perspective was adopted partly as a reaction against totalizing discourses of ethnic absolutism and belonging which fail to recognize the syncretic processes at work in the expression of contemporary cultural identities. In the specific context of discourses surrounding Asian identity in Britain, the articulation of ethnic absolutism is particularly problematic (Modood 1988, 1994 and 1997) and bound up in often stereotypically defined studies of separation and 'community' (Khan 1977; Modood 1997). The tendency for researchers to regard racial or ethnic categories as unproblematic damages our understanding of the flexible and dynamic articulation of self-identity for groups and individuals by pandering to what Stanfield and Dennis have called the 'fallacy of homogeneity', which suggests that individuals within minority groups (particularly non-whites) have no differential identities (Stanfield and Dennis 1992: 22). In order to avoid falling into what Silverman has called the 'trap of absolutism' (Silverman 1993: 5) it is therefore necessary in a study of this sort to focus on the specific experiences of individuals in some detail rather than utilizing discourses of ethnic absolutism or, in this case, 'community'. By examining in detail the experiences of specific individuals in particular settings, my intention is to show how a sense of Asian identity is one that is not fixed and rigid but one which is negotiated and dynamic. By focusing on just four bands I have been able to examine in depth the complex negotiations of identity and ethnicity which can only be understood by embarking on extensive and qualitative research. As Mann has written, particularly complex research projects are such that it is necessary to focus on a small group of 'key participants' in order to gather material of any insight:

> It may well be that a particular piece of research needs to be focused on selected people for information and the information gained from them will be fitted together in a coherent way with virtually no percentages and significant tests at all. (1993: 111)

These concerns were instrumental in the focus of my research on individuals rather than on a broadly defined social group; I purposely avoided gathering information from any 'community' sources in order to get away from discourses of ethnic identity which present Britain's diverse Asian population as a fixed and culturally isolated grouping. For this reason I have also kept away from gathering data about the ethnic make-up of the audiences that these bands play to, since it is rather reductive to judge the significance of these artists by measuring their success within the community. As I have stated, although the focus of the research is on Asian bands, I did not embark on this project with the notion of constructing a definitive or representative account of British Asian identity, but rather to examine the ambiguities and complexities of multi-accented identities. For this reason the research is intended not merely to provide specific accounts of Asian identity, but to shed light on what Stuart Hall has called the 'crisis of identity' (1992b) that is representative of late modernity. The decline of metanarratives in late modernity which has seen the erosion of old identities and allegiances is such that the politics of identity and belonging have become increasingly contentious (Harvey 1989; Lash 1990). The fragmentation of old sureties and allegiances has meant that particular modes of identity and political agency – not just those surrounding ethnicity but also those based around issues of gender, sexuality, class and generation – have become ever-intensified sites of struggle and negotiation. Rallying cries around notions of ethnicity and cultural authenticity have become particularly strident in attempting to reassert old allegiances and yet, at the same time, the manifestation of multi-accented and syncretic identities becomes increasingly hard to ignore. The ambiguous and reflexive nature of identities in flux during this period is such that it is hard to maintain any definitive or absolute model of ethnicity and identity without ignoring the dynamic processes of cultural change and syncretism that are becoming such an integral part of contemporary multi-ethnic society. This is not to say that specific cultural allegiances and histories do not have any specific bearing on the articulation of individual and group identities; far from it in fact. As the experiences of the musicians interviewed show, the cultural resource provided by their various Asian backgrounds are significant features in the articulation of their sense of self and belonging, but this resource does not have an absolute or fixed influence on their lives. As Wallman has recognized, the importance of the ethnic 'resource' is extremely flexible according to individual experiences and contexts and cannot be assumed to represent a dominant mode of self in all circumstances (Wallman 1981). We need to be able to recognize the combined importance of the dynamic and shifting processes of syncretism and cultural change as well as the pragmatic maintenance of a sense of cultural heritage and belonging. These two processes are not mutually exclusive: they co-exist and combine in a way that represents the complexity of ever-shifting concepts of self and belonging. This does not present us with an easy model of identity, but nevertheless reflects the intricacies of the cultural processes at work in the functioning of multi-ethnic societies in late modernity. This study is not intended to represent a definitive model of such a society but merely reflects the complex negotiations that are present in contemporary articulations of self and belonging. Although this is a terrain which is fraught with much difficulty and contention, it also reveals the vibrant and transformative potential of an environment which is marked by the dynamic processes of inter-cultural exchange and syncretism.

Writing music

The second question that needs attention is that of the music itself; how to write meaningfully about a medium that quite simply cannot be represented in words. Descriptions of the sound of music are inevitably subjective and tied into the ability of the author to convey what can be the most ephemeral or profound sonic and emotional nuances. Furthermore I have always felt that analysis of musical notation and lyrics is something of a cold and abstract tool; particularly when considering such complex issues as that of ethnicity and cultural identity. The close study of musical texts is undoubtedly a useful method and can uncover some important insights about both the author and the society that produced them, but ultimately they are limited insomuch as they are bound by the interpretative powers of the critic. The examination of lyrics is a particularly favoured source of analysis within popular music, but one which has limited value since it not only isolates particular passages and words but also excises them from the overall context where sound and language are fused. In the end, whatever is uncovered by such scrutiny must always be considered with caution; too often are meanings ascribed to lyrical texts that are alien or even anathema to authors themselves. It is troubling that many studies of identity and ethnicity that concentrate on music have based their analysis simply on musical texts such as records or videos, decoding them as unproblematic and unambiguous messages and statements, all too often ascribing meanings to these texts which may or may not be intended by the musicians in question. Any study of musical meaning and cultural significance taken from a musical text must be counterbalanced by consideration of the avowed intentions of the artists themselves. It is therefore crucial to allow the members of the bands in question to air their own voices and opinions, partly because of the complexity of the subject matter involved, but also because of the lack of such material in many others studies in this area (Hesmondhalgh 1995; Sharma, Hutnyk and Sharma 1996). This is not to say that artists are not prone to their own interpretative shortcomings, and the poetic or even abstract nature of many lyrical texts is such that they may escape neat analysis or understanding.

So from the outset I was suspicious of the value of textual analysis with regard to the music produced by these bands, and I soon realized that this book was not actually about the nature of the music created by Asian musicians but about how such music acted as a pivot around which notions of cultural allegiance and ethnic identity were established and negotiated. In that sense the actual music itself is not of primary importance; how it is used, interpreted and reported is the real source of interest. Music, like identity itself, does not come simply from within and, although both emerge from the individual, they find meaning and contestation in wider society. So, although I have drawn on various musical texts, my prime source of information has been the musicians themselves. While the music and lyrics they produce are certainly important and provide a necessary and valuable resource for this book, I have been more concerned with their reception; how others have interpreted them and how the musicians have responded to this. Musical meaning then, like a sense of self, is something that is contingent on and negotiated in relation to the outside world and that represents an ongoing process of identity construction and maintenance. The specific arena of musical performance and production is a particularly rich area through which to explore these issues as it provides a space where identities are presented, distorted and transgressed. The notion of cultural identity as *process* is mirrored by the development and articulation of musical styles and performances which are in a constant state of flux and re-evaluation. By prioritizing the importance of musical production as a significant site of cultural interaction and change I have sought to problematize much previous work in youth studies which have tended to relegate music as simply an adjunct of style (Cohen 1972; Hebdige 1976), preferring to assert its importance as a significant area of social and cultural transformation. Frith (1996: 109) has correctly identified the importance of music-making in the articulation of a dynamic and shifting sense of self and has stated that 'Identity is not a thing but a process – an experiential process which is most vividly grasped *as music*.'

By privileging music as a site of cultural negotiation and change, where identities are performed and transformed, I intend to show how the experiences of the musicians in this study represent part of the processes of transition and change that are transforming contemporary British society in ways which reflect the complex articulations of cultural syncretism at play in a multi-ethnic setting.

The bands

The bands that I have focused on all originated in the early 1990s and represent the influence of a wide array of musical cultures; in this sense they are characterized more by the diversity of their output than by their ethnic background. They were chosen because they happened to be some of the earliest Asian bands on the scene and, as it turns out, they have also been among the most successful and have enjoyed careers that were still developing some ten years later. Although all these artists have experienced a great deal of success both in the UK and internationally, I recognize that not everybody will be familiar with their work.

Therefore I have provided a short description of each for the edification of the reader. These descriptions are a somewhat brief overview of sometimes complicated careers, but it is hoped that they will provide a rough outline and backdrop to the subsequent interview data. The artists are listed in alphabetical order; this does not reflect their degree of success or indeed the musical preferences of the author.

Black Star Liner

This band was formed in 1994 in Leeds and consisted of three members: Choque Hosein, Chris Harrop and Tom Salmon. From the outset the band's music incorporated a fusion of elements drawn from a wide range of sources. Aspects of dub reggae and rock guitar were merged with a variety of instruments from Asia and the Middle East to create a deeply textured and unique sound by a process whereby the band (and various collaborators) recorded instruments and voices live and then manipulated and remixed them into the final musical text. As such, the band's recorded output differed markedly from live performances, which tended to rely on a more direct, 'rock and roll' approach.

Black Star Liner's first record, *Smoke the prophets*, was released on their own Soundclash Sound label in 1994 and was made single of the week in the Vibes section of *New Musical Express* (13 November 1992). Following the release of *High Turkish influence* in 1995 they were signed to the independent label EXP, which led to their debut album *Yemen cutta connection* the following year. It was a significant critical success – named as dance album of the week by *The Guardian* newspaper (23 August 1996) and the preceding record, *Haláal rock*, became single of the week in *Melody Maker* (10 August 1996). The latter included a collaboration with Cornershop's Tjinder Singh (see below), who provided vocals on the track 'Dhuggie Dhol', and the two bands would later appear together on the BBC's *India 5-O* live broadcast in 1997. By this time EXP records had collapsed and Black Star Liner subsequently signed a three-album deal with Warner Music UK. The deal in fact produced just a single album, *Bengali bantam youth experience*, which was released in 1999 to much critical acclaim and nominated for the coveted Mercury Music Award. The breakdown of relations between the band and the new management at Warner Music UK resulted in legal wranglings which meant that Black Star Liner did not release any further records for four years, although in 2003 Choque Hosein, the sole remaining member, was about to sign with a new label and finally to start releasing records again.

Cornershop

Previously named General Havoc, Cornershop emerged in Preston in 1992 around the nucleus of Tjinder Singh and Ben Ayres, who met while studying at Lancashire Polytechnic in the late 1980s and who have remained the key members of the band ever since. Tjinder's brother Avtar, David Chambers and Anthony Saffrey completed the line-up. The band was quickly signed to the London-based independent label Wiiija, through which they released their first records *In the days of Ford Cortina* and *Lock, stock and double barrel*, the latter being chosen as single of the week by *NME* (27 November 1992). Musically Cornershop began as an archetypal indie/rock band, favouring a three-guitar line-up betraying energy and enthusiasm over musical ability. The band courted controversy early in their career by burning a picture of former Smiths' vocalist Morrissey outside the London offices of his record label EMI in protest at the singer's supposed flirtation with far-right nationalist sentiments. This act garnered a lot of attention in the press and did much to label the band as an angry and explicitly political group, despite the fact that this was not always apparent in the band's lyrical content.

Following the release of Cornershop's debut album *Hold on it hurts* in 1993, the band began to experiment with new sounds, drawing on a wider range of influences and sounds, including greater use of Asian instruments such as the sitar and the dholki. The band's second album *Woman's gotta have it* (1995) reflected these changes and went on to gather widespread critical acclaim in the USA following a licensing deal with David Byrne's Luaka Bop label. Cornershop's increasingly eclectic and innovative approach came of age in 1997 with the release of their third album *When I was born for the 7th time*, which not only featured the number one single 'Brimful of Asha' but was also nominated for the prestigious Mercury Music Award. The combination of rock, hip-hop, funk, country and Asian sounds resulted in an album which was radically different from the band's initial output and Cornershop have since built on the success of this approach with the release in 2002 of *Handcream for a generation*, to almost universal critical acclaim. The band have continued to work around the songwriting ability of lead singer Tjinder Singh and, until 2003, remained under the auspices of Wiiija Records.

Fun^Da^Mental

Fun^Da^Mental were formed in London in 1991 around the core membership of PropaGhandi (aka Aki Nawaz), Lallaman and Goldfinger and released their debut single 'Janaam: righteous preacher' the following year on Nation Records – a label co-founded by Aki Nawaz. The band rapidly gained a reputation for the outspoken political content of their early records, as epitomized by their first album *Seize the time* which dealt with issues such as racism, vigilantism and the global arms industry. The controversial lyrics rapped over dense hip-hop beats and enhanced with provocative samples drawn from film, television and political speeches – *Seize the time* includes dialogue from the film *Gandhi* (1982), a documentary by Australian journalist John Pilger on the international arms industry and the speeches of Louis Farrakhan of the Nation of Islam – led the band to be described in some quarters as 'the Asian Public Enemy' (Sullivan 1993). Such was the force of the band's political approach, that their music was often under-reported early on, even though the fusion of hip-hop beats with samples of south Asian instrumentation was an innovative and original development in British music.

Fun^Da^Mental's subsequent output has reflected a continuing commitment to raising controversial political subjects (as in the case of their 1999 release *Why America will go to hell*, which speaks out against the issue of rape as a weapon of war in the CD's liner notes) as well as a process of musical discovery which has produced a diverse body of work. Since *Seize the time* Fun^Da^Mental have released an entirely instrumental album, *With intent to pervert the cause of injustice*, the dissonant, industrial *Erotic terrorism* and the almost world music sounding *There shall be love!* All of these releases have sought to widen the band's musical base through collaboration with musicians from as far afield as New Zealand, South Africa and Pakistan. Although the band has gone through several changes of personnel, Aki Nawaz has remained the chief creative force and co-ordinator, continuing to shape projects and seek out collaborators from within Nation Records in London.

Voodoo Queens/Anjali

Voodoo Queens were formed in London in 1992 by sisters Anjali and Rajni Bhatia, Anjula Bhasker, Ella Dragulis and Stefania. After playing live for the first time they were offered a John Peel session on BBC Radio One, broadcast in January of the following year. After further live performances the band were signed by London independent label Too Pure and released their first single 'Supermodel, superficial', which was a critical and commercial success. The song's lyrics presented a stinging critique of the beauty industry and the pressure put on young girls to diet and this, combined with the slogan 'Who needs boys when you've got guitars?', led to Voodoo Queens being associated with the UK's nascent Riot Grrrl scene. The band adopted a raw guitar-based style in garage/punk tradition and live shows were characterized by high-energy performance and aggression. Their musical approach, and the fact that several members of the band were of Asian descent, led them to be described in some quarters as the 'female Cornershop' – a label rejected by Voodoo Queens and certainly not borne out in any considered musical comparison between the two bands. In 1994 the band released their only album *Chocolate revenge* and embarked on a successful UK promotional tour. The following year saw Voodoo Queens leave Too Pure records because of musical differences and lead singer/songwriter Anjali Bhatia set up the short-lived Voodoo record label to release the band's last single 'Eat the germs' on limited edition 7-inch vinyl.

Following this Voodoo Queens disbanded and Anjali set out to re-invent herself as a solo artist, signing to Wiiija Records in 1996. Having begun working as a DJ and embracing a more technological approach, Anjali set up a studio in her home in order to write and produce her own material. Her new output was in marked contrast to that of Voodoo Queens, using sampling technology to create a decidedly more laid-back musical style, and her first single 'Maharani' was released in 1998. The incorporation of Asian instrumentation with soul and funk influences and the use of samples of 1960s exotica enabled Anjali to establish herself as a solo artist of some note. Her eponymous album released in 2000 was successful both in the UK and in Europe and the 2003 follow-up, *The world of Lady A*, looked set to build her reputation further.

Throughout the 1990s and beyond members of each group have allowed themselves to be questioned by me and have been gracious, open and thought-provoking in their responses. The interviews were open-ended and semi-structured, which enabled the respondents to raise a number of ideas and issues that undoubtedly played important roles in shaping the structure and key concerns of the final text. I also spoke to a number of journalists and record company personnel in order to widen the perspective of the study; a full list of all interviewees, including the dates of each interview, is included in Appendix 1.

At the time of writing (spring 2003), all the musicians I spoke to were active within the music industry, playing live, writing material and releasing records that continue to reflect the energy and enthusiasm that has enabled them to survive and prosper for well over a decade. I would whole-heartedly recommend any reader interested in the subjects raised by this work to seek out the recorded material of these diverse artists. Such is the variety of their music that there is no single compilation album that features them all and, although I would have liked to have included one with this book, the practicalities of doing so and the strict legislature of music copyright law prevent me from doing so. Needless to say, the music produced by these artists is not to everyone's taste, but the sheer weight of ideas and innovations they reflect would provoke the interest of even the most jaded of listeners.

Structure

In order to understand the particular experiences of the small number of Asian bands and musicians focused on here, it is important to establish an overall conceptual map of the specific environment from which these individuals have emerged. In the following chapter I will examine contemporary debates surrounding the articulation of ethnicity in the UK, paying particular attention to the experiences of Asian people. I will focus on the specific experiences of migration and settlement in the post-war period and examine subsequent attempts to construct 'authentic' discourses of identity and belonging. In doing so I will highlight the tension between absolutist and syncretic discourses of cultural and ethnic identity and examine the central role of the artist in the establishment of new understandings of self and belonging. In Chapter 3, I will summarize previous attempts to analyse the significance of youth culture in forging new identifies, focusing on the role assigned to music. Thus I will attempt to assert the central importance of music in the construction and transformation of youthful identities, particularly in the context of a multi-ethnic environment. As well as stressing the transformative potential of music-making in this context, I will also examine some of the pressures and expectations put upon Asian musicians by cultural commentators and elements of the music industry. Before I finally move on to examine the experiences of the musicians interviewed in some detail, Chapter 4 will look at the post-war history of Asian influences and involvement in popular music in the UK. Here I will examine the construction and maintenance of a number of delimiting stereotypes of Asian music and culture which have had a particular effect on the careers of contemporary Asian bands.

Having established the historical and theoretical background for this study I will then look at the experiences of the four Asian bands selected for this study in depth by focusing mainly on information gathered from personal interviews. Chapter 5 will examine how these bands have negotiated their sense of Asian identity as emergent artists in an industry that promotes notions of novelty and exoticism. It will focus on the reaction of the national music press to the emergence of Asian bands in the 1990s and examine how subsequently the musicians in these bands have attempted to transgress stereotypical interpretations of their music and identity, particularly those pertaining to notions of eastern mysticism and 'exotic' politics.

Chapter 6 will examine the importance of political issues in the music of these bands and focus on the pressures brought to bear on Asian musicians by the 'burden of representation', from both commercial and 'community' sources. Here, I focus on the importance of ideological and financial independence for these bands and examine the flexible and pragmatic tactics adopted by them in order to survive and flourish within such an arduous environment.

Finally, Chapter 7 focuses on the articulation of syncretic modes of cultural expression and identity, highlighting the ability of young Asian musicians to successfully manipulate a number of cultural inputs and resources. This chapter analyses a range of influences that were significant in the emergence of Asian bands in the 1990s and examines the combination of traditional Asian, global and Western influences that have combined to produce new, syncretic manifestations of cultural expression and identity. By examining the response of the musicians to existing categories of ethnicity and identity this chapter will conclude by highlighting the ability of these young people to articulate a multi-accented sense of self and belonging – one which is both flexible and able to incorporate a range of cultural inputs and allegiances.

The specific experiences of these few bands can never hope to deliver a definitive understanding of what it means to be Asian in the UK at the start of a new millennium, but can provide us with a vivid and enlightening snapshot of the transformative potential of life in a contemporary multi-ethnic setting. The ability of these individuals to balance a range of cultural inputs and articulate modes of self and belonging that are dynamic and multi-accented is evidence that we can perhaps begin to move away from the limiting discourses of absolutism and 'authenticity' which seek to stifle the ever-growing manifestations of cultural exchange and syncretism. The experiences of these musicians teach us that, despite the many pressures and expectations of contemporary life, it is possible to embrace a multitude of cultural inputs and influences and, with vitality and drive, transfix and transform the society from which they emerged.

Chapter 2

Negotiating difference: ethnicity and identity in contemporary Britain

This study is grounded in the context of what we might call a 'multi-ethnic' society as it exists in the contemporary setting of Britain at the beginning of a new century. The migration and settlement of brown and black people from the former colonies in the immediate post-war period radically altered the composition and character of British life in ways which continue to throw up new and ever-changing cultural forms and practices. For the settlers themselves, and in particular their offspring, issues of identity and belonging have been paramount in the functioning of their everyday lives. Widespread experiences of prejudice and racism (Fryer 1984; Solomos 1987) have meant that notions of ethnic and racial identity have taken on much importance for Britain's so-called 'ethnic minorities' and continue to play a central part in notions of identity and belonging. The maintenance and assertion of a sense of distinct ethnic identity, often with significant links (both real and symbolic) to the country of origin, have been important resources in establishing a positive and assertive role in contemporary British society. Of course any kind of positive expression of ethnic particularity cannot function in isolation, and the multi-ethnic nature of contemporary British life is such that the inevitable processes of cross-cultural dialogue and exchange challenge the maintenance of a closed or 'pure' sense of ethnic identity. Current debates on issues of ethnicity and identity therefore need to focus on the tension between the desire to retain a sense of ethnic particularity and the dynamic processes of cross-cultural exchange through which new modes of identity are realized.

It is in order to examine these dialogues that I have chosen to examine how a small group of individuals have negotiated their sense of 'Asian'[1] identity throughout the 1990s and beyond. I have focused on a small sample of Asian bands in the UK whose experiences represent both the vitality and creativity of a contemporary multi-ethnic nation, as well as highlighting many of its tensions and contradictions. The importance of expressive cultural forms and practices are central to any articulation of ethnic identity, and music is perhaps the most vivid and dynamic of these forms (Gilroy 1993a; Back 1996). The music of these young people embodies what Paul Gilroy has called, 'kaleidoscopic formulations of cultural syncretism' (Gilroy 1988: 45) which begin to realize the positive potential of a contemporary multi-ethnic pluralism, but is counterbalanced by the need to reassert and reinterpret a sense of ethnic identity which is bound closely to specific cultural histories. The need to marry these two elements of identity – that which represents the possibilities of the new and syncretic with that which refers to tradition and the past – is negotiated through a complex discourse of categorization, exclusivity and belonging which posits as many questions as it seeks to answer. These young people are making their way across hazardous terrain, trying to steer a path between the extremes of ethnic essentialism and the empty shell of the fractured self. This should not be viewed as an analysis of marginal 'ethnics' or exotic 'others'. In order to make sense of the expressions of self represented by the experiences of those examined in this book, we need to consider the question of ethnicity and identification in an open way which allows us to recognize that the processes at work here are the same ones that are changing *all* our lives in a world of ever-increasing diversification and fluidity.

This chapter will examine contemporary debates around ethnic identification in multi-ethnic Britain and focus on the importance of processes of intercultural exchange. First, I shall examine the tension between essentialist notions of ethnic identity and theories of cross-cultural syncretism as well as focusing on the contingent and contextual importance of the ethnic resource. Second, recent debates surrounding the attempt to construct 'authentic' political identities around definitions of black and Asian identity will be re-evaluated. By examining the complex processes of migration and settlement, combined with the diverse home backgrounds of non-white and Asian settlers in the UK, I shall then argue that notions of syncretism are an important resource in challenging the assertion of essentialized ethnic identities since they readily accept and acknowledge processes of cultural transformation and change. Finally I will look at the central role of the artist in the expression of these new and syncretic modes of identity and focus on the particular pressures placed upon black and Asian cultural workers living and struggling in Britain in the 1990s, as well as celebrating their innovative potential.

Ethnicity in the 1990s: locating the syncretic

The identities of the individuals in this study are grounded in a particular historical context of migration and settlement in what has become a multi-ethnic society. The younger generations of the UK's post-war black and Asian settler communities are forging new paths where identities are disrupted, intermingled and reassembled, yet at the same time we are witnessing the increasing use of a system of language and categorization which seeks to totalize and rationalize ethnicity as an absolute defining criteria for identity. This retreat into what Gilroy has termed the 'dubious comfort of ethnic particularity' (1993a: 31) is harmful on a number of fronts, not least because it panders to the pseudo-biological culturalism of the so-called 'new' racists (Barker 1981), but also in its failure to recognize the liberating potential of emergent, syncretic cultural forms and experiences. For the individuals in this book the articulation of new modes of self-identification which are thrown up by the contemporary realities of multi-ethnic Britain has to be negotiated against stifling theories of a regressive sense of 'Asian' identity. The restrictive rules of belonging to such ethnically 'pure' group identities are such that the creative processes of syncretism and cultural dynamism of individuals is stifled and devalued and where, as Gilroy has highlighted:

> Culture is conceived along ethnically absolute lines, not as something intrinsically fluid, changing, unstable and dynamic, but as fixed property of social groups rather than a relational field in which they encounter one another and live out social, historical relationships. (1993b: 35)

This tendency towards cultural absolutism ignores the dynamic and reflexive negotiations at work in the expression of ethnicity and identity within both groups and individuals. Ethnicity is undoubtedly a significant resource of self-identification for black and Asian people in contemporary Britain, particularly in contexts where prejudice and racism are prevalent, but to fail to recognize the ability of so-called ethnic minorities to operationalize a complex and fluid sense of identity damages our understanding of Britain's developing multi-ethnic society. If this fluidity is ignored, then new modes and ways of expressing a sense of ethnicity are devalued, since they are deemed to contravene the 'rules' of belonging that exist at the heart of absolutist notions of culture. Although the cultural heritage of their parents and families is an important resource for young, second- and third-generation black and Asian people in the UK, this does not preclude the emergence of new modes of identity which reflect the contemporary realities of their everyday lives. The reflexive and multi-accented processes at work in the development of self-identity enable individuals to express new modes of being, while simultaneously maintaining and re-evaluating links with their cultural past. The emergence of new, cross-cultural forms of self-identification based on the contemporary workings of a multi-ethnic environment does not necessarily erode the specificity of any sense of Asian identity, but can be understood as an extension of it; one which is flexible and dynamic rather than fixed and absolute.

What I hope to show by examining the experiences of the musicians in this study is the ability of individuals (and, by association, groups) to simultaneously forge new multi-accented identities while maintaining strong links to their cultural past. As Stuart Hall has said of black and Asian migrants and their descendants:

> These 'hybrids' retain strong links to and identifications with the traditions and places of their 'origin'. But they are without the illusion of any 'actual' return to the past ... there is no going 'home' again. (1994: 362)

The notion of hybridity is a useful one in this context since it recognizes the ability of groups and individuals to adapt and absorb a range of cultural inputs in new circumstances, opening up what Bhabha has called a 'third space' (Bhabha 1990) where new modes of identity can be lived out:

> Here the transformational value of change lies in the re-articulation, or translation, of elements that are neither the One nor the Other but something else besides which contests the terms and territories of both. (Bhabha 1988:13)

The processes at work in migration and settlement are such that any notion of cultural 'purity' is undermined by the lived realities of the migrants as they function within the new environment of the 'host' society. The subsequent articulation of self-identity for migrants, and in particular their descendents, becomes a process of negotiation between the cultural heritage of their ancestry and the lived realities of their contemporary multi-ethnic setting.

Despite its usefulness in this context, the notion of hybridity is also problematic in so much as it suggests a relationship between two 'pure' and pre-existing forms of cultural or ethnic identity; in this case 'Asian' and 'British'. This is problematic because it fails to recognize the complexities that exist within these seemingly discrete categories, as well as the long historical relationship between Britain and the Indian subcontinent. Since the concept of hybridity focuses on the boundaries between seemingly distinct cultural and ethnic groups (Wallman 1986; Bhabha 1988) it is easy to lose sight of the complicated processes at work in the construction of these 'original' identities and also to ignore the importance of other significant modes of identity such as gender, class and sexuality. There is a danger that the language of hybridity, rather than challenging cultural essentialism, actually places itself at the heart of such discourses where 'pure' and distinct identities are privileged and where cross-cultural dialogues could be interpreted as damaging fractures to the continuity of ethno-cultural particularity.

The socio-cultural diversity of both Britain (with its long history of inward migration and regional differences) and the Indian subcontinent (with its multiplicity of regional, religious and linguistic traditions) immediately challenges the notion of two separate and pure identities. The colonial history of the British Raj also does damage to the idea that 'British' and 'Asian' existed as separate and discrete entities prior to post-war settlement, when in fact they have been deeply entwined for at least 200 years. I therefore intend to operationalize the terminology of syncretism which allows us to understand the functioning of ethnicity and identity as part of an ongoing process which is both reflexive and dynamic. The use of syncretist language is not meant to detract from the importance of a sense of Asian identity and heritage in favour of a free-flowing model of non-specific diversification or assimilation, but is intended to highlight a complex position of negotiation where individuals are able to incorporate and make sense of a range of cultural inputs. As Becquer and Gatti have written:

> Syncretic relations are … traversed by a double movement of both alliance and critique. Syncretism involves neither 'flagrant compromise' (ultimately a transposition of the logic of contradiction to a quantitative transaction), nor 'uncritical acceptance' (i.e. pluralist inclusion), but rather a process which articulates elements in a manner that modifies their intelligibility and transforms their combinatory spaces. (1991: 68)

By utilizing the language of the syncretic we can begin to undermine the reductive notions of culture and ethnicity as absolute and discrete markers of identity. Rather than privileging the notion of a 'third space' (Bhabha 1990) which simplifies the process of cross-cultural interaction as the simple combination of two well-defined and 'pure' identities, the terminology of the syncretic allows us to examine identity as an ongoing process – one which incorporates both continuity and change within its continual and dynamic development.

As I have already suggested, it is important to recognize that ethnicity is not the only factor at play in identity construction and this is as true for the individuals featured in this book as it is for everybody else. We need to understand that a sense of ethnic or cultural heritage is only one of several factors that combine to construct any individual's sense of self and being. Although the ethnic 'resource' is undoubtedly a vital element in the expression of identity for most people, and is particularly important for black and Asian settlers in British society, it should not eclipse other equally important modes of identity. Ethnicity is not the be-all and end-all of identity for anybody; its importance is regulated by the specific contexts within which groups and individuals function. Sandra Wallman states:

> Depending on the perception of the actors involved and the constraints and opportunities of the context in which they act, ethnicity may be an essential resource, an utter irrelevance or a crippling liability. (1981: 4)

As we shall see, the contextual importance of ethnicity is reflected in the lived experiences of the individuals discussed in this book. The negotiation of a sense of Asianness by the young musicians interviewed forms part of a complicated process of self-realization which has to balance and make sense of a bewildering array of inputs and expectations. As Stuart Hall has quite rightly stated:

> … identities are never unified and, in late modern times, increasingly fragmented and fractured; never singular but multiples constructed across different, often intersecting and antagonizing discourses, practices and positions. They are subject to a radical historicization and are constantly in the process of change and transformation. (1996: 4)

Against this understanding of the fluidity of identity is the frustrating tendency for the bands in this study to be labelled solely in terms of what is perceived to be their 'absolute' ethnic identity. As we shall see, the categorization of these groups within the music industry as 'Asian bands' is a source of much contention and is resisted by the musicians involved, who exhibit all the flexible and dynamic processes of identity formation discussed above. It is important then to account for the contextual importance of a sense of Asianness in relation to other important modes of identity such as class, gender and generation.

For the purposes of this book I am also making use of the terminology 'Asian band', but do this in a pragmatic fashion and in order to help deconstruct rather than perpetuate essentialist notions of Asian identity. When we recognize that the personnel of the bands in question from a variety of backgrounds – non-Asian as well as Asian (indeed only one of Cornershop's five members in 2003 could be described as 'Asian') – we can further problematize the labelling of such groups as Asian bands. Since a vocabulary of ethnic difference and distinction has widespread currency in contemporary Britain I have consciously utilized this terminology as a starting point from which to examine and deconstruct essentialist dialogues of ethnic particularity. I shall go on to look at the problems of using such language later in this chapter but, as I have stated, I do not wish to denigrate completely the importance of the ethnic resource, but to examine its importance as a flexible and dynamic component of a wider process of self-realization and transformation.

It is only by understanding the negotiation of identity as a process which is able to simultaneously incorporate the full complexity of cultural inputs at play while maintaining a strong sense of cultural heritage that we can begin to make sense of the lived experiences of the young people focused on here and attempt to understand better the developing complexities of developing multi-ethnic societies.

The politics of ethnicity: articulating black and Asian identity

Although this study is intended to reflect the process of syncretic culture and identity, it is important to recognize the particular social context that provides the backdrop for the actors involved. If we accept that the ethnic resource is an element of self-identification that has varying significance at different times and settings, we need to understand the historical processes that have combined to construct current debates surrounding the notions of ethno-cultural authenticity and belonging. As I have already stated, we need to understand ethnic and cultural identity as something that is constantly in flux; as a process rather than as a fixed and permanent marker of self. Of course this process does not unfold in a vacuum and has to incorporate a variety of inputs and influences that are imposed from an array of societal forces. For Britain's black and Asian minorities the common experiences of prejudice and racism have meant that a sense of cultural and ethnic identity has assumed a particularly important role in many aspects of everyday life. The political significance of maintaining a positive and assertive sense of ethno-cultural identity and cohesion has been a primary factor in shaping contemporary debates surrounding issues of identity and belonging. In particular, the attempt to construct a unified public identity which can throw its weight behind an anti-racist political agenda has led to much debate within and around Britain's 'non-white'[2] settler communities. This desire to present a united front against racism, allied to the relatively small proportion of black and Asian people within the population,[3] has meant that the desire for a broad-based political identity has been paramount. This has given rise to the attempt to construct a political category out of 'black' terminology; a category that seeks to incorporate all non-white groups and individuals.

The impetus behind the construction of an inclusive and politicized notion of black identity arose out of the specific historical and social conditions of post-war immigration and settlement into the UK. Although we can identify two broad sources of this migration (the Caribbean and the Indian subcontinent), non-white settlers in the UK came from a variety of cultural and ethnic backgrounds. In the Caribbean these differences were marked particularly by inter-island loyalties, while people from the Indian subcontinent were differentiated by a variety of regional, religious and linguistic differences (Watson 1977). The sheer diversity of cultural identities represented by the mass of non-white settlers during the post-war period would seem to preclude any attempt to construct a unifying discourse of black identity; but the common experience of prejudice and racism experienced by black and brown people settled in the 'mother country' provided the basis for a potentially unifying rallying point. Furthermore, Paul Gilroy and others have argued that the shared experience of anti-colonial struggle under the yoke of the British Empire also provided common ground for the general mass of non-white settlers in the post-war period and therefore helped bolster the legitimacy of establishing a broad-based black political identity. Paul Gilroy has stated that:

> These non-European elements must be noted and their distinctive resonance must be accounted for. Some derive from the immediate history of empire and colonisation in Africa, the Caribbean and the Indian sub-continent from where post-war settlers brought both the methods and the memories of their battles for citizenship, justice and independence. (1988: 156)

The idea of unity based around a common experience of racism was used by many to mobilize anti-racist political action throughout the 1970s and 1980s under the umbrella term of 'black'. Despite the intention to operationalize a black identity as a unifying and rallying cry, it is clear that in practice this highly politicized discourse contained significant areas of absence and silence. Many of those supposedly represented by this political discourse either rejected out of hand the label of black identity or found themselves marginalized within its confines. The rejection of a sense of black identity by many groups and individuals reflects the processes of contestation that have surrounded the meaning of the term during the latter part of the 20th century. The use of 'black' as a unifying political concept emerged partly from the work of cultural activists in the late 1960s and early 1970s who (re)claimed the word as a moniker representing pride and achievement rather than as a mark of racial subordination and inferiority (Malcolm X 1996; Cleaver 1968; Hraba and Grant 1970).

Despite the positive aspects of locating blackness as a source of strength and assertion, it is important to recognize that the terminology is open to a number of competing interpretations. The inability of a significant proportion of non-white groups and individuals to identify with the label black ('I'm not black, I'm Pakistani!') significantly undermined the unifying potential of political blackness, as did the inability of others to use the term in an inclusive manner ('You're not black, you're Pakistani!'). For many of the older generations of settlers to the UK the term black was associated with all of the negative aspects of colour-based racism. This was particularly marked by the unwillingness of many Asians to be represented in this way; the use of the term black was more likely to be regarded as an insult rather than as a marker of political solidarity. As Tariq Modood has argued, many Asians were alienated further by the tendency of black anti-racist politics to become entwined with a sense of an African diasporic ethnic identity (1997: 159). The privileging of an Afro-Caribbean perspective within much anti-racist politics of the 1970s and 1980s undoubtedly served to disenfranchise the Asian voice within black politics. As Stuart Hall has written (1991: 56): 'The truth is that in relation to certain things, the question of Black, in Britain, [also] has its silences. It had a certain way of silencing the very specific experiences of Asian people.'

For people from an Afro-Caribbean background the mobilization of 'political' blackness was able to function as both a political and cultural focus, but simultaneously this created a vacuum for Asians who seemingly had only one facet of black identity subscribed to them: an exclusively political one. Tariq Modood and others have argued (Modood 1990 and 1994) that Asians were sold short by political blackness because of the way the term privileged the experiences and needs of people from an Afro-Caribbean background. Asian concerns were seemingly sidelined by the political usage of black, in a hierarchy where the significance of Asian culture was rendered invisible: 'while mobilisation to secure rights requires a dynamic of group pride, "black" serves to obscure Asian identities and smother the basis of ethnic pride' (Modood 1994: 869). According to Modood, the question of racism cannot be addressed without recognizing the important role that specific cultural stereotypes play in the expression of a range of racist behaviours and practices. He has argued that racism towards Asian people exhibits an explicitly culturalist agenda which is often overlooked by the more generalized language of political blackness:

> An emphasis on discrimination against 'black' people systematically obscures the cultural antipathy to Asians (and, no doubt, others), how Asian cultures and

> religions have been racialised, and the elements of discrimination that Asians (and others) suffer. (Ibid.: 865)

These weaknesses displayed within the discourse of black anti-racist politics have encouraged many to seek out more particular modes of cultural strength and unity. The retreat towards more specific sites of ethnicity such as that denoted by 'Asian', does not, however, guarantee the emergence of more democratic politics of identity, but may exhibit many of the problems associated with political blackness; and these 'new' categories bring with them their own silences.

Tariq Modood talks of the need for 'we Asians' to develop and articulate an 'authentic public identity' in order to ensure a more balanced cultural-political agenda (1988: 401); but who exactly are 'we Asians' and what exactly is an 'authentic' public identity? In order to address these questions we need to look at the variety of discrete identities claimed by the category of Asian and also to consider the ways in which a sense of ethnicity is mediated and transformed by the experiences of migration and settlement in a multi-ethnic environment.

Who are 'we Asians'?

The desire to assert an 'authentic' Asian identity in contemporary Britain is fraught with a number of significant problems. The diverse composition of the UK's Asian population is such that it is hard to identity a common source of unity. As I have already stated, Asian settlers in Britain, while broadly sharing a common source of origin (that is, the Indian subcontinent), display a complicated array of regional, linguistic and religious affiliations. These differences mean that any attempt to construct an all-embracing and authentic sense of Asian identity, often expressed via the language of 'community' is somewhat flawed and fails to serve adequately the individuals it seeks to embrace (Anwar 1979; Modood 1994). Furthermore, the syncretic processes at work in a multi-ethnic environment are such that, for younger generations of Asians in Britain, the essence and meaning of Asianness is open to the forces of change and negotiation.

The application of a common sense of Asian identity inevitably has the potential to create its own silences, since there is little to unite Asians as a cohesive whole other that what is perceived as their common origins. Peter Jackson has talked of the 'myth' of Asian identity as a concept that has its roots in the perceptions of the UK's mainly white 'host' society, which is unable to recognize the diversity of Asian experiences:

> There is no uniform Asian life-style or culture ... Differences of nationality, religion, language suggest that the only thing Asian people have is common is being regarded as members of a single ethnic group by the majority society. (1989: 147)

Indeed, this is a key factor in Modood's argument (1997) for claiming an Asian identity that is distinct from a sense of blackness; he claims that racism towards Asians exhibits a particularly 'culturalist' slant which differs from other forms of racism experienced, say, by people of Afro-Caribbean origin. This has a number of worrying implications, not least that the more easily 'socially assimilated' (1997: 164) Afro-Caribbean population would appear to exhibit a relative lack of cultural identity that could be subjected to particular forms of cultural racism. Modood asserts that Asians suffer specific forms of discrimination arising from their religious practices, ways of dressing and speech, suggesting that these forms are particular to the Asian experience of racism. This would seem to ignore that similar forms of discrimination are also experienced by Afro-Caribbeans (and others); wearing hair in dreadlocks and talking in Jamaican patois is as likely to draw out cultural racism as dressing in a sari and speaking with a Punjabi accent. There are many ways of expressing and experiencing racism which focus on particular cultural specifities, but all are nearly always predicated by the primary indicator of skin colour, since the essence of any racist discourse is the linking of biology to behaviour or, in this case, colour to culture (Barker 1981; Miles 1989).

Modood suggests that an authentic public Asian identity should focus on what he perceives to be the more positive elements of Asian culture in Britain:

> An identity which can earn us the respect due to us in British society by virtue of the hard work and disciplined commitment that we or our parents have made in establishing ourselves in this country, and by virtue of our growing contribution in the many areas of commerce, law, medicine, science, technology and so on. (1988: 403)

These positive attributes of Asian success, based on notions of hard work, studious behaviour and self-discipline, are in themselves stereotypes that do little to challenge or displace the expression of culturalist forms of racism. By focusing on a range of essentially conservative values Modood is reinscribing a range of stereotypes of 'success' (themselves a source of much bitterness and attack by racists) associated with the Asian 'community' and, in doing so, he creates his own silences; sportspeople, writers, film-makers and musicians are all noted by their absence.

The 'celebration' of the ex-boxer Frank Bruno as a 'Great Briton' is cited by Modood (1997: 163) as an example of the assimilation and acceptance of Afro-Caribbean people by white society that is apparently not open to Asians; and yet what are we then to make of the success of Nasser Hussain – who is seen as the embodiment of the 'Bulldog spirit' – as the former captain of the England cricket team? Modood also ignores the success of writers and performers such as Hanif Kureishi, Meera Syal and Jimi Mistry, all of whom represent a generation of young Asians who do not adhere to the stereotypes expressed by either racists or critics such as Modood and who assert their own cultural and political agendas. There is also a notable absence of recognition for the vibrant and exciting musical developments being created by young Asians that are transforming not just Asian culture but British culture too (Back 1996; Mishra 1996). In fact it seems ironic that, despite all his assertions to the contrary, there is precious little 'culture' in Modood's aspirant 'authentic' public identity.

The search for an authentic public identity which seeks to construct an absolute sense of Asian identity risks stumbling over many of the pitfalls that the articulation of 'political' blackness suffered from. Modood once criticized the expression of political blackness because it suggested a 'false essentialism' (1994: 467), and yet the authentic public identity that he suggests for Asians is flawed in these same terms. The tendency for Modood to equate cultural racism towards Asians with what he terms 'Islamaphobia' (1997: 155)[4] could be seen to collapse the category of Asian into one of Muslim. Such slippages serve to undermine Modood's project of creating an authentic public identity for Asians, since significant groups of people are silenced by this focus on British Muslims.

Perhaps, inevitably then, we are witnessing a further fractioning of the terminology of Asian into increasingly specific modes of ethno-cultural particularity. This is perhaps exemplified by the 'banning' by Sunrise Radio (a leading London 'ethnic minority' station) of the term 'Asian' from its news bulletins in response to the fallout from the September 11th bombings in America. According to the chief executive of Sunrise, Avtar Lit:

> In the wake of September 11th and also following the race riots last year we have had a lot of calls from Sikhs and Hindus worried that in many people's eyes the word Asian links them to events involving Muslims. Hindus and Sikhs feel that Muslims are bringing the Asian community into disrepute in Britain and do not want to be put in the same bracket as them. (Britten 2002: 14)

This desire by some Asians to distance themselves from Muslims appears partly to be a response to the Islamaphobia that Modood refers to, but it would be a mistake to think that racists equate all Asians with Muslims.[5] It is rather the case that anti-Muslim sentiments are a convenient tool with which to espouse racist views and behaviour. It is worrying then to read in *The Daily Telegraph* in November 2001 that a group of Sikhs and Hindus from London had engaged in talks with the right-wing British National Party (BNP) to counter the threat they perceived that Muslims were posing to society. This somewhat disturbing development reflects the dangers of seeking a more particular and exclusive definition of ethnic or cultural identity; such a discourse can lead ultimately to cultural chauvinism and separation.

The move away from Asian as a catch-all category, however, has apparently been encouraged by some Muslims[6] although, once again, it is debatable how useful such a label may be; the Muslim community itself is of course an extremely heterogeneous group – a fact that we need to bear in mind when considering the media statements of so-called 'community leaders' and bodies such as the unelected and unrepresentative 'Muslim Parliament' which was so vociferous during the crisis of the *fatwa* issued against Salman Rushdie following his controversial novel of 1988, *The Satanic Verses*.[7] The benefits of adopting more (seemingly) particular ethno-cultural public identities seem rather debatable since such language lends support to damaging discourses of absolute cultural difference and separation.

Realizing then that 'Asian' is a particularly troublesome and oft-contested term, nevertheless I have decided to make use of it for the purposes of this book. I do this partly because of, rather than despite, the tensions and contradictions associated with its use. As I have already stated, the construction and maintenance of cultural identity need to be considered as a *process*, not something that is fixed and absolute. No sense of identity is formed in a vacuum; how others view an individual – label an individual – is crucial to the development of a sense of self. The origins of this study arise out of the increasing recognition within the music industry and associated media of 'Asian bands' in Britain, and two of the first questions to arise were 'What exactly is an Asian band?' and 'What exactly does that mean?' So I have adopted Asian as an 'operational' term; its use in this book is partly because of its inclusiveness (that is, it refers to all people with origins in the Indian subcontinent); and partly because it offers an opportunity to tackle some of the problems and intricacies of living out a sense of ethnic identity in both private and public. My intention is not then to assert a definitive or authentic sense of Asian identity, but to interrogate and explore the possibilities of the term as it is lived out in a contemporary multi-ethnic setting.

Migration, mobility and diaspora

As I have already suggested, any attempt to reach an understanding of what it means to be Asian in Britain today needs to take into account the complex identities that are negotiated and mediated through migration and settlement. We need to recognize that these processes are dynamic and transformational, representing the emergence of new cultural and ethnic identities. The physical realities of migration and settlement into a new host society inevitably changes people's lifestyles and, as much research has shown, 'transplanted' communities are subject to processes of continual adaptation and change (Watson 1977). As George Lipsitz has suggested, the pragmatic realities of migration and settlement can have a profound effect on the self-image of the immigrants:

> Through self-active struggles for recognition and power they often realise that the act of immigration itself changes both the immigrants and their host countries, that ethnic and national identities are floating equilibria that are constantly being constructed, negotiated and changed. (1994: 121)

Arjun Appadurai (1991) states that the process of what he calls 'deterritorialization', which characterizes much of the contemporary landscape of international relations, has had a significant effect on how individuals and groups rationalize their sense of self and being. The processes of dislocation and resettlement that reflect the immigrant experience has an inevitable effect on cultural and ethnic identity and makes the expression of 'original' modes of identity hard to maintain (Gopinath 1995). According to Appadurai:

> The landscapes of group identity – the ethnoscapes – around the world are no longer familiar anthropological objects, insofar as groups are no longer tightly territorialised, spacially bounded, historically unselfconscious, or culturally homogenous. (1991: 191)

The migration and settlement of Asians into the UK during the post-war years is part of a long history of global migration from South Asia and this diaspora, which has spread throughout Africa, Europe and the Americas, provides us with a clear example of Appadurai's deterritorialization in action. It is important to recognize that the existence of an Asian population in the UK does not simply represent the relocation of South Asian identities into a new setting, but is part of a complex diasporic and global network. The advent and expansion of advanced communications technologies such as satellite television, international phone networks and the Internet, combined with the relative ease of global travel facilitated by increasingly affordable flights has resulted in the compression of space and time which has a profound effect on the development of diasporic identities (Hall and DuGay 1996; Giddens 1991). No longer are groups and individuals geographically isolated, they are in fact able to retain links not only to their point of origin but also to other nodes within the global diaspora. Asians living in the UK do not exist as an isolated pocket but have access to a diasporic consciousness that has spread throughout the world.

The importance of this Asian diaspora has often been undervalued in the past, particularly when contrasted with work focusing on the Black/African diaspora as cited by Paul Gilroy in his thesis on the 'Black Atlantic' (1993b). Gilroy makes a convincing case for the importance of the Black/African diaspora on the development of modern Western culture, but in doing so fails to acknowledge the importance or even existence of an Asian diaspora, even going so far as to reduce contemporary Asian musical developments as mere adjuncts of black culture.[8] Despite Gilroy's overall intention to reject notions of ethnic absolutism with regard to black culture, his inability to recognize the importance of the Asian diaspora (which has, of course, intersected with the black diaspora in Africa, the Caribbean and in the UK) leaves him vulnerable to criticisms of Afrocentrism (Chrisman 1997). As others have suggested (Back 1996; Gopinath 1995), the coming together of elements of Asian and African diasporas in the UK represents an important intersection in the creation and development of new syncretic identities, rather than the subordination of the former by the latter. With regard to the formation of new syncretic musical forms Les Back has written:

> This process takes on further transnational nuances when South Asian lexical and cultural elements are introduced into these syncretic processes. The modes of expression that are produced possess a kind of triple consciousness that is simultaneously the child of Africa, Asia and Europe. (1996: 185)

The dynamics of migration and diaspora are essential in illuminating our understanding of the processes of identity construction and maintenance in the contemporary setting of post-war Britain. The desire to preserve the cultural identity of the homeland, particularly for first-generation settlers, is extremely strong and can result in the construction of rigid and idealized notions of cultural belonging and identity. As Vijay Mishra has noted (1996), these idealized notions of 'home' are often far removed from the realities of the point of origin and fail to take into account the changing environment of the 'homeland' itself, which continues to develop after the migrant has departed. The so-called 'myth of return' (Khan 1977; Anwar 1979) expressed by many first-generation settlers reflects the desire of migrants to retain a sense of continuity and belonging with the point of origin, but is fatally undermined by the inability of many migrants to recognize that the homeland remains 'pure' and unchanged only in their own minds. The contemporary realities of the homeland, transformed over time, can never match up to the 'diasporic imaginary' (Appadurai 1991) so that, as Stuart Hall has suggested, 'there is no returning home' (1991: 46), since home as it is remembered in the mind of the migrant no longer exists. The desire to retain an authentic sense of cultural identity that maintains links with a homeland is particularly acute in times of crisis and, in the context of the UK – where racism has been such a powerful factor in the life of black and Asian settlers – this has heralded a tendency for some to construct absolutist notions of ethnic and cultural identity. This defensive positioning is also encouraged by the pressures of assimilation; a discourse often allied with anti-immigration rhetoric and one which seeks to absorb and make invisible people from 'alien' cultures.

It is somewhat ironic that the need to assert an authentic ethno-cultural identity linked with the homeland may in itself result in the expression of similarly racist ideas, as Mishra has illustrated:

> To be able to preserve that loss, diasporas very often construct racist fictions of purity as a kind of jouissance, a joy, a pleasure around which anti-miscegenation narratives of homelands are constructed against the reality of the homelands themselves. (1996: 422)

This somewhat regressive rationalization of cultural heritage and identity is inherently problematic since it fails to accept or incorporate the processes of change and syncretism that lie at the heart of identity formation. The multi-accented and syncretic processes at work within any diaspora are such that the overarching significance of a pure place of origin in constructing a cohesive group identity becomes increasingly difficult to maintain. The expression of new and syncretic modes of identity, shaped by specific local conditions and fed back through diasporic networks, are able to 'displace[s] the "home" country from its privileged position as originary site and redeploy[s] it as but one of many diasporic locations' (Gopinath 1995: 304). Any attempt to construct a meaningful category of 'Asian' based on a sense of common origin is extremely problematic not only because of the diversity of identities and allegiances present at the 'source', but also because it fails to take into account the significance of transformative and syncretic processes of identity formation engendered by migratory practices and diaspora.

Although some have responded to the experience of migration by attempting to construct a defensive and restrictive model of Asian identity, others – particularly younger generations of British-born Asians – have sought to articulate a more dynamic and productive sense of cultural identity. As already stated, processes of migration and settlement have a profound effect on the intricacies of self-identification experienced by settlers, but it is also important to recognize the significant impact that these processes have on the host society. As George Lipsitz has stated:

> Once immigrants from the Indian sub-continent or the Caribbean arrive in the UK, they transform the nature of British society and culture in many ways, changing the nature of the 'inside' into which newer immigrants are expected to assimilate. (1994: 126)

What takes place during this process is not simply a struggle where individuals fight to retain an authentic and original sense of ethnicity, or else fall victim to the evils of assimilation and cultural subordination; but rather the negotiation of a number of cultural inputs which are incorporated and interlinked to form new modes of identity and being. As Stuart Hall has said, ethnicity is not 'once and for all' (1990: 226), and the experiences of migration and settlement seem to point to a more open and flexible understanding of identity. Negotiating between the culture of the homeland and that of the host society need not represent a gladiatorial conflict in which only one side conquers, as reflected by Khan's observation (1977: 82) of Pakistani migrants settled in Bradford during the 1970s: 'It is not an either/or situation, individuals vary in ability and desire to manipulate two different cultural traditions.'

For the subsequent younger generations of settlers the processes of negotiation and cross-cultural exchange are inevitably enhanced by the particular dynamics of a multi-ethnic environment. The expression of diverse and complex identities by young Asians living in Britain is based on an ability to absorb and process a complicated array of cultural resources that can be seen to challenge totalizing discourses of self-identification. This ability is not limited to any specific group or country however; it is representative of the shifting realities of the contemporary world in late modernity:

> Throughout the world today, immigrants reject binary oppositions that force them either to give up their cultural identities completely or that force them to cling to them eternally, with no opportunity for transformation or change. (Lipsitz 1994: 120)

This rejection of totalizing binary oppositions reflects the dynamism of identity formation which is constructed as an ongoing process, one that is constantly analysing and incorporating a range of cultural inputs and influences. If we are to reach a useful understanding of what it means to be Asian in Britain today we need to recognize these processes at work, rather than adopting absolutist positions of ethnic particularity which are unable to come to terms with the shifting terrain of a multi-ethnic environment.

Is the actor happy? Negotiating art and ethnicity

As I have already suggested, the development of new modes of syncretic identity is particularly present in the experiences and expressions of younger generations of black and Asian people, many of whom were born and raised in the UK. For these young people the cultural arena of the arts – of music, film and literature – has been an important site of self-expression that has produced an exciting array of new creative forms and practices. The area of art and culture is significant not merely as a site where pre-existing identities are displayed but where new modes of self and being are contested and negotiated. As George Lipsitz has stated (1994: 137): 'Culture enables people to rehearse identities, stances, and social relations not yet permissible in politics ... popular culture does not just reflect reality it helps constitute it.'

The production and performance of musical styles and genres plays a central role in the development of cultural and social life, and the focus of this study is partially a reflection of this. The expression of new musical forms and new modes of cultural identity goes hand in hand since both are experienced as a *process*, and illustrates the importance of the dynamic and syncretic in the construction of self. The complex expressions of self reflected through music production and performance enables us to recognize the combined importance of elements of continuity and change in the development of cultural identities. As Paul Gilroy has suggested:

> Music and its rituals can be used to create a model whereby identity can be understood neither as fixed essence nor as vague and utterly contingent construction to be reinvented by the will of aesthetes, symbolists and language gamers. (1992b: 102)

The recent emergence of a number of often high-profile Asian musicians and bands onto the British music scene provides us with an ideal case-study through which we can interrogate and analyse the processes of cross-cultural change and the emergence of new, syncretic modes of identity. It is clear that, as part of an emerging phenomenon, these artists have to negotiate and balance a number of complex influences and allegiances. Not only are they bringing forward new artistic concepts and expressions through their music, but they are also picking their way through the complicated discourses of ethnic, national and individual identity.

Stuart Hall has suggested that artists have to function simultaneously on two fronts: both as expressive artists and as representatives of 'community' (1988: 253). As Julien and Mercer have highlighted in their work on black film, artists from ethnic minorities find that each cultural text is burdened with the added pressure to somehow be representative of a black constituency (1996: 453). As we shall see in the case of the musicians in this book, their music is similarly laden with the burden of Asian representation, with individuals expected to act as role models for some imagined community. This creates extra pressures for the artists in question since their work is often regarded as the expression of the social group rather than that of the indivudual. The idea of an absolute notion of Asianness, in this way, can have a stifling effect on the output of artists since:

> Individual subjectivity is denied because the black subject is positioned as a mouthpiece, a ventriloquist for an entire social category which is seen to be 'typified' by its representative. Acknowledgment of the diversity of black experiences and subject positions is thereby foreclosed. (Julien and Mercer 1996: 454)

This burden of representation is one which is foisted upon the individuals concerned whether they like it or not, and the musicians in this book have had to negotiate particular strategies to manoeuvre between private and public modes of identity and self. The positioning of these individuals in a highly public sphere where they are subject to competing discourses of authenticity and belonging means that an extremely flexible and contextualized subjectivity needs to be adopted. According to George Lipsitz:

> Unable to experience either simple assimilation or complete separation from dominant groups, ethnic cultures accustom themselves to a bifocality reflective of both the ways they view themselves and the way they are viewed by others. (1990: 135)

The position that provides the focus of this study presents us with clear examples of the processes of syncretism and cross-cultural dialogue, and the very nature of the subjects' artistic endeavours means that they have had to do their 'growing up' very much in public. The new modes of identity created and performed by these individuals are subject to much public scrutiny and necessitate a highly reflexive and dynamic negotiation of cultural inputs which sheds new light on the development of *all* our multi-ethnic futures.

Conclusion: new ethnicities, new identities

There can be no escaping the growing reality of cultural syncretism in contemporary British society, and the musical expression considered within this study is just one of many of the fruits borne by the collision and intermingling of different cultural histories and allegiances. These emergent forms and practices – which represent much of the positive potential of a multi-ethnic setting – should be regarded as a celebration of a dynamic society in transition and can be drawn upon to resist any attempt to retreat into entrenched positions of fixed and unchanging ethnic particularity. I have no desire to romanticize contemporary life in multi-ethnic Britain; racism and ethnic tensions still exact a heavy price on those who feel the brunt of discrimination on a regular basis. Racism and inequality need to be challenged constantly, but in a way that asserts the moral strengths of inclusive anti-racist politics rather than falling back on rigid constructions of ethnic particularity.

An anti-racist 'community' politics such as that suggested by Modood – one that promotes the notion of a fixed and absolute sense of Asian identity – is likely to fail because it does not recognize the full diversity of experiences and positions of the subjects it wishes to serve. We must not forget that the propagation of such a 'fallacy of homogeneity' (Stanfield and Dennis 1993: 19) has historically been such a key part of racist thought and action. Discourses of cultural insiderism and ethnic exclusivity can never hope to liberate the people that they claim to serve because, not only do they fail to acknowledge diversity and difference, but they also risk slipping into dangerously racialized language. Paul Gilroy notes:

> A commitment to the mystique of cultural insiderism and the myths of cultural homogeneity is alive not just amongst the Brit-nationalist and racist but among the anti-racists who strive to answer them. (1993b: 101)

A more flexible and open understanding of ethnicity and identity gives individuals more room to manoeuvre and express themselves in a celebratory way, while simultaneously challenging biological notions of ethno-cultural belonging. As George Lipsitz has commented:

> To think of identities as interchangeable or infinitely open does violence to the historical and social constraints imposed on us by structures of exploitation and privilege. But to posit innate and immobile identities for ourselves or others confuses history for nature; and denies the possibility of change. (1994: 62)

Sadly, the move away from the assertion of political blackness has done little to ensure that individual Asians are represented by a more consensual definition of what is intended to be an authentic public identity. The attempt to assert a more particular mode of Asian identity fails because it seeks to assert rigid and absolute 'rules' of belonging which are both inappropriate and inadequate for those young people whose lives are marked by the realities of intercultural dialogue and exchange. The inability of discourse on ethnic particularity to recognize and include these dynamic processes has potentially grave consequences not just within minority communities, but also affects the way in which contemporary society itself functions. Novelist Hanif Kureishi, who has provided many an illustration of syncretism and social change, has written of this need to recognize and embrace these processes as an integral part of all our futures:

> British isn't what it was. Now there is a more complex thing, involving new elements. So there must be a fresh way of seeing Britain and the choices it faces: and a new way of being British after all of this time ... This decision is not about a small group of irrelevant people who can be contemptuously described as 'minorities'. It is about the direction of British society. (1986: 38)

The contemporary realities of intercultural exchange and syncretism means that the old certainties of ethnic belonging are being undermined and eroded as young generations of Britons emerge having known nothing but a multi-ethnic environment. In such an environment it becomes increasingly difficult for, and unreasonable to expect, individuals to assert an identity which claims total allegiance to any kind of absolute essence. This necessarily does not make for an easy cultural politics, and we must not forget that this multi-ethnic society continues to be riven with inequalities justified via discourses of racial and ethnic difference. In his discussion of the Black diaspora Stuart Hall wrote:

> Third generation young Black men and women know that they come from the Caribbean, know that they are Black, know that they are British. They want to speak from all three identities. They are not prepared to give up any one of them ... This is not a politics which invites easy identification – it has a politics which is grounded on the complexity of identifications at work. (1991: 59)

These comments are equally true of Asians living in Britain today; they speak from a multi-accented centre of identity, one that resists the simplifications of ethnic particularity and exclusion. This would seem to suggest that, aside from the experience of racism, all black and Asian individuals share a common sense of multi-accented cultural identity which is grounded in the specific experiences of migration, settlement and diaspora. This does not mean the abandonment of inherited modes of cultural identity, but represents the ability of individuals and groups to develop and express new modes of identity while simultaneously reasserting and reinterpreting the links to their cultural past. Of course these processes are not restricted to the experiences of black or Asian people, but are part of the ongoing transformation of British life in general; and if we are to look to the future with any hope we need to be able to recognize the significant impact of syncretism on the cultural life of the entire nation.

Notes

1. This in itself is a contested and sometimes problematic term, the use of which I will discuss later in this chapter.
2. I am using this term to speak broadly of the so-called 'New Commonwealth' immigrants and their offspring in the post-war period (Solomos 1988); those who came to Britain from the old colonial dominions in the Caribbean and the Indian subcontinent. 'White' will be used to denote people whose (predominantly European) origins predate this origin, as well as referring – broadly speaking – to skin colour.
3. According to the 2001/02 census the size of the UK's 'minority ethnic population' was 4.5 million, or 7.6 per cent of the total population. Just over half of the total minority ethnic population were of Indian, Pakistani, Bangladeshi or other Asian origin.
4. Modood's almost exclusive focus on anti-Muslim sentiments (which have certainly grown in the wake of the September 11th bombings) seeks to obscure the arguably more prevalent expression of racism directed at Asians, based on stereotypes of dress, cuisine (that is curries), speech patterns and, of course, colour.
5. Gurmel Bolla, vice-president of a Sikh temple in Derby, reflects this:

   > I have been knocked off my bike by white people after the race riots and the attacks on America because people see Asians as one community, when Sikhs were not involved in either incident. If one group of people is causing trouble then others who are not involved should not have to take the blame as well. (Britten 2002)

   The implication that one group (that is Muslims) should take the blame for the actions of a number of individuals is rather disturbing here.
6. Iqbal Sacranie of the Muslim Council of Britain supported the move by saying 'It will give a clear recognition of how communities are identified, which is about faith' (Britten 2002).
7. The undemocratic and sometimes authoritarian nature of the Muslim Parliament ultimately led to its decline and the body folded in 1998 (Siddiqi 2000).
8. In his book *The Black Atlantic* Gilroy dismisses the importance of emergent Asian music cultures in a single, short passage:

   > In re-inventing their own ethnicity, some of Britain's Asian settlers have also borrowed the sound system culture of the Caribbean and the soul and hip-hop styles of black America, as well as techniques like mixing, scratching, and sampling as part of their invention of a new mode of cultural expression and identity to match. (1993b)

Chapter 3

Music, culture and identity

In the previous chapter I examined the importance of the ethnic resource in the lives of black and Asian people in the context of multi-ethnic Britain. I have suggested that the processes of identity negotiation and syncretism are particularly pronounced in the lives of creative artists; in this chapter I will specifically focus on the realm of music. Music, as a mode of cultural expression, is one of the most important and immediate outlets of human social activity. Although music arouses a sensual pleasure on the part of both listener and performer, it is also a means of cultural dialogue; a medium through which issues of politics and identity can be articulated and developed.

The contemporary cultural landscape of Britain in the late 20th and early 21st centuries has been shaped significantly by the syncretic processes at work in the production and performance of new forms of popular music. These forms not only represent the spontaneous arrival of novel sounds, but also reflect the emergence of new modes of cultural identity and allegiance. Popular music then should not be marginalized because of its 'frivolous' entertainment value (Adorno 1991; Strinati 1995); neither should it be considered outside wider debates on identity and belonging. In fact music is central to these issues since it provides a channel where identities can be asserted, consolidated and negotiated. In this way popular music can be used to challenge and deconstruct rigid notions of ethnic particularity that are propagated by both black separatists and white racists. As I have stated, the purpose of studying a range of Asian bands is not to cement all these groups together to form some definitive understanding of an authentic Asian identity, but to show the diversity of their experiences and aspirations. What I hope to show is that, while 'traditional' modes of ethnicity are often important resources in daily lives, they are supplemented and transformed by processes of cross-cultural exchange and syncretism. Music, much like identity, is best understood as an ongoing process, whereby existing identities are not only expressed and re-inscribed but also transformed and made anew.

This chapter will examine and re-evaluate a number of existing theories of music and identity in order to uncover the transformative processes at work in this particular realm of cultural activity. I shall begin by considering ideas that emerged from the Centre for Contemporary Cultural Studies (CCCS) at the University of Birmingham in the 1970s and 1980s. The importance given to the creative potential of musical expression by the CCCS is significant but not without its deficiencies; I will also consider more recent studies within this tradition which offer a more flexible approach towards identity and music.

Second, the relationship between music and community will be focused on in order to examine the relationship between tradition and novel forms of cultural expression. The immediacy and vitality of musical forms is such that they provide us with an ideal model through which we can examine the development of syncretic identities in a contemporary multi-ethnic setting. Third, recent debates surrounding authenticity and ownership of particular musical forms will be examined, with particular emphasis on the tension between the often politicized readings of non-white musical forms on the one hand and narratives of intercultural exchange and syncretism on the other. Finally, I shall consider the importance of the highly commercialized international music industry as the specific context within which the subjects of this book, and indeed all musicians, have to function. Emergent cultural identities expressed through music, at some time or other, have to come to terms with the marketplace which, as we will see, can frustrate and constrain the expression of new cultural sensibilities. Although the marketplace can be used to disseminate new forms of ethnic and cultural identity, it is also where stereotypes and novelty abound, representing a site of struggle and negotiation.

Music and subculture: style, authenticity and resistance

The development of subcultural theory at the University of Birmingham's Centre for Contemporary Cultural Studies (CCCS) is a useful place to start when re-evaluating the role assigned to music in the creation and maintenance of youthful identities. The work of the CCCS is significant insomuch as it recognizes the creative potential of youthful music-making and performance in the formation and maintenance of group identities (Hall and Jefferson 1976; Hebdige 1979). Despite the progressive nature of much of the work done by the CCCS, some of the assumptions established within this tradition are somewhat problematic. Music is generally perceived by early subcultural theorists as one of several contributory elements in the construction of youth subcultures. I would argue that the importance of music is somewhat de-emphasized and undervalued in favour of an elevated, almost obsessive, fascination with the concept of 'style' (Cohen 1972; Hebdige 1979). Phil Cohen, one of the originators of subcultural theory, identifies music as one of four contributory 'modes for the generation of subcultural style', the others being dress, ritual and argot (1972: 54). The fundamental and central importance of music as the major stimulus for the development of subcultural identities is sidelined in favour of the notion of style. In fact it is music that gives these subcultural groups the initial stimulus for ways of dressing, acting and speaking; indeed style emerges from and is promoted through music. Music and musicians provide the raw materials for the creation and maintenance of subcultural identities; they represent both the origins and the development of subculture style – a point recognized by David Muggleton (2000:

69) who comments that 'the interest in a particular music is *primary*, preceding and leading to a related subcultural affiliation.'

The vitally expressive nature of musical performance and production is such that the modes of dress, ritual and argot are deeply rooted in and influenced by the innovations of musicians, songwriters and producers. Instead, many subcultural theorists preferred to focus on the more 'stylistic' elements of youth culture, such as fashion and dance which could be interpreted as symbolic expressions of cultural 'resistance'; the meanings of which were decoded and inscribed with meaning by self-appointed 'experts' on the outside (Clark 1981: 87). As Muggleton has written (2000: 13): 'Style is read as text, and only the semiotician is entrusted to crack the code. There is, in other words, an academic "elitism" implicit in this method.'

The undervaluing of music within the work of the CCCS is reflected further by the exclusive focus on young people as consumers, rather than producers, of popular music. Musicians themselves are not considered to any degree; they are portrayed almost as if they exist *outside* the groups that they inspire and, in part, represent. Members of bands are also members of subcultural groups and, as such, are often the originators of particular styles and identities, since the medium through which they work is so expressive. This is not to suggest that music fans are not creatively involved in the construction and maintenance of subcultural identities – on the contrary, they are essential to these processes; but it is significant that they often work with the raw materials supplied by innovative musicians. Furthermore, the separation of musician and fan is misleading, we need to accept that musicians are fans of other bands and that fans often become musicians themselves.[1]

Bands such as The Who during the 1960s and The Sex Pistols during the 1970s illustrate the central role that music and musicians have played in the development of two of the archetypes of subcultural style: mod and punk respectively.[2] The musicians in these bands not only provide a springboard for the establishment of subcultural styles but also continue to develop these over time. This reflects another of the shortcomings of subcultural theory, which often ignores the dynamic nature of youth cultures – instead presenting a picture of discrete and inflexible groups. As Gary Clark has noted (1981: 82), these groups are portrayed as 'static and rigid anthropological entities where in fact such reified and pure subcultures exist only at the Centre's [CCCS] level of abstraction.'

The constantly shifting character of subcultural identities is such that it is extremely difficult to assert any sense of uniformity within any given group. We need to consider the way that identities are sustained and transformed over time; processes that blur any attempt to construct definitive subcultural groupings. As David Muggleton has suggested (1995: 18): 'Tendencies towards diffusion, diversification and fragmentation have always been intrinsic to subcultural development.' He also suggests that the fragmentary and multi-accented nature of youthful subcultural activity is such that what he calls the 'sociological concept' of subcultures is becoming increasingly obsolete (Ibid.: 7)

This tendency to set up the notion of fixed and rigid subcultural categories is partly the result of a certain fascination with the idea of the 'authentic' in youth culture. In his influential text *Subculture: The Meaning of Style* (1979: 84) Dick Hebdige focuses on authenticity to such an extent that he not only divides members of subcultural groups into 'originals' and 'hangers-on' but also identifies and privileges what he calls the 'subcultural moment'. This would seem to limit the syncretic and dynamic processes at work and, as Gary Clark has commented:

> The Centre's [CCCS] paradigm of examining the 'authentic' subcultures in a synthetic moment of frozen historical time ... results in an essentialist and non-contradictory picture ... the descriptions of the processes by which they are sustained, transformed, and interwoven are absent. (1981: 83)

The construction of subcultural groups as discrete and static entities is further compounded in the work of the CCCS by the adoption of a somewhat rigidly Marxist framework which privileges class over all other constituent elements of cultural identity. This manifests itself in the fact that, almost without exception, all of the subcultural groups examined are identified as 'authentic' working-class arbiters of 'resistance'. Apart from simplifying the complexity of youthful expressions of cultural identity, this focus inevitably ignores and silences the experience of other important modes of self. First, a distinction is drawn between members of subcultures and the 'mainstream'; the former are defined by their active and authentic resistance and the latter as passive and manipulated. Not only does this privilege the role of authentic working-class males (women are notably absent in much subcultural theory), it also denies the ability of 'straights' (members of mainstream society) to contribute meaningfully to the development of cultural production and expression. According to James Lull:

> The contrast of the social impact of mainstream culture and subculture, of mainstream media and alternative media, should not be drawn too sharply. Most audiences have been influenced by both. (1987: 25)

It is often very difficult to mark out a clear boundary between mainstream and alternative cultural forms and practices and, as we shall see when examining the distinction between independent and major record labels, this is representative of a much more complicated model of syncretic cultural development and change.

There are other areas of silence that result from the class-based focus of much subcultural theory. As I have already mentioned, women are effectively sidelined, as are middle-class youth movements (such as hippies) and – most significantly in terms of this study – the experiences of black and Asian youth is marginalized. This is not to say that black cultures are absent from the work of the CCCS but, where they are present, they are afforded little attention in themselves. For someone like Dick Hebdige black culture is a vital element of the development of subcultural style. Elements of black, Afro-Caribbean[3] cultures are readily acknowledged, but their significance is only granted as an *influence* on white, working-class subcultures. The simplified notion of black culture in this way ignores the significance of black cultural styles in their own right and hence the processes of syncretism at work there; and also fails to analyse the influence and confluence of black culture on straight or mainstream society. Interestingly, the significance that Hebdige acknowledges in relation to the 'influence' of black culture is largely based around musical styles whose significant role seemed to be simply to stimulate and develop white, working-class subcultures.

All the failings of subcultural theory that I have briefly highlighted above are compounded by the lack of empirical data. With a few notable exceptions (such as Paul Willis's *Profane Culture*, 1977) all the writings that initially came out of the CCCS were theoretical exercises based on largely secondary or anecdotal observations.[4] Subsequent research – that which draws significantly upon the actual views and experiences of the 'subculturalists' themselves – has revealed that such groups are less well defined than suggested by the work of the CCCS. Furthermore, those often perceived by outsiders as belonging to particular subcultural groups reject being labelled in such terms and have a much more ambiguous relationship towards group allegiance and identity (Muggleton 1995 and 2000; Thornton 1995). Indeed, a sense of individuality forms an essential part of subcultural identity, as Muggleton's exemplary research has highlighted:

> Group identifications are [therefore] resisted because they carry connotations of collective conformity, suggesting a concomitant loss of individuality that renders their members inauthentic. (2000: 78)

In order to move on from 'traditional' subcultural theory we need to develop a more flexible and less deterministic way of looking at the construction of youthful identities in the contemporary world. This new perspective needs to recognize the combined importance of factors such as gender, sexuality and ethnicity and not seek to shape manifestations of youth culture to fit any predefined ideological positions. The development of more in-depth and flexible studies on manifestations of youth culture and music has begun to establish a much more complex way of examining processes of identity formation and transformation in the lives of young people in contemporary settings (Gilroy 1993b; Thornton 1995; Back 1996; Muggleton 2000). These studies have recognized the sheer range of complex factors and interactions that impact on the transient and sometimes contradictory manifestations of identity that emerge from dynamic and ever-changing music cultures. It is apparent that in our contemporary world it has become increasingly difficult to categorize young people in terms of neatly defined, distinct subcultural groups, such is the diversity of influences and identities at play; we need to recognize the multi-accented and shifting character of youthful identities, as Muggleton has suggested (2000: 128): 'individuality, mobility and diversity are central characteristics upon which any adequate explanation of subcultures must be founded.' Bearing this in mind, we need not only to pay careful attention to the actual views and experiences of individual subjects, but also to recognize that a medium such as music reflects the negotiation and transformation of old and new identities – not as a mere adjunct to discrete group allegiances based around rigid notions of style and resistance. As we shall see in considering the artistic lives of the musicians in this study, processes of identity formation and maintenance cannot easily be filed away into such discretely bound categories.

Music, identity and community

The bands examined in this study represent the marriage of two vital processes in the expression and development of cultural identities. First, these bands, to a certain degree, can be seen to represent and reflect cultural backgrounds from which the musicians originate. As I have already stated, music is a central part of cultural expression and reproduction, and Paul Theberge's definition of musical groups as 'images of community' (1989: 99) is useful in this respect. In the context of the experiences of post-war black and Asian settlers in the UK the importance of music as a means of cultural expression and the assertion of ethnic identity became increasingly paramount. Given the disruptive nature of migration and settlement in a foreign land, particularly when compounded by processes of racism and discrimination which sought to isolate and marginalize non-white migrants, the role of music as a means of positive self-expression was vital as a tool of survival. Paul Gilroy (1993a: 82) recognized that 'musical heritage gradually became an important factor in facilitating the transition of diverse settlers to a distinct mode of lived blackness.'

The existence of prejudice and often open hostility towards non-white settlers during the post-war period has often meant that music has become arguably one of the most important ways to express a positive sense of ethnic identity, as well as a means to raise a dissenting voice. Second, while recognizing the importance of music as a means of expressing a positive sense of self-identity and community, we must be careful not to portray music as a 'pure' reflection of a fixed and unchanging essence. As Martin Stokes has written (1994: 4): 'Music does not [then] simply provide a marker in a prestructured social space, but the means by which this space can be transformed.'

Music played by black people in the UK does not simply reflect some idealized notion of a pure and essential origin, it forms part of an ongoing dialogue which, while rooted in the experiences of the past, also makes sense of the present and begins to shape the future. The expression of cultural identities through music reveals the transformation of tradition and the emergence of new, multi-accented modes of being and becoming. Musical groups do not present us with an image of a fixed and unchanging community, but rather reflect the syncretic and dynamic manifestation of new ethnicities and identities. The music of the post-war settlers and their descendants expresses a range of identities that have maintained cultural allegiances to the past but have also continued to grow within the context of a multi-ethnic setting. The processes of intercultural dialogue and exchange that arise here are particularly important for younger generations of black people whose experiences are not restricted by the confines of some imaginary fixed community. As Simon Frith has rightly pointed out:

> ... identity is mobile, a process not a thing, a becoming not a being ... our experience of music-making and music-listening is best understood as an experience of this *self in process*. (1996: 109)

Although all of the bands featured in this study are frequently described as Asian, it is clear by listening to their music and lyrics that they do not present us with simple or reductive expressions of a pure or authentic Asian identity. The rumbling bass and Middle-Eastern instrumentation of Black Star Liner celebrate the goal-scoring prowess (for the 1995/6 season at least) of Leeds United football club's Ghanaian striker Tony Yeboah,[5] Cornershop evoke memories forged *In the days of Ford Cortina*, a single released on 'curry-coloured vinyl' (see Figure 3.1)[6] and Fun^Da^Mental sample (among others) the speeches of Louis Farrakhan, the thuggish threats of Combat 18[7] and the home-spun philosophies of Alan Clark.[8] All of these bands are rooted (by varying degrees) to certain aspects of their Asian cultural heritage, but they also speak from and to national and international metropolitan constituencies, making a nonsense of any attempt to define or assert a unifying sense of Asianness. This process is developed further by the fact that none of the bands I have mentioned is 100 per cent Asian; all of them include and work with musicians from a variety of ethnic and cultural backgrounds.

What we are witnessing in bands like these are the dynamic workings of identity construction and reconstruction through music that reflects the continuing transformation of British cultural life. The syncretic processes at work in the production and performance of such contemporary music helps us to understand the shifting nature of multi-ethnic society in a way that challenges discourses of cultural exclusivity and offers us a vision of the future that is full of vibrancy and vitality.

Exotic politics? Essentialism vs syncretism

Despite the syncretic processes at work in music, many musicians and social commentators have attempted to claim music as an unproblematic marker of

Fig. 3.1 The cover artwork for Cornershop's *In the days of Ford Cortina*

essentialism and difference. This is often partly a defensive reaction on the part of non-white minority groups, grounded in the bitter experiences of prejudice and racism (Solomos 1988; Miles 1989). The assertion of a positive sense of ethnic identity is extremely important in these circumstances, but is undermined when expressed as an assertion of essentialism and cultural separatism. Although certain musical forms can be seen to have strong elements of origin in particular groups, the desire to claim ownership and somehow keep these forms pure ignores the processes of intercultural exchange and syncretism that drive the creativity at the heart of music-making of any kind. Music is best understood as an open-ended and ongoing dialogue, and we can no longer talk of pure or original sources in a world where music-making is driven by the aesthetics of the syncretic and the crossover (Hall 1991; Lipsitz 1994).

Despite the self-evident dynamism and reflexivity of contemporary music there are those who have attempted to lay claim to the ownership of particular musical forms and styles (Swedenberg 1989; Allinson 1994). The desire to assert a sense of ownership over a particular musical form works on two fronts; it not only claims the music as the authentic property of one group, but it also excludes and discredits the involvement of 'others', whether they be producers or consumers of any particular genre. This means that a commentator such as Ewan Allinson can make the claim that rap music is an exclusively black art form and that it is impossible for whites to either contribute to or make sense of the genre. In his own words (1994: 44), rap music 'Serves to deny whites on a very obvious level ... Not only the content, but the delivery itself is foreign to non-whites.'

This essentialist (but not uncommon) reading of the genre not only serves to ignore the influence of other non-white groups – the significance of Latino rap for instance is overlooked[9] – but also fails to take into account the importance of 'white' influences like European 'electro-pop' (in particular the highly influential impact of the German band Kraftwerk) and rock music (Rose 1994). It is ironic that a musical form that is characterized by its ability to absorb and reinterpret a range of cultural sources can also be used to assert essentialist notions of cultural exclusivity. The constantly transformative and dynamic processes at work in the construction of both musical forms and ethno-cultural modes of identity is such that it becomes increasingly difficult to hold on to notions of absolute cultural identity. As George Lipsitz (1994: 124) has commented, 'Music is nothing but dialogic, the product of an ongoing historical conversation in which no-one has the first or last word.' Attempts to deny the importance of this dialogue, which seek to define music as an essence rather than a process, become isolated with the need to defend cultural forms that have been frozen in an imaginary pure location. In this way the widespread influence of black musical forms and genres is not celebrated but frowned upon, which has led US film-maker Spike Lee to lament 'It's a shame that the more we progress as a people, the more diluted the music gets' (Gilroy 1993a: 96).

This view is understandable perhaps when we consider the long history of the subverting of black musical forms in the recent history of popular music in the West. The 'whitening' down of rock and roll is well documented of course, whereby 'safe' white stars (such as Pat Boone and Tab Hunter) were promoted by the major record labels in the USA in order to present a more favourable alternative to the actual, often black, innovators (such as Little Richard and Chuck Berry) who were viewed, for a number of reasons (race being paramount) by corporate America as an undesirable influence on the nation's (white) youth. More recently rap music has witnessed a similar crisis with the short-lived but phenomenal success of white rappers such as Vanilla Ice, who presented a global audience with a somewhat sanitized simulacrum of the genre.[10] Of course some would argue that black artists (for example MC Hammer) have played a sizeable role in this process of 'dilution'. While there is undoubtedly some cause for concern when considering the effect of corporate marketing strategies (more of which later) we must not overstate the extent of this problem. The stadium rap of MC Hammer may well have garnered much attention (and riches), but this has coincided with the long-term success of uncompromising and hardcore rap acts such as Public Enemy, who are seldom described as diluted and, incidentally, have made use of the directing skills of a certain Spike Lee. One of the important elements in the success of Public Enemy has been their cultivation of a diverse audience that cuts across ethnic and musical boundaries, as illustrated by their highly successful tours with heavy metal band Anthrax in the USA.[11]

Interestingly, black musicians working within 'white' genres such as rock and metal have been frowned upon by the cultural essentialists, since they do not conform to a fixed and essential definition of blackness. As Michael Odell has highlighted, UK bands as diverse as Dub War, Audioweb and Skunk Anansie have all told of the pressure to conform to restrictive stereotypes of what black music is supposed to be, but choose to ignore this in favour of playing and producing musical styles that celebrate the diversity of their experiences and influences (Odell 1996). What these bands (and those featured in this study) represent is an ongoing process whereby identities are expressed, reflected and ultimately transformed through musical production and performance. As Line Grenier has written, 'music is said not only to express differences but also to articulate them creatively, affecting social and cultural realities while at the same time being shaped by them' (1989: 137).

While recognizing the importance of significance of difference in musical expressions, we need to be wary of slipping into stereotypical definitions of the 'different' cultures and identities being expressed. In particular there has been a tendency to stereotype the music of non-white musicians in Western societies simply as the articulation of an authentic expression of anti-racist politics. The privileging of non-white ethnicities within discourses of anti-racism has often led to a one-dimensional reading of black music(s) which is valued only for its seemingly authentic politics.

The legacy of the CCCS's model of resistance in youth cultures is central to this process, only now the importance or authenticity of ethnicity is privileged rather than that of class. The reification of ethnicity as an authentic marker of progressive political resistance is such that we can identify what I have termed 'exotic politics'. What this term reflects is the process by which the cultural expressions of non-white minority groups are romanticized, stereotyped and interpreted as authentic articulations of a radical political vanguard. For the people in the bands featured in this study there is as much likelihood that they will be exoticized in terms of their supposed political radicalism than in terms of any link with the fixed stereotypes of mystical India. This does not mean that issues of anti-racism and politics do not play a significant role in the lives of these musicians; quite clearly they often do, but it is nevertheless important to recognize that these bands are often portrayed only in terms of what is perceived to be their political radicalism. This is closely tied to fixed and romanticized notions of ethnicity and identity reflecting what Paul Gilroy has called the 'glamour of purity' (1993a: 30). This denies non-white musicians the full range of experiences and influences that are readily open to other, white musicians; instead they are perceived as the 'exotic other'.

We can identify the articulation of exotic politics in two significant domains: in the national media and in the academic world. This is nowhere more apparent than in the national music press, in particular in the weekly *New Musical Express* (*NME*) and (the now defunct) *Melody Maker*. These two publications have played a significant and influential role in shaping the popular music scene in the UK in the post-war period and, as Tony Mitchell has pointed out, the extent of this influence was as pronounced as ever during the 1990s:

> The various trends in British popular music are largely signalled by the weekly music papers *New Musical Express* and *Melody Maker*, two vastly influential organs who initiate new styles, break new bands, dictate taste, and establish the credentials of what style magazine *The Face*, has called a 'righteous pop nation'. (1996: 19)

Significantly, many of the journalists writing for such publications emerged from the cultural upheaval of punk in the late 1970s, perhaps the most celebrated instance of subcultural style and resistance. This is reflected in the coverage of bands like Fun^Da^Mental and Cornershop, insomuch as it is the politics of the groups that provides the focus, often at the expense of their music. A telling manifestation of this tendency can be seen in the response to the release of Fun^Da^Mental's instrumental LP *With intent to pervert the cause of injustice* in 1995. Prior to this release the band had been best known for their uncompromising political rap lyrics as expressed in their debut LP *Seize the time* in 1994, of which *With intent to pervert the cause of injustice* was a reinterpretation. Although the latter was still intended to contain elements of politics (as reflected by the album's liner notes – see Appendix 2), one of the main purposes of releasing a lyric-less record was to focus primarily on the group's *music*. This focus, however, was all but lost in subsequent reviews of the LP in the national music press: *Melody Maker* virtually ignored the album's musical content in favour of perpetuating the somewhat one-dimensional stereotype of Fun^Da^Mental simply as a forum for a radical political agenda. The review, written by David Bennun (1995: 35), was headed in bold type with the statement 'The very great Fun^Da^Mental have released an LP of instrumentals. But, never mind that, here's David Bennun on the politics of global exploitation.'

This clearly reflects the focus of this 'review' only one sentence of which actually refers to the LP itself – which, incidentally, consists of 12 tracks and runs for 72 minutes.[12] Here clearly the exotic politicization of the band is elevated to such a degree that the actual musical expression seems almost insignificant. As we shall see, this somewhat one-dimensional portrayal of Fun^Da^Mental is a source of irritation for the band, who quite rightly perceive themselves in a more complex way. Bands like Fun^Da^Mental are often reviewed and interpreted in a relatively crude manner, with an overemphasis on selective and seemingly radical lyrical content; hence the inability of *Melody Maker* to adequately review the band's instrumental album. This process does not give a fully rounded impression of any band and, as Roy Shuker has commented (1994: 140): 'Songs create identifications through their emotional appeal, but this does not necessarily mean that they can be reduced to a simple slogan or message.'

Despite being a less obviously political band than Fun^Da^Mental, Cornershop have also been portrayed in a similar and stereotypical way. In a 1993 piece in *NME* Cornershop were hailed as 'the voice of disaffected Asian youth' despite the fact that three of the band were white and that they tried to distance themselves from any organized political agenda. Although there is undoubtedly a political element in Cornershop's music (albeit it in a less obvious and confrontational way than Fun^Da^Mental's) it is a mistake to portray the band as somehow representative of the national constituency of 'Asian youth', a concept with which the band's songwriter Tjinder (as we shall see) finds it hard to identify. This burden of representation is something that all the bands in the study have had to deal with and is a symptomatic manifestation of exotic politics.

These bands have also attracted a similar degree of attention within some academic writing, where the simplistic stereotyping of Asian bands as essentially exotic and political groups has also been present. The 1996 work *Dis-orienting rhythms: the politics of the new Asian dance music* (Sharma, Hutnyk and Sharma 1996) features many examples of the practice of portraying Asian bands as models of authentic political resistance. As Ted Swedenburg has written:

> When 'other' cultural forms of expression are considered, they all too often serve simply to confirm already established models of resistance and thereby function as further instances of the same. (1989: 59)

Despite recognizing the pitfalls of essentialist categorization of Asianness, the books' authors nevertheless do not resist the temptation to valorize what they interpret as the political agenda of bands such as Fun^Da^Mental and Asian Dub Foundation in a way that ignores the complexity of the multiple identities and articulations at play. There is no consideration of music as *pleasure* [13] for these bands, or of music as a means of cultivating success and status; these bands are only allowed to function as the resistive voice of an aggrieved community; music making is seen as 'a means of articulating a radical politics within organisational struggle against resurgent racism in Britain, and across Europe and the USA' (Sharma, Hutnyk and Sharma 1996: 153).

All of the musicians interviewed for this study expressed a broadly anti-racist position, although not all of them reflected this in their music; and there were certainly no uniform political agendas shared between the bands. As we shall see, however, even a band like Fun^Da^Mental, who often privilege a radical political agenda in their music, reject the notion that there is nothing else going on in the band; hence their release of an instrumental album. The authors of *Dis-orienting rhythms* base their conclusions almost entirely on their own, highly selective, reading of the lyrical texts of bands like Fun^Da^Mental and Hustlers HC. This selective and subjective reading of one particular aspect of musical expression not only ignores and reduces the importance of other areas (such as the actual 'sound' of the music) but also fails to recognize the contingent and contextual nature of reading such texts and, as Jonathan Fornäs has pointed out (1992: 158): 'Texts have various use values in relation to different individuals and groups in specific contexts. Use values cannot be quantitatively measured but only qualitatively interpreted.' In order to attempt to reach such a meaningful qualitative understanding of the bands in question it is necessary to take into account the views of the musicians themselves, to understand their motivations and rationales, which, as we shall see, do not always confirm literal readings of musical 'texts'.

The tendency to view these bands only in terms of an expression of a radical political agenda is compounded further by attempts to establish a rather disingenuous linkage with organized political groups of the past and present, claiming that these musicians:

> ... have drawn from the organisational practice of the Indian Workers Association (IWA) and of Asian Youth Movements (AYMs) – where politics and music were meshed in a deliberate political-cultural programme. (Kalra, Hutnyk and Sharma 1996: 153)

Although there is some evidence that there has been a degree of involvement in youth groups by some bands (most notably Asian Dub Foundation who are involved in the Community Music project in East London) it would be a mistake to claim that the musicians in these bands see themselves as part of a community-based organizational politics. As we shall see, all of the musicians I interviewed reject both the notions of continuity and representation of any narrowly defined Asian community in their music. They certainly have not expressed any linkage or inspiration gleaned from the work of the IWA; indeed there is no reference available to suggest such an explicit link as the authors of *Dis-orienting rhythms* seem to suggest. They contend that:

> ... contemporary Asian-based bands such as Fun^Da^Mental, Hustlers MC and Kaliphz are doing cultural and political work drawn in part from earlier Asian political formations like the IWA and AYMs of the 1970s. (Kalra, Hutnyk and Sharma 1996: 153)

This is rather misleading and is not substantiated by any empirical evidence from the musicians in question. Such attempts to impose a sense of political continuity based on preconceived notions of authenticity and radical resistance sell short the actors it seeks to represent. John Hutnyk for one is certainly unapologetic about his focus on the politics of Asian musicians, stating (2000: 118) 'I'd more readily celebrate groups like Asian Dub Foundation or Fun^Da^Mental for their politics than their ethnic flavour.'

The problem is that for critics such as Hutnyk it is exactly this fascination with their 'ethnic flavour' that leads to an overbearing focus on the politics of such bands. These people are denied the right to be regarded as fully rounded social beings who articulate a range of emotions, passions and identities. Instead these musicians and other 'cultural workers' are ghettoized as purely political and reactive representatives of some fixed notion of a pure, ethnically defined community – a position which suggests that individuals are defined *only* in terms of their race or ethnicity. This is a problematic position that does little to break away from stereotypes based on ethnic and cultural identity. According to Paul Gilroy (1993b: 97): 'This defensive reaction to racism can be said to have taken over its evident appetite for sameness and symmetry from the discourse of the oppressor.'

The stereotypical tendencies embodied by exotic politics – whether expressed by journalists or academics, Asian or otherwise – serves to limit and constrict our understanding of the complex workings of ethno-cultural expressions of identity and belonging. The dynamic and fragmented cultural manifestations produced and performed by contemporary Asian bands do not fit neatly into any fixed or stereotypical definitions of what represents authentic Asian culture, whether defined in terms of an exotic politics or a mystical/spiritual heritage. In fact these stereotypes are undermined and transformed through the diverse musical practices of young Asian bands who seek to disrupt neat and cosy definitions of identity, opening up the possibility of a new understanding of the dynamics of ethnicity and identity. As we have seen, this process does not take place in a vacuum: music and its meanings are taken up and interpreted by various sources and in different ways – often contrary to the intentions of its creators. It is for this reason, therefore, that the rest of this chapter is dedicated to looking at the significance of the structure of the national and international music industry, which uncovers the pragmatic and contextual processes at work within musical expressions of cultural and ethnic identity.

Music and identity: selling difference

In order to appreciate fully the complex processes at work in the performance and production of music we need to take into account the commercial aspect of any musical endeavour. At the heart of all musical production is the need to be heard; the audience is an essential element common to all forms of musical expression. In the context of this study, for those whose primary role is to produce music and hopefully make a living from this, the audience is invariably a paying one. In a capitalist society such as the UK it is impossible for any individual musician or group to survive and flourish without having to grapple successfully with the machinations of the national and international music industry. Whether they like it or not, all musicians must come to terms with the fact that their music is treated as a commodity and is subject to the whims and vagaries of the marketplace. In the marketplace identities become commodities; exoticism and novelty are engaged as marketing strategies, all based on the notion that *difference sells*.

Globally the music industry is dominated by four major record consortiums,[14] which have access to the huge resources of multinational parent companies that make up some of the most powerful financial institutions on the planet. These huge companies seek to maximize profit by maintaining the global market saturation of massive stars like Michael Jackson and Madonna while simultaneously seeking out and absorbing new musical trends and performers. These few 'super' major record labels (Robinson 1991) are thought to dominate between 70 and 90 percent of the (legitimate) international music industry (Negus 1992), representing a multibillion-dollar market. Despite these figures the international music market is notoriously unpredictable and, for these major record labels, a large amount of time and money is spent on tapping into the 'next big thing'. This is done by investing vast quantities of money in the grooming and production of new would-be stars and is accompanied by the process of incorporating established bands on more specialized scenes which, more often than not, brings them into contact with independent record labels.

The existence of small, specialized independent record labels seems an ideal counterpoint to the machinations of the global super major labels. In reality, of course, the demands of the marketplace mean that the degree of interlinkage and co-operation between major and what Negus calls 'minor' record labels (1992: 17) is such that it becomes hard to define exactly what is meant by 'independent'. The archetype of an independent company is the label created on a small scale, at street level where financial considerations are less important than the ability to produce and provide an outlet for new and often uncompromising music. Gottlieb and Wald's study of the LA 'Riot Grrrl'[15] scene reflects such a definition of independent which is constructed in direct opposition to the insidious and cynical practices of the majors:

> Independent labels are often tiny (run from someone's kitchen), have limited funds and minimal distribution (primarily through mail order), and have to choose the least expensive recording technologies and media – most often the 7-inch single, or, more recently; cassette. Majors plunder indies for talent and trends, and therefore are viewed with scepticism and frequently loathing among the rock underground. (1994: 251)

This attitude embodies much of the philosophy of the punk era with its focus on anti-professionalism and self-sufficiency. In the UK labels such as Stiff were partly responsible for nurturing and developing punk by putting music before financial considerations. We can see this attitude reflected more recently with labels such as Sarah Records of Bristol, which traded successfully throughout the 1980s and 1990s by maintaining a fiercely non-corporate identity culminating in the self-closure of the label in September 1995 – an act which was presented as the 'most gorgeous pop art statement' (*NME* 23 September 1995). These labels were not run primarily to make huge profits, but focused more on the task of producing and distributing unconventional musical material. James Lull (1987: 23) has commented on this role by saying that 'Small, independent companies in the US, England, and elsewhere record and distribute music that falls outside conventional textual and lyrical constructions.'

Within such an environment the role of the musicians themselves is felt to be uninhibited by the overriding commercial pressures that are present within the confines of major labels. This is often a major issue for musicians concerned with musical or political independence, and in many cases bands set up labels to distribute their own music, thereby cutting out the need to convince a corporate institution before disseminating material to the public. All the bands featured in this study have at some time released records on independent labels, although this involves a variety of different practices.

Some small labels are set up by bands simply to release their own material, building on the do-it-yourself (DIY) ethic of punk, an approach adopted by Voodoo Queens who, following their time with Too Pure records, released their last single 'Eat the germs' on their own, purpose-built Voodoo label. In the case of Nation Records, founded and owned by Fun^Da^Mental's Aki Nawaz, the label has maintained a profile that provides an outlet for bands with unusual and non-conformist political and musical approaches. Nation's fiercely independent basis is combined, however, with a hard-headed pragmatism that recognizes the need to function as a business in a highly competitive industry. During the mid-1980s Beggars Banquet, a larger and more established independent label, invested in Nation Records in return for a minority share of the label. Its support helped to steer Nation Records through a period of financial instability but not at the expense of the independence of the smaller label, whose owners retain absolute control over the day-to-day running of the business. The alliance between these two enterprises is perhaps not surprising, since Beggars Banquet (under the management of Martin Mills) has been one of the most successful proponents of the ideology of independence that was so influential during the 1980s. More surprisingly, however, Nation Records has been involved with some of the largest corporations in the music industry and, despite being highly critical of the more destructive elements of global capitalism, the label has also had dealings with at least two of the five major record companies. TransGlobal Underground, Nation's most successful band (in terms of sales), have released two of their LPs through Nation but with licensing deals first with Sony and also with BMG. Similarly, indie stalwart Wiiija Records worked with David Byrne's

Luaka Bop label (a subsidiary of Warner Brothers) to distribute Cornershop's output in the USA.

As we shall see, the practicalities of running a small business are such that even a highly politicized label such as Nation Records sometimes reaches a compromise merely in order to fulfil its market potential. The size of an independent company (a measure of its success in the marketplace) is vitally important and, once well established, such labels will inevitably attract attention from the majors. As Simon Frith has commented:

> Eventually, [though] returns are sufficient to attract the majors and the new practices are routinized, and the independents are bought out, absorbed, driven out by unfair competition. (1983: 90)

So, ironically, the success of an independent label can in fact lead to its demise; co-opted by the majors it once challenged. The majors have no qualms about buying up and selling even the 'ideologically' based labels, since the major concern is to shift units. More often than not, however, major labels will do deals with smaller labels with regard to specific and successful bands who have a proven record on the independent scene, as was the case with TransGlobal Underground in the early 1990s. This process of co-operation rather than co-option ensures the continued existence of many independent labels which are able to subsidize less successful bands with the profits gained from licensing more marketable acts to the majors.[16]

The significant point here is that the major labels will finance and distribute any form of music deemed to be profitable, almost regardless of the musical or lyrical content.[17] If anti-establishment music sells, then it will be sold by the major labels. As Eisen has written (1978: 170): 'There is no consensus in the industry other than to sell, and they will sell antiwar songs and good poetry just as easily as they will sell the schlock.'

Marketing the authentic

The phenomenal success of rap music, which has spawned the global success of highly politicized black nationalist groups like Public Enemy and nihilistic anti-establishment rappers such as Ice-Cube, shows the extent to which major labels are willing to accept and promote potentially incendiary music because of its profitability. Although initially suspicious of rap music, once the genre had proved to have access to a huge national (and later international) market, the major labels showed no qualms in signing up rap artists (Rose 1994). Indeed, any aura of political authenticity can be turned to commercial use, and this is often conferred partly by association with independent labels. It is ironic that the anti-commercial and anti-establishment attitude of many independent labels can itself become simply another marketing tool. The authenticity conferred by independents is that they are closer to 'the street' and have access to new, pure sounds that are uncontaminated by the commercial concerns of a major corporation. Whilst it is undoubtedly true that independent labels are often at the forefront of discovering and developing new musical styles and trends,[18] there is often a romanticized view of such labels which may be little more that small-scale business ventures, with no ideological or musical agendas (Harker 1980; Frith 1983). Nevertheless, this view of independent labels is such that the authenticity they generate has itself become a recognizably marketable commodity. This is so much so that all the major labels have been involved in the setting up of 'bogus' (Negus 1992) independent labels which attempt to confer some of the aura of authenticity associated with the smaller labels.[19]

As we have seen, the focus on the exotic politics is such that a marketable sense of authenticity is conferred upon Asian bands often at the expense of a more considered understanding of the music itself. This is compounded by a similar process which presents Asian bands in a way which taps into an established stereotype of the 'East' as exotic and mystical. This is analysed in more detail the following chapter, when we shall see that this romantic and exotic notion of difference is deeply rooted and provides the music industry with another mode of difference which can be used to market and promote certain artists.

In the post-war period in the UK Asian musicians had the lowest of profiles, but since the late 1990s major record labels have become more aware of the potential marketability of the exotic East. The very lack of a high profile for Asian music has increased the novelty potential of 'exotic' Asian bands, as, above all, they appear *different*. But although the increased profile of Asian musicians in the UK since the 1990s has forced the music industry to take note, more often than not new Asian music has been trivialized and packaged as an exotic novelty. The 1990s wave of Asian bands gave rise to the idea of 'New Asian Kool' (Morris 1993) – a notion which many bands of the time rejected – and more recently there has been a similar amount of attention afforded to the so-called 'New Asian Underground' (Simpson 1997). The articulation of a sense of Eastern exoticism often goes hand in hand with more overtly demeaning stereotypes of Asian culture, and although there is an increasing awareness within the industry, and the music press in particular, of the need to challenge and ridicule established stereotypes of Asianness, there are still endless references to saris, curries and Bombay mix.[20] The development of Asian music (and its attendant stereotypes) in contemporary Britain is discussed in greater depth in the following chapter, but the important point to stress here is that the perception of Asian music and Asian bands as exotic and different at the hands of the major record labels can be used as one way of promoting such acts as financially viable and marketable commodities.

Before 1990 no Asian artists were signed to major record labels, but throughout the decade that followed there were many – Apache Indian, Bally

Sagoo, Trickbaby and Talvin Singh to name but a few – although the success of some was more short-lived than others. Progress has been slow, largely because it has taken the major record labels a long time to become convinced of the marketability of Asian music. Ironically though, Cornershop have survived throughout this period and their patient endeavour finally paid off in 1998 in the shape of the number one single 'Brimful of Asha' released on one of the stalwarts of the independent record scene, Wiiija – undoubtedly to the delight of the company's personnel and perhaps to the chagrin of many a major record label scout. The cautious approach usually adopted by the majors is well documented by many, such as James Lull, who points out that:

> When alternative music first develops it is resisted by the industry primarily on financial grounds, then is reluctantly accommodated by them when profit potential is more clear, and is finally brought under their financial and artistic control, a process that almost always demands substantial modification of the music itself. (1987: 21)

It remains to be seen, of course, how long the industry's interest will last and whether or not Asian bands and artists can establish themselves as ongoing concerns within the larger companies; several of the artists mentioned above are no longer signed with the major labels. Although the relationships between innovative new musicians and the corporate body of major labels is undoubtedly full of pitfalls it would be a mistake to overemphasize the negative aspects of such relationships. Writers such as Harker (1980) have extensively documented the perils that musicians face when entering into a relationship with a major label to such an extent that any positive factors are ignored and the bands in question are dismissed as having sold out to the exploitative forces of international capital.

As I have stated, by making deals with major labels independents are able to tap into a vast resource network, enabling them to reach a huge market, and also to divert extra profits back into the development of new bands and artists. It is not only financial support that the majors can offer independent labels; more importantly they have access to huge structural resources, ranging from recording studios and record-pressing facilities to global distribution and publicity networks. Alan McGee, founder of Creation, one of the UK's most influential independent labels (home to Oasis) – which in the 1990s was part-owned by Sony (now the sole owners) explains how this process works:

> Last year Creation gave The Weather Prophets £3,000 to live on; this year WEA through Elevation is giving them £100,000. Equally, if their new LP had come out on Creation it would have sold about 40,000 copies. On Elevation I reckon it'll do somewhere between 100 and 150,000 copies. (Kelly 1987: 30)

Co-operation between independent and major labels is increasingly the order of the day; licensing deals are struck rather than takeovers mounted. This benefits both parties: the majors are able to pick and choose the most successful independent artists to invest in, and the independents are able to expand their market with relatively little interference and channel excess funds back into the label. The increasing extent of this type of co-operation between the major companies and the independents has led to a blurring of label identities, making it increasingly difficult to distinguish clearly between the two. This 'symbiosis' (Frith 1987) between the independents and corporate giants has created what Negus (1992) describes as 'webs of major and minor'[21] record labels that represent a pragmatic and contingent relationship that ensures benefits for both parties. In this context there is not necessarily a great deal of pressure on unconventional or politically controversial artists to tone down their musical or lyrical output; in fact, as Lull (1987: 23) has recognized, 'the musicians themselves exercise considerable control over the social impact of their work.' As we shall see, the ability of artists to express radical musical or political messages in their music takes on a potentially greater significance when combined with increased access to the global music market.

A global perspective

Apart from financial benefits and associated economies of scale, co-operation between major and independent labels has another significant effect, that which accords localized music access to global flows of communication. By using the international communication networks set up to serve the global markets, of which the music industry is but one, individuals and groups can facilitate the processes of cultural syncretism and exchange on a global scale. These international networks, as well as enabling major corporations to maximize their profits, are also responsible for transporting local styles and sounds around the globe. In this way the very structures set up by major corporations to maximize profits and the flow of international capital have become proactive in the development of new dynamic musical forms and the emergence of new syncretic manifestations of cultural identity. As Wallis and Malm have recognized:

> On the local level, musicians are influenced not only by their own cultural traditions but also by the transnational standards of the record industry regarding music content and 'sound'. The result is the production of various hybrid forms, either of local music with a transnational flavor, or transnational music with a local flavor. (1987: 127)

This process allows music to rebound and resound around the globe, picking up antiphonic responses that continually express and re-articulate the syncretic manifestation of cultural identities. The dynamic forces at work in the development of new, multi-accented musical forms on an international scale damages the notion of ethno-cultural purity, since they constantly disrupt and undermine any assertions of absolute cultural ownership. According to Paul Gilroy (1993b: 110): 'The calls and responses no longer converge in the tidy patterns of secret, ethnically encoded dialogue. The original call is becoming harder to locate.'

The transfer of musical and cultural identities along what George Lipsitz terms 'conduits of commodity' (1994: 153) goes hand in hand with the expression of disparate and localized political agendas. As we have seen, there is no given tension between non-conformist political expressions and marketability in the music industry, and the conduits along which international capital flow can also be used to transmit the dissenting voice of often isolated and oppressed minority groups. The flow of musical styles around the globe can offer new opportunities for political expression by aggrieved local populations, as Lipsitz explains:

> ... because popular music functions as a node in a network of international capital it sometimes offers subordinate populations opportunities to escape the limits of their own societies, to find new alliances and allies by appealing to an international market and embarrassing local authorities by exposing them to international censure and ridicule. (1994: 138)

If we look at the example of rap music we can see how this works in practice. From its origins in the urban centres of America, rap has become a global phenomenon and its association with the expression of political dissent has meant that the genre has become a global language of resistance. By making use of the global networks of international capital, rap music has given a voice to local populations the world over, uncovering and highlighting issues like poverty, racism and police brutality in countries as disparate as Italy, South Africa and Australia (Gilroy 1993b; Rose 1994; Mitchell 1996). The common language of rap music has been used to express locally specific political agendas on a global scale and, just as important, has been able to tap into a sense of global solidarity against oppression in general. Such 'families of resemblance' (Lipsitz 1994: 180) are of particular importance for extremely isolated minority groups, who are able to draw strength from the globally perceived sense of solidarity (Lipsitz 1994; Davies 1993).

Fun^Da^Mental can be seen to be part of this process, drawing not only on the local context of contemporary British society but also on influences from black America, Europe and Asia. Founder member Aki Nawaz states that one of the main stimuli behind the formation of both Fun^Da^Mental and Nation Records was a trip he made to the USA in 1990 which helped bring home the stark reality of contemporary racism in the West. Since 1994 he has travelled around the world combining music-making with the establishment of contacts with localized community projects and record labels. These journeys have encompassed various countries in Europe, Asia, Africa and Australasia where music and politics were combined in order to establish a common bond with local communities. In South Africa this resulted in a number of performances with local rap collective

Prophets of Da City (a band noted for their uncompromising stance on the political injustices heaped upon the people of the townships, both prior to and after the dismantling of apartheid), who eventually signed with Nation Records and released their debut LP with the label in 1995.

The influence on the music of Fun^Da^Mental itself has been significant and has resulted in many collaborations (both live and recorded) with musicians from around the world, as reflected in *There shall be love!* (2001), which features artists from Pakistan and South Africa, as well as from Wembley and Bradford in the UK. Fun^Da^Mental reflect the positive potential that exists within the functioning of international flows of commodity which allow previously isolated local communities to interact with other like-minded groups. The band have shown that this process has a dual impact, affecting and transforming the nature of musical and cultural identities as well as providing a global forum for political dissent. The construction of a global collectivity which unites the disparate voices of the oppressed and dispossessed is an important source of alternative communication in an increasingly globalized world. For these previously marginalized voices this is particularly significant and, as George Lipsitz has suggested:

> The populations best prepared for cultural conflict and political contestation in a globalized world economy may well be the diasporic communities of displaced Africans, Asians, and Latin Americans created by the machinations of world capitalism over the centuries. These populations, long accustomed to code switching, syncreticism, and hybridity may prove far more important for what they possess in cultural terms than what they appear to lack in the political lexicon of the nation state. (1994: 30)

Although it is difficult to discern any direct effect of a single band like Fun^Da^Mental on any contemporary national or international political landscape, their experiences do show how groups and individuals can exploit the potential benefits of working within the international music industry by adopting a pragmatic and flexible approach to their artistic and business practices.

Conclusion: making music, remaking identity

The role of music as a medium through which identities are expressed and negotiated is particularly significant in the context of a multi-ethnic society, but should not be taken as representing or reflecting any fixed definition of cultural identity and belonging. The shifting musical forms and practices that we hear on a daily basis mirror the complex processes of intercultural exchange that reflects both the modification of existing cultural allegiances and the emergence of new and multi-accented modes of identity. Undoubtedly, the importance of music as a vital means of cultural expression is particularly important for the UK's non-white settler population; and for young Asian bands in the 1990s and beyond it is a medium where both old and new identities are forged and contested. These manifestations of cultural expression and identity do not take place in a vacuum, however, and we need to recognize the significant impact that competing interpretations and appropriations have on these developing musical forms. Only by taking into account the full range of subjective positions and external pressures surrounding the production of these musical expressions can we come to a better understanding of the complex processes at work in the development of syncretic cultural forms and identities.

The music of the Asian bands in this study, like all other music, has to function and interact with the outside world and, as such, can often be appropriated and operationalized in ways not intended by the musicians themselves. As we have seen, the music of these bands has been evaluated, colonized and reshaped by a range of political, commercial and academic interests which have sought to make often unsubstantiated claims – largely based on what are deemed to be the 'authentic' qualities of the music – about the political and representative agency of the musicians involved. The harsh realities of the external forces that come to bear on the musical forms presented by these bands are an inevitable part of musical production and performance; in particular the specific context of the highly commercialized music industry plays an important role in the way that this music is heard and consumed. In order to survive and function as professional or semi-professional musicians, the individuals in these bands have to come to terms with the practical considerations of functioning within an industry based largely on the pursuit of profit. Such an environment encourages the pursuit of novelty, and the pressure to conform to seemingly 'authentic' stereotypes of Asian culture and music is one that these young Asian bands constantly have to negotiate – and one that many attempt to transgress. Despite the fact that prior to the 1990s Asian bands enjoyed an almost non-existent profile on the UK music scene, there does exist a strong tradition of the interpretation and appropriation of Asian musical forms within popular music in the West, as well as a recent history of 'underground' Asian music forms which have failed to impact significantly on the mainstream. In the following chapter I will examine and evaluate the impact of these influences and interventions on popular music cultures in the UK during the post-war period and highlight the significance that associated stereotypes of Asian music and culture have had, and continue to have, on contemporary Asian bands.

Notes

1. Noel Gallagher (songwriter and guitarist with Oasis) was a fan before he was a 'star', indeed he was a roadie for the Inspiral Carpets some years before going on to join Oasis.
2. The songs 'My Generation' by The Who (1965) and 'Anarchy in the UK' by the Sex

Pistols (1976) remain the most emblematic and influential expressions of the subcultural development of mod and punk respectively.

3. Many of the theorists from the subcultural tradition often use simplistic and problematic definitions of 'black' culture, as Gary Clark has illustrated (1981: 89) 'Hebdige tends to equate black culture with a Jamaican culture (Asians are noted by their absence) which is unproblematically imported.'
4. Muggleton suggests that for the CCCS '[their] most serious theoretical inadequacy is their failure to take seriously enough the subjective viewpoints of the youth subculturalists themselves.' (2000: 3)
5. 'Yeboah's jawz' on the *Haláal rock* EP (EXP 1996).
6. Single released on Wiiija Records in 1992.
7. Combat 18, a violent right-wing organization formed in 1992 out of the security wing of the British National Party, take their name from the numerical value of Adolf Hitler's initials – the first and eighth letters of the alphabet. The group advocates hate and violence against black people in general, as well as against any white people who, in their eyes, appear to support the notion of a multi-ethnic Britain. In a series of high-profile hate campaigns they have targetted (white) public figures such as the former Olympic swimmer Sharron Davies (ex-wife of the black athelete Derek Redmond), the broadcaster Anna Ford and politicians such as former Liberal Democrat leader Paddy Ashdown and Labour MP Peter Hain.
8. Before his death in 1999 politician Alan Clark was a maverick right-wing Conservative who was renowned as much for his outspoken views and philandering lifestyle as for his role in Parliament. He was MP for Plymouth for 18 years from 1974 (later representing Kensington and Chelsea) and in the early 1990s served under Margaret Thatcher as a minister in the departments of Employment and Trade. But he was at his most controversial and outspoken during his time at the Ministry of Defence, when he was criticized for his role in the arms-for-Iraq affair.
9. Kid Frost, a pioneering LA Latino rap artist, has challenged the notion that rap is an exclusively black phenomenon by asserting that 'Rap is not a black art form, rap is an *urban* art form' (Stephens 1992: 74).
10. The more recent and apparently sustainable success of Eminem draws heavily on the 'authenticity' of the artist's biography. His deprived and troubled 'white trash' upbringing (as fictionalized in the 2002 film *8 Mile* directed by Curtis Hanson) combined with his relationship with black hip-hop luminary Dr Dre has been central to the establishment and maintenance of the artist's credibility within the genre.
11. Similarly, the success of rock and roll has not led to the dilution of the 'original' forms. As well as the ultimately elevated status of the black originators of rock and roll, it is worth noting how this has led to a strengthening of interest in one of the 'original' sources of the genre, that is the blues. Blues music in its purer forms has continued to thrive alongside rock and roll and its offshoots, as evidenced in the successful career of John Lee Hooker spanning four decades.
12. The sentence read:

    > But this record is essentially a clutch of instrumental takes on the band's greatest moments, peppered with intercontinental samples – agreeable enough but lacking the lump-hammer force of Fun-Da-Mental proper. (Bennun 1995: 35)

13. As DJ Mitts from Asian hip-hop combo Hustlers HC has commented, 'We're not thinking about racism 24 hours a day, we want to go to clubs and have a good time' (Morton 1994: 11).

14. They are: Sony Music Entertainment, Warner Music International, Polygram and Bertlesmann Music Group (BMG).
15. Riot Grrrl was a neo-feminist punk music subculture that emerged in the early 1990s and was concerned with asserting the position of female rock groups in a traditionally male-dominated industry. Groups such as Bikini Kill in the US and Huggy Bear in the UK have stressed the need for females to set up their own labels and throw off the constraints of such patriarchy.
16. The global success of Nirvana is a case in point. The licensing deal struck by Nirvana's original independent label Sub-Pop with Geffen (part of MCA International) provided a much-needed financial boost which in fact staved off bankruptcy and continues to give the label a stable financial base from which to uncover and promote new artists.
17. There are limits, of course, and for an account of some of these see *The Ice Opinion* (Ice-T 1994), which chronicles the controversy over Ice-T's lyrical and musical imagery (most notably surrounding the track 'Cop killer' which featured on the eponymous debut album of the singer's thrash-metal combo *Body Count* in 1992). This controversy played a large part in his eventual departure from Warner Brothers.
18. Two examples of this would be London-based Stiff Records in the UK in relation to punk in the late 1970s and, in the USA, Seattle-based Sub-Pop which was instrumental in promoting the grunge scene in the late 1980s and early 1990s.
19. During the success of Britpop in the mid-1990s for example, bands such as Sleeper and Salad released their records on the independent-seeming Indolent label, which is in fact a subsidiary of BMG.
20. The rather jaded pun 'Keep taking the tablas' for instance has been doing the rounds for a number of years and has been used in reviews of the Anohka compilation CD, psych-rock band Saddar Bazaar (on at least two occasions) and articles on Black Star Liner, Cornershop and jazz-fusionist Nitin Sawhney.
21. Defined in his words as 'external links between large corporate labels and small companies through investment arrangements, licensing deals and joint ventures' (Negus 1992: 17).

Chapter 4

Asian influences on pop and rock in the UK

The dynamism and creativity of the post-war music scene in Britain represents one of the country's most telling contributions to contemporary culture. Along with that of the USA, British music culture has played a particularly influential role on the experiences and aspirations of both listeners and artists throughout the world. Key to the development of these musical innovations has been the interaction between young people from different and previously distant ethnic and cultural traditions. Patterns of post-war immigration and settlement have been central to this growth of new musical forms that have had a significant cultural impact on both a national and international scale. The influence of black settlers from the Caribbean in the development of new musical genres is widely recognized and well documented but, in contrast, the impact of Asian settlers appears less clear and perhaps harder to pin down. Although in the past Asians have had an extremely low public profile on the UK music scene, more subtle but nonetheless significant influences have played an important part in shaping modern pop and rock sensibilities.

The practically non-existent public profile of Asians in British popular music in the past can be contrasted with an unprecedented upsurge of Asian bands in the 1990s and beyond, many of whom have enjoyed a certain degree of both critical and commercial success. The rise of Asian bands, mirrored by the revival of Asian influences on popular rock and dance genres, has occurred despite a number of negative and reductive stereotypes of Asian culture and identity which are highly resilient and often have deep historical roots. These stereotypes play an important part in the way that Asian musicians live out their sense of ethnic identity and also influence how audiences perceive and consume Asian bands and music.

First, stereotypes regarding the supposedly joyless and conservative nature of the Asian 'community' in the West have sought to establish an image of Asian youth that renders them incompatible with the glamorous world of pop and rock. As Rupa Huq has written: 'Asians have simply never assumed a principal place in Top Of The Pops/MTV youth culture mythology, instead they have been perennially considered unhip' (1996: 63).

Young Asians have previously been perceived as essentially conservative figures, bound by the strict conventions of community and more likely to be doing schoolwork or toiling in the local corner shop than playing or enjoying pop music. This is in marked contrast to the fetishization of black, Afro-Caribbean youth, who have been considered perennially cool and hip by white, mainstream society (Hebdige 1979) – although this is often accompanied by attendant stereotypes of physicality and criminality (Fryer 1984, Solomos 1988).[1]

This 'uncool' stereotype is supplanted by an exoticized notion of Asianness that is associated with the perceived mysticism of the East (Reck 1978; Said 1978) feeding into wider processes of 'othering' in the Western world. According to George Lipsitz:

> Modernist literature, art and music in Western countries has consistently spectacularised difference, titillating 'respectable' audiences with sensational portrayals of 'primitive', 'exotic' and 'oriental' outsiders. (1994: 4)

As we shall see, the notion of the East as mystical and exotic has been particularly influential in shaping Western interpretations of Asian music during the post-war period, and contemporary Asian bands have had to struggle to counter such stereotypes as they attempt to produce new musical forms and other innovations. These stereotypes have combined to make Asians all but invisible within youth culture and rendered the work of Asian bands seemingly incompatible within the context of the popular music scene. For emergent Asian musicians in the 1990s the existence of these reductive notions of Asian music and culture has created a significant site of struggle and negotiation, and many have tried to counter and subvert such resilient stereotypes.

In this chapter the historical terrain over which these stereotypes have been asserted, developed and contested will be examined. First, I shall focus on the use of Eastern cultural and musical influences by popular musicians in the West during the late 1960s. It will be argued that such interpretations were based on an Orientalist understanding of the East which constructed an exotic and mythical notion of an imaginary 'India' that has dominated Western understanding of Asian music. Second, the production and consumption of Asian music through the genres of world music and bhangra will be considered, focusing on how stereotypes of Asianness have affected both the financial success of the former and the failure of the latter to cross over into the popular mainstream. Finally, I shall look at the impact of Asian music on the popular music scene in the UK during the 1990s, focusing on the resurgence of interest in Asian music as well as on the rise of Asian bands themselves, and examining how the individuals in these groups seek to challenge and resist existing and resilient stereotypes of Asianness.

The shadow of the 1960s: George Harrison and the 'sitar explosion'

> George Harrison has a lot to answer for. All those tedious sitar passages you skip over on The Beatles albums are not designed to dispose an audience favourably to

> Indian sounds. And the muzak played in Indian restaurants doesn't help either. (*The Independent* 15 July 1992: 14).

Although there have been many attempts to introduce and adapt Asian musical forms in a Western context, most notably by jazz musicians in the 1950s (Farrell 1988), it was not until the late 1960s that the 'Indian sound' reached a widespread audience. The so-called 'sitar explosion' (Shankar 1968: 2) was initiated as early as 1965 by The Beatles, or more specifically by George Harrison who contributed a rudimentary sitar piece on 'Norwegian wood' which appeared on the band's influential *Rubber soul* LP.

Over the next few years Harrison developed his fascination with Indian classical music via the musical output of The Beatles, culminating with the track 'Within you, without you' from the seminal *Sgt. Pepper's lonely hearts club band* which was released in 1967 and became the unofficial soundtrack of the summer of love.[2] By this stage he had immersed himself in Indian classical music, which is reflected in the fact that the track features stringed instruments such as dilurba, tanbura and svarmandal, and tablas, as well as the sitar. Harrison at this point had become a pupil of sitar virtuoso Ravi Shankar who, in the 1950s, had been involved in attempts to fuse Indian classical music with jazz (Farrell 1988). Shankar became a global superstar during the late 1960s, playing at rock festivals (most notably Monterey in 1967 and Woodstock in 1970) alongside such luminaries as the Jimi Hendrix Experience, The Who and Janis Joplin. Throughout this period the influence of Indian sounds, mainly represented by the use of sitar, became widespread through-out the British music scene. Most famously The Rolling Stones employed the sitar (as played by Brian Jones) on their single 'Paint it black' (1966) but other bands, including Traffic, Pretty Things and the Yardbirds, also incorporated Eastern influences into their music. It is also worth noting the important influence that Indian music had on the development of progressive or acid rock during the late 1960s and early 1970s. The meandering and improvisational guitar workouts of bands such as the Grateful Dead, Cream and The Jimi Hendrix Experience were directly influenced by Indian musical practices – particularly the semi-improvisational form of raga (which spawned the term 'raga rock' to denote lengthy guitar workouts) – and, although these influences are less obvious than the actual, physical use of Indian instruments, they nevertheless perceptibly altered the direction of contemporary rock and pop in the West (Farrell 1997: 188).

Although this period marks the first significant incorporation of Eastern musical forms into Western pop and rock music, it would be a mistake to acknowledge without qualification the music of this time simply as a celebration of syncretic, cross-cultural interaction. Gerry Farrell has documented the manifestation of Indian influences on Western pop music during this period in some detail[3] and usefully provides us with examples of dissenting voices (such as that of Steve Marriott from The Small Faces and Paul Jones of Manfred Mann) who regarded the use of Indian sounds as 'little more than a tawdry fad' (Farrell 1997: 174). The borrowing of 'surface' elements of Indian music to provide Western pop bands with an exotic frisson aimed at achieving a short-lived novelty appeal brings into question the 'legitimacy' and balance of power at the heart of such seemingly syncretic musical endeavours.

The question of cultural power is important here, as musicians in the West have enjoyed a freedom of expression and access that has been shaped by a history of colonial and imperial dominance which has maintained an unequal system of political and economic control between East and West. As Edward Said wrote in *Orientalism*, his classic reading of colonialism:

> A certain freedom of intercourse was always the westerner's privilege; because his was the stronger culture, he could penetrate, he could wrestle with, he could give shape and meaning to the great Asiatic mystery, as Disraeli once called it. (1978: 46)

This freedom of intercourse was vital in the development of the Indian sound in Western pop because it allowed Western musicians not only to relocate Indian sounds and instrumentation into the West, but also to mould the cultural meanings associated with these sounds.

The musical influences of Indian classical music during this period were inextricably linked to a romanticized notion of a mythic India, a place of profound spirituality, ancient knowledge and deep sensuality. As Reck has noted, this mythical image of India (and the East in general) is a 'peculiarly Western' one (1978: 5) and is extremely selective in its choice of cultural markers. This sense of the exotic East became an important part of the hippy culture of this period and deeply woven into the philosophies of free love, peace and transcendence through drugs. The Beatles were of course instrumental in this process, best illustrated by their homage to the Indian spiritual guru par excellence, Maharishi Mahesh Yogi. The pilgrimage The Beatles made to India to pay homage to the Maharishi in 1968 was very much a journey to seek out an authentic representative of the mythologized image of the East. Ironically the Maharishi was so successful in selling his own brand of accessible, Westernized Indian mysticism, that he was able to adopt many of the luxurious manifestations of stardom enjoyed by many of his pilgrims (which included movie stars, business people and other members of the jet-set as well as rock stars like The Beatles). The teachings of the Maharishi had less to do with the actual cultural traditions of the East, and more to do with catering for the Orientalist gaze of wealthy Westerners. As David Reck points out:

> While the famous Yogi was, beyond doubt, Indian, the expensive trappings (the same as for a pop or rock star), the high-powered Madison Avenue hype (ditto), the corporation like organisation and planning systems as well as the philosophical/religious vagueness … are Amercanisations, Western cultural overlays. In short, Indian philosophy or religion (but not real, practised Hinduism) became one more of many spangled, glittering elements in the chic and pop world. (1978: 9)

As Said has indicated, such forays into the East as that represented by The Beatles are less to do with the East – or, to use Said's phrase, the Orient – than to do with the West (1978: 49). The mythic interpretation of the East is manufactured and maintained in order to 'serve' the Orientalist gaze of the West and the Maharishi can be see as representative of this process. The siting of this image of the East in an imaginary spatial and temporal location means that it is very resilient over time and appeals to a romanticized notion of 'other' societies as fixed, authentic and traditional. As Stuart Hall has commented:

> The idea that these are 'closed' places – ethnically pure, culturally traditional, undisturbed until yesterday by the ruptures of modernity – is a Western fantasy about 'otherness': a 'colonial' fantasy maintained *about the* periphery *by* the West, which tends to like its natives 'pure' and its exotic places 'untouched'. (1992b: 305)

For young Asian musicians operating on the contemporary music scene this fantasy of exotic difference is such that they are constantly having to negotiate and challenge such notions of an exotic and mystical sense of otherness in order to be taken seriously as artists rather than as exponents of an 'authentic' and antiquated culture.

The period of the mid- to late 1960s exemplified by The Beatles represents arguably the most significant stage of Indian influence on popular music in the UK and the West in general (at least until the 1990s); it is therefore important to recognize the overarching effect that this has had on the perception of Asians as musicians as well as on the consumption of music influenced by Indian sounds. The impact of The Beatles and others of their ilk on conceptions of Indian music during the mid- to late 1960s over subsequent decades can be divided into two broad but interrelated areas. First, the selective use of Indian instruments and sounds as adornments for Western tunes in a tokenistic way establishes the notion of Indian music as an 'exotic novelty' undervaluing its worth both as a distinct musical form (or forms) and also its potential in the formation of new hybrid musical forms. Emma Cook writing in *The Independent on Sunday* has commented on this by stating that:

> It seems that the British concept of Asian music is still relatively clichéd – one that is still conditioned to expect a traditional fare of tablas and sitars usually tacked onto a distinctly Western sound. (1996: 32)

Second, the articulation of a mystical and exotic image of the East at the heart of 1960s experiments with Indian music has led to a long-lasting and resilient association between Indian music and hippy culture: 'Part of the problem is that since The Beatles first romanticised Asian music over 30 years ago, the sound is more usually associated with hippy nostalgia' (Ibid.).

The musical and cultural legacy of the late 1960s in terms of expressions of Asian music in the UK has been such that it has been, and continues to be, extremely difficult for bands either using Asian sounds or featuring Asian musicians to break away from these long-established stereotypes of 'Indian' mysticism and other-world spirituality. Indeed it can be argued that, until recently, Asian musical influences on pop and rock have been filtered almost exclusively through the perceptions and practices of white musicians rather than Asians. Only those Asian musicians that appear to represent the supposed Orient of antiquity – particularly those 'discovered' by Western musicians/experts – have experienced a degree of success. Ravi Shankar, playing music derived from India's classical heritage and patronized by George Harrison and The Beatles, can be seen as one such example.[4] The focus on a mythical India fixed somewhere in the past helps to render the contemporary Asian invisible, only existing in antiquity, whereas the Western 'expert' is free to discover and make sense of this almost archaeological culture (Said 1993).

The subsequent history of Asian music in the UK has been dogged by the shadow of the 1960s and many have found it hard to escape from this legacy. In the late 1990s many of the UK's biggest bands, such as Oasis[5] and Kula Shaker, looked to the 1960s and 1970s for their inspiration, often in a rather derivative fashion. For Kula Shaker in particular a significant part of their homage to this period is their re-articulation of notions of the mythical, mystical East. As Gerry Farrell has suggested (1997: 1), the way that 'Indian' music has been used to represent the exotic and the 'other' in the West has been so resilient that 'Indian music has continued to be unknown in the West, and is continually being "discovered" over and over, as if for the first time.' Kula Shaker's use of Hindu iconography and the employment of Sanskrit in songs such as 'Tattva' and 'Govinda'[6] (Top 10 singles in 1996 and 1997 respectively) can be understood both as a familiar re-articulation of the mysticism of The Beatles and their hippy counterparts and also as part of an ongoing historical process of 'othering' which has dominated Western interpretations of Indian music throughout much of recent history (Farrell 1997). Predictable though Kula Shaker's vision may be, it was extremely successful and, until their demise in the late 1990s, they were one of the most successful rock bands in the UK, suggesting perhaps that the mythic image of Asianness is particularly marketable when interpreted by a group of nice young white boys, rather than by contemporary Asian bands and musicians.

Such stereotypical interpretations of Asian music and culture do not escape criticism, however,[7] and one significant difference between the late 1960s and the 1990s is the existence of a number of British Asian bands and musicians seeking to disrupt the retro-Orientalism of bands like Kula Shaker. Choque Hosein has been particularly scathing in his criticism of Kula Shaker and, as we shall see, uses the music of his band Black Star Liner to disrupt stereotypical readings of Asian music and culture. In an interview for the *NME* in 1996 he said that:

Fig. 4.1 Black Star Liner circa 1997: (from left to right) Chris Harrop, Choque Hosein and Tom Salmon

> Somebody played Kula Shaker to me, and it's the same kind of, right, let's put the Indian bit in now, here we go. Thank you very much, goodnight. It's almost like *It Ain't Half Hot Mum*[8] on record. I've got a fuckin' house in Leeds, y'know, which isn't full of fuckin' woven carpets by some sad fuckin' woman in a caravan. (Bennun 1996: 23)

In 1998 Madonna, perhaps the most influential female artist in pop history, was also inspired by the ancient and exotic East, which she put to work on her career-revitalizing album *Ray of light*. As well as sporting the 'new' and, for a time, highly fashionable body art of henna on her hands and feet (the traditional adornment of Asian brides from a variety of religious backgrounds[9]), she also recorded the quasi-mystical lyrics of the track 'Shanti/Ashtangi' in ancient Sanskrit.[10] Once again we have witnessed the Western expert 'discovering' and making sense of the supposedly ancient and spiritual wisdom of the East. Although Madonna has since shifted her attention elsewhere[11] and Kula Shaker have since disbanded, their flirtation with Asian sounds and iconography reflects the continuing resilience of the mythic and mystic East within popular music cultures.

Home and away: Asian sounds in the 1980s

During the 1970s we can see how the influence of the 'Indian sound' became incorporated into the increasingly self-indulgent excesses of progressive rock – from the lengthy guitar solos of the Grateful Dead to the epic concept albums of Led Zeppelin. The backlash against highly technical, studio-bound progressive rock, as represented by the punk phenomenon in the late 1970s (summed up by Johnny Rotten's 'Never trust a hippy' T-shirt motif), meant that any use of Indian sounds became increasingly unfashionable. Apart from a number of exceptions such as the rather cheesy Coral electric sitar played on Abba's 1979 hit 'I have a dream', the UK's music charts remained largely free of Eastern flavours throughout the 1970s.

Although during the 1980s we did not witness the breakthrough of Asian music into the mainstream, in retrospect we can recognize the significance of musical styles such as bhangra in laying down foundations for the future. The 1980s represent a period when Asian musicians began to push tentatively towards the edges of the mainstream music industry, and many of the lessons learnt during this period have been important in forming the success of Asian artists in the 1990s. The 1980s saw stereotypes of Asian music maintained and articulated in ways that explicitly referred back to the 1960s mythology of Eastern sounds. The short-lived success of 'Indipop' in the early part of the decade reflects many of the problems that Asian artists faced when attempting to produce popular music during this period. Indipop (derived from the record label at the centre of this phenomenon) was a genre that attempted to fuse elements of Western pop with Eastern sounds and that enjoyed a brief spell of popularity in the early 1980s

(Farrell 1997). It involved both white and Asian youth and is probably best remembered for the success of Monsoon's Top 20 hit 'Ever so lonely' in 1982. Indipop as a genre was consumed largely by non-Asian audiences in the West, most notably in Scandinavia, appealing particularly to those who already had an interest in 'Indian' music (Banerji and Baumann 1990). Undoubtedly the image projected by the group's vocalist, Sheila Chandra, pandered to a stereotype of erotic exoticism that has a long history in Orientalist tradition (Said 1978; Kabbani 1986). Sheila Chandra has subsequently embarked on a solo career and, after a number of increasingly experimental LPs, is now releasing records through Peter Gabriel's Realworld label which in the late 1980s was instrumental in establishing the success of world music as a new musical genre and a highly profitable marketing category that has had a significant influence on perceptions of Asian music in the West ever since.

World music: exotic sounds for a bored culture?

Although throughout the 1980s Asians maintained a relatively low profile on the UK music scene, the emergence of world music was a significant development in the consumption of certain musical forms from the East. The establishment of a niche market for traditional non-Western music for Western consumption has ensured that certain elements of Asian music have reached vast international audiences and become part of the highly commercialized global music industry. Although we can identify the origins of this market in the 1950s through albums recorded in the field by Western anthropologists, it was not until the late 1980s that world music was established as a discrete marketing category which drew together a number of disparate 'native' musical forms and packaged them for Western consumption. According to Tony Mitchell (1996: 53), world music can be defined as 'a generalising marketing tag referring to popular music originating in countries outside the normal Western (and predominantly Anglo-American) trade routes of popular music.'

It was in 1987 that world music emerged as a recognizable genre when a number of independent record labels first operationalized the term as a specific marketing category (Barrett 1996; Mitchell 1996). These labels (such as Oval Records and Globestyle) produced recordings of a range of traditional and popular musical forms drawn largely from a disparate range of Third World sources and marketed them successfully in the West. Inherent to the appeal and marketing success of world music is the notion of authentic cultural purity related to a celebration of traditional, unspoilt musical forms. As Paul Gilroy has stated:

> Authenticity enhances the appeal of selected cultural commodities and has become an important element in the mechanism of the mode of racialisation necessary to making non-European and non-American musics acceptable items in an expanded pop market. The discourse of authenticity has been a notable presence in the mass marketing of successive black folk-cultural forms to white audiences. (1993a: 99)

The prerequisite of authenticity at the heart of the genre means that the archive of world music may be drawn from a range of cultural traditions from around the world and incorporates a variety of styles and genres from as far afield as Africa, the Middle East and South America as well as from Asia, and then packaged for consumption in the West. Although Asian styles and artists make up only a part of the world music archive, there are certain parallels between the consumption of this contemporary genre and that of the 'Indian sound' in the late 1960s, both of which are facilitated by the othering gaze.

If we look at the role of Ravi Shankar in popularizing the sitar in the late 1960s we can see him as a prototype world musician; in fact he has become one of the genre's most successful exponents. The mysticism and exoticism associated with sitar music at this time shares much of the appeal based on authenticity that is associated with world music. Simon Frith has commented that, as world music developed as a commercial genre, 'It was soon clear that "the authentic" worked in retail terms as a redescription of the exotic' (2000: 308). In this way we can see how a great deal of world music is packaged and marketed in a way that appeals to stereotypical notions of the primitive and exotic which have little to do with the actual contemporary practices of the musicians in question. Frith continues: 'such music is made in local contexts of mobility, migration, the constant writing out and blurring of class and ethnic difference; tradition is always a matter of invention and reinvention' (p. 311).

This is exemplified by the career of one of world music's biggest stars, Nusrat Fateh Ali Khan, a Pakistani exponent of qawwali – a form of devotional folk music popular throughout the Indian subcontinent. This is a genre that has developed and mutated over hundreds of years and Nusrat was known for his innovative and contemporary style that was very much his own reinterpretation of a tradition handed down through generations of his own family.[12] Despite the modern nature of Nusrat's music, to the untrained ear his qawwali meets many of the criteria of exoticism and authenticity associated with world music. Qawwali is usually performed by a troupe using only their voices and a few acoustic instruments, suggesting a sense of unspoilt tradition which is at the heart of world music's appeal. As James Barrett (1996: 240) suggests, consumers in the West are able to turn their 'touristic gaze' on to a musical form that appears to be a pure exponent of a distant and exotic culture that is transported to and consumed by the West.[13] As Tony Mitchell has commented, 'The more extreme forms of exoticisation in world music recordings and videos position the viewer and listener as privy to a synthetic form of imaginary global travel' (1996: 73).

Covers and titles of world music appeal to what Barrett calls a 'National Geographic' mentality which seeks to consume distant and 'other' cultural forms.[14] The origins of qawwali in the Sufi tradition within Islam also appeals to vague notions of spirituality associated with the East. The fact that qawwali is performed mostly in Urdu and Punjabi means that the specific meaning of the lyrics (which are often in praise of Allah) are largely unintelligible to a Western audience, who nevertheless derive a degree of pleasure from their proximity to an exotic and alien spiritualism (Farrell 1997). As Barrett noted, 'it is as though world music serves as spiritualism for atheists' (1996: 243). In this way world music is evoked in order to import a sense of spirituality into the West to fill the void left by the abandonment of traditional religious practices. The commodification of seemingly traditional non-Western forms within world music indicates a broader process in which Third World cultures are plundered by the West in order to feed a desire for all things pure and authentic.

World music can then perhaps be thought of as the import of new sounds for a bored culture, an audience which is disillusioned by the corporate predictability of music in the West and looks increasingly farther afield in search of musical difference and integrity. This is exemplified by the efforts of a number of Western musicians to revitalize flagging careers by incorporating 'other' exotic musical forms in their output. One such example is the 1986 album *Graceland* which used musicians and musical styles from South Africa to spice up Paul Simon's fading pop sensibilities and resulted in a global hit (Lipsitz 1994; Mitchell 1996). In defence of accusations of exploitation (having worked on his album in South Africa during the apartheid regime), Simon claimed that the African musicians not only benefited financially from the album but were also exposed to a wider global audience that resulted in the revitalization of traditional South African musical forms. As Lazarus has pointed out, however, the interest in 'traditional' and 'authentic' African music(s) stimulated by the huge international success of *Graceland* meant that record companies in the West encouraged African musicians to focus on musical forms that they had previously abandoned, resulting in a stifling effect on the development of new and innovative musical practices in Africa (Lazarus 1994; Lipsitz 1994). In this way the financial profitability of world music and the emphasis placed on pure and authentic music helps to perpetuate the myth of the non-white other as primitive and exotic. Although world music as a distinct genre represents a profitable niche market in the international music industry, there has been little mainstream chart success for its artists in their own right. Despite the fact that Nusrat Fateh Ali Khan has had notable success as a featured artist on film soundtracks[15] and that his albums on the Real World label represent some of the best-selling world music recordings, he has never featured in the singles chart. The Senegalese singer Youssou N'Dour did manage this feat when '7 seconds' (recorded as a duet with Neneh Cherry) charted in the UK in 1994, but it is notable that this song was sung in English and remains his solitary mainstream success.

The processes at work within world music are akin to those discussed in relation to The Beatles' experimentations with Indian music in the late 1960s and can be seen as a part of an ongoing process whereby the East is constructed and 'othered' by the domineering gaze of the West (Said 1978). Indeed, the re-emergence of hippy values through some forms of contemporary dance music (including associations with drugs and spiritual transcendence) is marked by the incorporation of elements of world music (usually in the form of samples and loops) and the iconography of exoticized otherness. The fixing of world music to notions of tradition and cultural authenticity promotes an inappropriate image of areas in the Third World (in this case the East) as well as rendering Asians settled in the West invisible with regard to contemporary musical practices. According to Barrett:

> It [world music] renders the authentic indigene terminally incompatible with the developed world, while sentimentalising aboriginal music as the true expression of human primacy. (1996: 243)

In this way the experiences and cultural practices of contemporary Asians, both on the subcontinent and in the West, are often overlooked unless they conform to Western constructions of authenticity and cultural purity. It would be a mistake, however, to overstate the cultural imperialism thesis with regard to the growth and continuing success of world music. First, we must recognize that notions of difference and authenticity play a central role in the artistic and commercial success of many musical genres. Indeed the introduction of diverse and non-Western musical styles and sounds on to a global music scene previously dominated by an Anglo-American axis is to be celebrated, whatever reservations we might have about the some of the problems this raises. Furthermore, to portray all world musicians merely as victims of Western capital and consumption is a somewhat paternalistic and patronizing practice in itself; we must recognize their ability to challenge and manipulate the system that seeks to profit from their artistry.

As stated earlier, the very networks of international capital set up to maximize profits for retailers and provide a perhaps jaded Western audience with novel and exotic sounds can also have a nurturing effect on the synthesis of new cultural forms and allegiances. As well as revitalizing localized musical forms by opening them up to a global market, the superhighways of international, organized capital can facilitate the emergence and growth of new syncretic musical forms and practices. The music of Nusrat Fateh Ali Khan (who suffered an untimely death in 1997) not only raised the profile of qawwali in his native Pakistan but also had a significant influence on the development of new musical forms throughout the Asian diaspora. In the UK, where Nusrat performed regularly, his influence is particularly marked and many of the young Asian performers who have emerged during the 1990s have cited the singer as a source of inspiration. This influence culminated in the release of *Star rise* in 1997, a CD of remixes of Nusrat's collaborative work with Canadian composer Michael Brook. The album features contributions from a range of young contemporary British Asian musicians, including Aki Nawaz, Black Star Liner and Asian Dub Foundation who, through their reinterpretation of Nusrat's work, highlight the importance of both continuity and change in the expression of diasporic identity.[16]

If we accept that the production and marketing of world music originates in the desire of Western audiences to consume novel and exotic commodities, we must also accept that the international flows set up to exploit this genre can also facilitate the development of new and syncretic cultural forms and practices. The re-articulation and incorporation of Nusrat's work by young Asian musicians in the UK reflects the importance of a diasporic heritage which can be drawn on to construct new modes of ethnic and cultural identity in a contemporary, multi-ethnic environment and is, in part, facilitated by the international networks of the global music industry (Gopinath 1995). These international conduits do not simply enable diasporic allegiances to maintain a sense of purity and linkage with the point of origin, but facilitate the development of new manifestations of cultural identity. Despite the music of Nusrat Fateh Ali Khan having its origins in a particular variation of Islam, his work has acted as a focus for many Asian musicians in the UK from a range of different cultural heritages; *Star rise* features artists from Hindu and Sikh backgrounds as well as Muslims, which, in a time where religious differences and communal tensions are starkly pronounced, offers the possibility of a more inclusive sense of Asian identity within the global collective.

It would be a mistake to suggest, however, that such music only has influence within the bounds of the Asian community; as well as his collaborations with Michael Brook and Peter Gabriel, Nusrat's work has been remixed and reworked by artists as diverse as Massive Attack and Nine Inch Nail's Trent Reznor. What this reflects is that, despite the deep ethical and political problems associated with the exploitation of Third World musical resources, there can be no corporate control over the eventual outcomes of such processes, out of which may emerge new cultural forms and allegiances.

Bhangra: the sound of the East in the West

We have seen how the appeal of both the Indian sound and world music is dependent partly on notions of exoticism and authenticity. This has facilitated a process of consumption whereby musicians and audiences in the West have sought out and utilized novel sounds and styles from the East; bringing them in from the periphery in order to be enjoyed in the comfort of more familiar surroundings. This has meant, particularly in the case of world music, that despite the involvement of many non-Western musicians, the focus of the music – its production, distribution and consumption – always tends to be on the Westerner; what then of the Easterner? As we know, there is a significant Asian presence in the UK as a result of post-war immigration and these settlers and their families have brought with them a range of rich and diverse musical traditions. The consumption of traditional and diasporic musical forms – such as ghazals, Bollywood film soundtracks and a variety of popular styles by Asians – has remained largely invisible to a mainstream that has showed comparatively little interest in these contemporary, populist forms which do not appear to have the same aura of the authentic and pure that fuels much of the consumption of world music. These forms have therefore had to flourish through an underground distribution network which has functioned independently of the national networks that compose the popular music charts. This parallel Asian network has flourished and continues to nurture a variety of musical styles that have occasionally drawn the attention of the established mainstream, as in the case of the contemporary bhangra scene.

Contemporary bhangra emerged in the UK during the mid-1980s from within urban Asian populations around the country and represents the development of a cultural form shaped by migration and diaspora. The music takes its name and origins from a form of Punjabi folk music that is commonly played to celebrate harvest festivals and is characterized by a distinctive percussive rhythm usually played on traditional drums such as tumbi or dholak. Bhangra was imported into the UK along with Asian settlers from the Indian subcontinent and became an important component of social gatherings, particularly weddings. In its contemporary form the traditional bhangra beats are fused with a variety of Western dance styles – taking in genres as diverse as disco, house, rap and ragga – often resulting in the description of musical hybrids such as 'bhangra-house' or 'bhangramuffin'. This illustrates a musical identity that is as much British as it is Asian (Huq 1996: 63). The success of this syncretic musical form is such that contemporary bhangra has become an important element in the cultural expression of Asian diaspora and has been exported not only back to the Indian subcontinent but also to diverse locations around the world where Asians have at some time settled, such as North America, Africa and the Caribbean. Set against this context it is interesting that bhangra is often classed as a sub-category of world music, showing that the othering gaze is equally significant when relocated in contemporary Western settings. Stephen Feld (1991: 134) has suggested that world music can be defined as 'any commercially available music of non-Western origin and circulation as well as ... all musics of dominated ethnic minorities within the Western world.' The perception of bhangra as an 'interior' form of world music, that is an alien cultural form based on traditional (authentic and antiquated) cultural practices, is one of many ways with which bhangra has been othered and arguably has been an important factor in its marginalization within mainstream British popular music.[17]

This process of othering can be seen in the way that bhangra is portrayed as *the* music for *all* Asian youth. Bhangra is often rationalized in this way as somehow being representative of Asian culture as a whole in the UK, which is linked to totalizing notions of the 'Asian community' (see Chapter 2), thus ignoring the diversity of the country's Asian population.[18] This association of bhangra as a cultural representation of a fixed community is a problem that is particularly pertinent to the decidedly non-bhangra acts featured in this study. All the groups I have interviewed felt the need to distance themselves from bhangra and resent any association with the genre, as Aki Nawaz from Fun^Da^Mental illustrated:

> I like the original bhangra but the stuff around now has no vision. It's all about getting paid, like show business or cabaret. They all want to be George Mohammed, like George Michael or something. The scene is petty and trivial and there's no experimentation. (Eshun 1994: 27)

Despite the 'the complex intertextuality and array of musical reference points available to Asian youth' (Huq 1996: 71) public portrayals of contemporary Asian music are centred around the notion of bhangra as *the* music of *the* 'community'. Media portrayals of bhangra in particular have been central to this unifying discourse and have used the musical phenomenon to perpetuate the myth of a separate and uniform Asian community. The emergence of bhangra as a cultural phenomenon associated with Asian youth was portrayed in the British media in ways that confirmed both the otherness of the music (linked explicitly to the notion of community) and many stereotypes of Asian culture and tradition. The phenomenon of daytime bhangra events was seized on by the media as confirming existing stereotypes of the Asian community by focusing on the 'un-Asian' activities of Asian youth. The attendance of all-day bhangra events, particularly by females, was portrayed as antithetical with regard to the traditional values of the Asian community, a community stereotyped as work- and education-oriented and with strict parental controls. Attendants at these events were associated with deviancy as represented by tales of truancy and disobedience. Rupa Huq illustrates this process:

> Notions of 'clandestine clubbers' defying parental authority and shaking the shackles of their traditional Asian upbringing satisfies this requirement, buttressing existing preconceptions and misconceptions of Asian youth. (1996: 67)

If we refer back to Stuart Hall's comments about the way the West perceives the periphery (as closed and pure) we can see how the Orientalist gaze works at 'home'. The stereotype of a closed and unitary Asian community renders Asian youth incompatible with contemporary youth cultures; bhangra is therefore portrayed primarily as an Asian (therefore peripheral) cultural phenomenon and also as a transgressive medium for Asian youth. This perpetuates two notions: that bhangra is specifically Asian (not for 'us' Westerners); and the separateness and incompatibility of Asians with Western cultural practices, as represented by narratives of culture clash and intergenerational strife – clandestine clubbers being a case in point.

The inability of bhangra to cross over into the mainstream via the national charts is a useful way of examining the operationalization of a number of stereotypes of Asianness. The huge audiences generated by bhangra, particularly during the late 1980s, stimulated a great deal of speculation that the genre had much crossover potential, particularly in the context of a revitalized dance scene. Although there have been a few notable crossover success stories (see below), during the height of the bhangra boom during the late 1980s and early 1990s the genre failed to achieve its potential, despite much media hype and speculation. The fact that bhangra lyrics are usually performed in Punjabi has undoubtedly acted as a significant stumbling block to gaining widespread appeal and bolsters the perception of bhangra as an alien cultural form within the UK. Attempts to skirt the language barrier by singing in English have, however, also failed to grasp the imagination of non-Asian audiences, who have remained largely unimpressed by bhangra as a popular British musical genre.

Despite this fact the sheer size of the Asian audience in the UK is such that the genre is an extremely profitable and viable business proposition; however, bhangra has had, until recently, a negligible impact on the national music charts. As Manjit Tamba from the Wolverhampton band Intermix points out, 'Asian groups have been selling thousands of albums for ages but they haven't been registering in the charts' (Simpson 1993: 43). The distribution of bhangra music within Asian communities on what has been called the 'cornershop circuit' has meant that sales are not registered in the national charts. Gallup – who collate the national LP and singles charts – take their chart returns by and large from large high-street chains and do not venture into more specialized Asian shops. Ninder Johal of Nachural Records, speaking in 1993, illustrates this point:

> To date, all sales of Asian acts have been registered in the Asian specialised distribution game. That means cornershops and grocers. Very few albums are sitting in the megastores. Asian shops don't believe in monitoring sales and, even if they did, mainstream organisations such as Gallup have never gone there. (Simpson 1993: 43)

Mainstream record companies and distribution chains have tended to be disinclined to stock music such as bhangra that is seen as having a limited Asian appeal. The financial potential of bhangra remained hidden partly because of its specialized distribution but also because of its perception as Asian music, therefore having no place on a major label or in a mainstream outlet. The fact that bhangra has remained hidden in terms of the charts, mainstream music outlets and therefore also in terms of national radio airplay has helped to perpetuate the stereotype of the genre as belonging to a specific alien community; it has also significantly reduced the ability of the music to be heard by non-Asian audiences. Nevertheless the sheer popularity and large audience for bhangra in the UK would appear to suggest that the genre had great potential to cross over into the mainstream and to make an impact on the national charts. It would seem that bhangra's 'alien' nature and its association with a separate and distinct community has much to do with its lack of crossover success. Even in the 1990s when there were more Asian artists than ever before (many with proven track records) there was still resistance by many within the mainstream record industry.

As Aki Nawaz has stated, 'Larger record shops often don't handle our records because they say no Asian people are buying them. That type of response makes me angry and that goes into the music' (Cook 1996: 32).

In the 1990s, however, by merging musical styles and embarking on carefully planned marketing strategies – usually with the hard-won backing of major labels who have at last been convinced of the marketing potential – bhangra has managed some degree of mainstream success,[19] which has occurred alongside an explosion of Asian artists and sounds across the entire spectrum of popular music in the UK.

Beyond bhangra: Asian sounds for the 1990s

Chart returns: Asians and the mainstream

This expansion across the musical spectrum, along with a revitalized interest in traditional Asian sounds and musical forms meant that bhangra eventually fulfilled its huge potential and began to make a gradual impact on the mainstream. Although the careers of artists such Apache Indian and Bally Sagoo have enjoyed a certain degree of success in the charts, their experiences illustrate some of the difficulties that bhangra acts and Asian artists in general have to negotiate. The emergence of Apache Indian in the early 1990s was heralded by many as the turning point for the involvement of Asians in the mainstream music industry. Undoubtedly Apache Indian's success (including Top 10 singles and the LP *No reservations* being nominated for the Mercury Music Prize in 1995) stimulated much interest in Asian musicians,[20] but his subsequent career has met with a number of difficulties. Apache Indian's success was based on the fusion of certain elements of bhangra onto ragga, which was dubbed bhangramuffin by many in the media (Back 1996). Although originally Apache played up the Asian aspect of his music and embraced the role of community spokesperson with great gusto, he later began to back away from this role, reflecting an increased awareness of the novelty element of his success. His 1996 album *Make way for the Indian* steers clear of 'Indian' issues (unlike his earlier records such as the single 'Arranged marriage' which was a Top 20 hit in 1995) and the music is almost completely devoid of Asian influences. Talking about his role as the 'Gandhi of Pop' in the early 1990s Apache said:

> It got kind of heavy that way, so I've kind of kept away consciously from specific Asian issues on this album. I think I don't have to keep waving the Indian flag all the time. Hopefully the tracks will just stand up: It's either a good hip-hop track or it's not, or a good reggae track or it's not, and afterwards you see it's an Asian guy. (Mitchell 1996: 64)

The burden of representation that Apache Indian clearly felt, combined with his realization of the novelty aspect of his perceived Asianness is something that eventually became tiresome for him, although earlier on he had appeared to embrace such a role. Interestingly enough many of the people I interviewed for this study sought to dismiss Apache Indian as a crass novelty act who did not represent the rich diversity of contemporary music being produced by Asians as Aki Nawaz illustrates:

> I'd prefer it if a mainstream act was actually acknowledged as an Asian thing and the music had some integrity and creativity. A lot of Asians feel that what's there is diluted and it's not what we're about. (Cook 1996: 33)

Another bhangra-influenced success has been the Midlands-based producer/performer Bally Sagoo. After reputedly selling over 100 000 copies of six albums of bhangra and Bollywood-inspired dance music released during the early 1990s on the cornershop distribution network, Sagoo was signed to Columbia Records in 1994 in a deal reputed to be worth £1.2 million. Columbia appeared to invest much money into promoting Sagoo, hoping to translate his massive underground sales into the mainstream. As Simon Reynolds wrote in *The Observer*, the deal represented:

> … a gamble for both Sagoo and Columbia, but the stakes are high: it could be that Asian music will have the same influence on Nineties pop that Jamaican reggae did on the Seventies. (1994: 8)

The breakthrough that Columbia hoped for in 1994 with the release of the LP *Bollywood flashback* failed to emerge and the success of the single 'Dil cheez' (which entered the UK charts at number 12 and resulted in TV appearances for Sagoo on *Top Of The Tops* and the *National Lottery Live*) was perhaps not of the scale hoped for; the record did not hang about in the charts for long. By stressing the need for Asian fans to buy his records from mainstream, chart-monitored outlets (Cook 1996) Sagoo was able to make some inroads into the music charts, but failed to build on his initial success and was dropped by Columbia within a year.

It is perhaps significant that the most notable Asian chart successes during the 1990s came from outside the genre of bhangra and two such acts experienced number one hits with their debut singles during this decade. In 1996 the glam-rock band Babylon Zoo, fronted by Jaz Mann (a musician of Indian extraction but brought up in Wolverhampton), went straight to number one with 'Spaceman', a feat matched in the following year by White Town's 'Your woman'. What is notable about both records is the lack of emphasis put on the Asianness of the musicians involved. Neither of these records has any noticeable Asian instrumentation and their promotion could be said to render the Asianness of their artists relatively invisible. The success of 'Spaceman' was largely based on the use of a remix of the song on a Levi's jeans advertising campaign that fixed the song in Britain's consciousness before anyone had actually seen the artist in question. Similarly White Town's single was able to build its success without breaching the anonymity of the band. In fact White Town is not a band but the project of musician Jyoti Mistri, an Indian-born mature student from Derby.[21] His song was produced by Mistri on a four-track porta-studio in his bedroom and was championed by the BBC DJ Mark Radcliffe on his late-night radio show and promoted with an abstract video that did not feature the artist himself. Initially Mistri refused to give interviews and subsequently the single reached number one without the actual musician being seen.

The anonymity of these big-selling artists compared to less successful but more overtly Asian artists may suggest that the otherness associated with being Asian can still be a burden in terms of marketing certain types of music, at least when performed by Asians. Both Babylon Zoo and White Town have drifted into obscurity since the initial success of their debut singles[22] and it may well be that their subsequent musical output simply did not match the quality of their chart-topping releases; but it may also be indicative of the poor marketability of an Asian image on the national music scene.

This point is emphasized by the career of Freddie Mercury – former lead singer with Queen - who not only managed to break into the mainstream of popular music in Britain, but also managed to become a global superstar with a career eventually spanning three decades. Although Mercury was born in Zanzibar – his name at birth was Farrokh Bulsara and he was brought up in India until the age of 16 – his public persona made little or no reference to his ethnic origins. This public denial of his background (along with a similar refutal of his homosexuality) reflects a man who certainly valued his private life but can also be viewed as part of a calculated and necessary career plan; being Asian and being gay did not sit well with the marketing image of the macho world of the rock star. The notion of an openly gay singer declaring 'Fat bottomed girls, you make my rocking world go round'[23] could be deemed to be alienating for the average heterosexual rock fan. Similarly, the essentially conservative and uncool stereotype of Asian men – more commonly thought of as hard-working shopkeepers or accountants – could be viewed as incompatible with the traditionally white-dominated world of pomp-rock.

By effectively erasing any trace of his ethnic origins Mercury was able to maintain an acceptable public persona that allowed a long and prosperous career, but he also perhaps avoided an opportunity to challenge existing perceptions of Asian culture and identity; although whether he could have enjoyed the same degree of success while asserting his Asianness is a moot point. As a consequence Freddie Mercury is seldom referred to as the most successful Asian musician in Britain's post-war period, and it is notable that his ethnic background is rarely mentioned in biographies, except to state the basic facts of his birth and early years (Jones 1998; Freestone and Evans 2000).[24] Since he is no longer with us (having died of an AIDS-related illness in 1991), it would be unfair to condemn Mercury as a serial 'denialist'; but his career does perhaps reflect the difficulties for Asian musicians to be taken seriously within certain realms of popular music.

The independent scene and the 'new Asian Kool'

The mainstream music industry in the UK as expressed by the weekly singles and LP charts does not, however, represent the full picture. The independent sector of the UK music scene is a vital component in the production and consumption of popular music on a national scale. This area is particularly important in the development of new bands and musical genres and is responsible for maintaining a vibrant live music scene in the UK as well as for producing recordings for retail sales. In the UK the independent sector has become a primary source of artists who have been able to cross over into the mainstream. The so-called Britpop phenomenon of the mid-1990s is indicative of this, with many of the UK's largest acts such as Oasis, Blur and Manic Street Preachers having their origins in the independent sector; indeed Oasis featured in the independent (as well as the mainstream) charts due to their association with Creation Records, despite the fact that Sony owned a major stake in the label and have since assumed total control. In this way the independent sector is seen as both the cutting edge of the music industry and also an indicator of future success and trends. This study has focused on the emergence of Asian bands on this national independent scene during the early- to mid-1990s in this context, as a realm of development and negotiation.

If we look at the emergence of Asian bands on the independent scene we can identify two broad areas, although there is a degree of slippage between them. The first can be defined in terms of what has been called 'Asian dance music' (Sharma, Hutnyk and Sharma 1996) which incorporates a wide range of musical genres such as hip-hop, house and techno. Bands such as Fun^Da^Mental, Asian Dub Foundation and Hustlers HC, emerged as purveyors of politically uncompromising hip-hop and dance, often fused with typically Asian sounds and samples. The emergence of bands such as these during the early 1990s alongside the high-profile success of Apache Indian sparked off a short-lived interest in the national press, resulting in many speculative articles and features in broadcast and printed media alike (Morris 1993). These bands have found a degree of success in the independent charts as well as a high media profile, featuring in many British broadsheets and particularly in the music weeklies *New Musical Express* and *Melody Maker*. Interest in these bands can be linked to the emergence of a dance genre associated with the idea of world music discussed earlier. What had been called 'Ethno-Trance', 'Global Dance' or 'World Dance Fusion' (WDF) fuses contemporary dance music with sounds and samples from Third World sources and is linked to both a burgeoning club and festival scene (Hesmondhalgh 1995). The use of Third World sounds has meant that this genre has often been welcomed by the world music fraternity, with bands such as

TransGlobal Underground regularly playing at the UK's high-profile annual WOMAD (World Music and Dance) festivals at Reading and Morecambe Bay.

The WDF genre makes use of many exotic sounds and iconography from the Third World, in particular the East. The fascination with transcendence, spirituality and mind-altering drugs is central to much of WDF and represents the emergence of a neo-hippy culture for the 1990s. This contemporary dance genre exhibits many of the interests and cultural forms previously associated with the hippies of the late 1960s, as illustrated by Iestyn George's somewhat cynical reading of the scene:

> Global house introduced African and Asian styles to an entirely different audience, inadvertently encouraging them to dabble with tie-dye clothing, nose-rings and Eastern spiritualism. Next thing you know, it's all 18–30 holiday packages to Goa and the inner-self. (1996: 65)

The commodification that surrounds this particular genre has also taken on the notion of the spiritual pilgrimage to India, although this practice has been transformed somewhat by the hedonistic pursuits of all-night clubbers. India has become an important focal point for this dance scene and Goa in particular has become a destination for neo-hippy 'dance-tourism', fêted as a site of easy access to drugs and a source of exciting nightlife. Asian bands such as Black Star Liner have sometimes been linked to this dance scene – much to the annoyance of the bands themselves – reflecting the continual tendency to associate Asian music with a mythic sense of the East that is invariably linked to 1960s hippy culture, as band member Choque Hosein has stated:

> We don't have to have a load of rhetorical hippy bollocks behind it … I found it really offensive that somebody said we were kind of like a hippy band. It's as if a band uses Asian music, well, we've got to be psychedelic. (Bennun 1996: 23)

Nation Records undoubtedly played a significant role in the development of WDF, particularly though the output of TransGlobal Underground, who have had some success in the mainstream album charts, and also through bands such as Loop Guru and Zuvuya. Other bands on the label such as Fun^Da^Mental and Asian Dub Foundation have not been associated with WDF or, if so, to a much lesser degree. For these bands, as well as being subject to familiar stereotypes of exoticism and difference they are also subject to analyses that emphasize their politics as the primary focus of study. Undoubtedly there is a political element to both of these bands but this has been often overemphasized by both journalists and academics at the expense of the music (Sullivan 1994; George 1994; Hutnyk 1996) which, as we shall see, is extremely frustrating for the musicians involved.

Within the wider independent scene political issues are undoubtedly a significant factor, since many smaller labels have their origins in the desire to produce music away from the overbearing power of the major corporations. During the

1980s the notion of independence was linked also to a specific musical tradition which merged and co-existed with the ideology of self-sufficiency which has its roots in the punk tradition of the late 1970s, when the DIY ethic was self-apparent in both the playing of music and the setting-up and running of record labels. Both Cornershop and Voodoo Queens emerged from what can be called this 'indie guitar' scene that had been notable, until their arrival, for the lack of both Asians and black people in general. Both bands can be seen as part of the tradition of guitar-based independent music that originated in punk and worked its way through a vibrant 1980s scene that spawned bands like The Smiths and the Jesus and Mary Chain. These bands produced noisy guitar-based music that was far less self-consciously Asian, although Cornershop made use of Indian instruments as part of an eclectic repertoire. Although there was, to a certain degree, a political aspect to these groups, this was only one element of their identity which was nevertheless seized upon by the press to portray the bands in certain, restricted ways. The inherent left-field political perspective that exists within the independent scene has meant that political issues have been an important feature of this sector of the music industry, as witnessed by the success of the Rock Against Racism movement in the late 1970s and early 1980s and in the deliberately provocative anti-establishment lyrics of bands like Chumbawumba and New Model Army.

The lack of explicit political references in the music of Cornershop and Voodoo Queens (with some notable exceptions) did not prevent the music press from portraying these bands as radically political, and both were linked to the Riot Grrrl scene that enjoyed a brief spell of notoriety during the early 1990s. Asian bands emerging on to a largely white indie-guitar scene often preoccupied with a vague leftish political agenda were seen as authentic figureheads for (in particular) anti-racist politics. As we shall see, this overemphasis on the political aspects of these bands is a source of some irritation for the musicians who have had to struggle to be heard as creative artists in their own right. The initial wave of publicity surrounding Asian bands during this period quickly faded, suggesting that a novelty appeal had been central to the media's interest; what Anjali Bhatia, singer-songwriter with Voodoo Queens called the 'Hey they're Asians!' effect (Huq 1996: 73). There has been an inability, both in the media and in academic writing, to separate the ethnicity of Asian musicians from their artistry (Glanvill 1996). Asian artists have found it difficult to express their ability as musicians without falling foul of stereotypes pertaining to either the quasi-mystical or notions of political authenticity.

Conclusion: syncretic soundscapes or sound stereotypes?

The recent history of Asian influences and Asian participation in popular music in the UK has been the story of an uphill struggle for recognition and respect. The almost non-existent public profile of Asian artists, combined with stereotypical representations of Asian culture and music, has made it difficult for Asians to make themselves heard within the popular mainstream. Throughout the 1990s and beyond we have, however, witnessed an increasing number of Asian bands and musicians establishing themselves on the national music scene. Towards the end of the decade, the rise of the so-called 'New Asian Underground' (Simpson 1997; Mir 1998) saw the emergence of artists at the cutting edge of British dance culture, as exemplified by Talvin Singh's ultra-hip *Anokha* club night at London's Blue Note. Singh, an accomplished tabla player who has worked with artists such as Massive Attack and Björk and been name-dropped by David Bowie, was included (along with Tjinder Singh) in *Select* magazine's list of 'The one hundred most important people in the world' (1997).

Towards the end of the 1990s the critical success of British Asian bands had reached a level that would have seemed unlikely, if not impossible, just a decade earlier. Between 1998 and 2000 five Asian bands/artists[25] were nominated for the Mercury Music Prize; Talvin Singh's debut album *OK* won it in 1999. This critical landmark, coming in the aftermath of Cornershop's chart-topping single 'Brimful of Asha' in 1998, is indicative of how far Asian musicians had moved on during the 1990s. By the end of the decade it could no longer be said that Asians were invisible on the wider UK music scene. The sheer number and diversity of Asian artists and music is such that it would be hard to imagine the future of popular music in Britain without them. This does not, however, represent the establishment of some multicultural utopia, as the experiences of these musicians continue to be shaped by deep-rooted stereotypes and assumptions that can stifle and frustrate any of these new artistic endeavours. The drive to assert new modes of cultural expression is not necessarily a simple matter of self-awareness but represents in part a process of negotiation between competing notions of Asian identity and culture. The articulation of new musical forms then is driven partly by the pressures and challenges of debates about what it means to be Asian in contemporary Britain and the following chapter will therefore begin to consider how some of these processes are lived out in practice.

Notes

1. It is interesting that as more 'cool' images of Asian youth (Jimi Mistry, Talvin Singh, etc.) have become more commonplace, so too have images of (mainly male) Asians as criminals and thugs, as evidenced by press reports of rioting or 'racist attacks' on white people in the north of England.
2. The preceding Beatles LP *Revolver* included the track 'Love you too' which utilized tablas, tanpura and sitar.
3. He summarizes the main features borrowed from Indian music by Western pop artists as:

    1) Drones, on sitar, and sometimes *tanpura*.

2) Partial use of specific Indian sounds, such as the *taraf* or sympathetic strings of the sitar being stroked in a descending scale.
3) Mimicking of certain types of vocal delivery perceived to be Indian in style – e.g. flat tone, with slides, slurs, etc.
4) The occasional use of additive rhythmic ideas based on *tals*.
5) Melodies based on modes which correspond to *thats* or Indian scale types.
6) Imitative questions and answers between instruments, like the *saval-javab* sections of Indian performances.
7) Instruments shadowing vocal lines in unison.
8) Mystical or quasi-religious lyrics.

(Farrell 1997: 182)

4. This point should not of course detract from the musical excellence of Shankar's work, nor his long and active role in seeking out musical innovations and exchanges with Western music.
5. Despite their clear admiration for The Beatles, Oasis have not drawn upon the Indian influence of George Harrison to any great extent, although they did achieve a number one hit with the single 'The Hindu Times' in 2002.
6. Both tracks taken from Kula Shaker's 1996 debut LP *K*.
7. Johnny Cigarettes' live review of the band in *NME* reflects the cynical approach of many music journalists towards Kula Shaker's appropriation of 'Indian' influences:

> So you have to admire their shamelessly maverick eccentricity when they get more and more Indian on us at the expense of trad-rock thrills. Except that we're getting bored already. A lava-lamp projected onto a duvet quilt on the backdrop, and a few lines off the back of a Sharwood's packet is no excuse for an extended cross-legged tabla-rock wank … if they want to start living in our hearts as well as the charts they better start saying something other than, 'We've been to India and we're gonna use it.' (1996: 43)

8. *It Ain't Half Hot Mum* was a successful BBC sitcom during the 1970s which focused on the lives of British army entertainers in India during the Second World War and has since become somewhat notorious for its use of racial stereotyping, with the lead Indian role (Rangi Ram) being played by 'browned-up' white actor Michael Bates.
9. A style sported by a number of celebrities, including Sting, Prince, Demi Moore and Gwen Stephani (*Q*, August 1998: 7).
10. A sample of the lyrics translates as: 'I worship the guru's lotus feet, Awakening the happiness of the self-revealed' ('Shanti/Ashtangi' from the 1998 LP *Ray of light*).
11. Madonna has sinced turned to the Jewish mystical tradition of Kabbalah for her spiritual needs and has continued to explore a range of fashion options, including a period of wearing Union Jack-festooned garments and accessories.
12. The qawwali of Nusrat Fateh Ali Khan is distinctive both in its intensity and the upbeat nature of its rhythms. This more forceful version of the genre has since been developed further by groups such as Rizwan Muazzam Qawal who have worked with Fun^Da^Mental and are described by Aki Nawaz as having a 'punk rock' attitude to their music.
13. Tony Mitchell refers to world music as 'sonic tourism' (1996: 68).
14. In his discussion of 'pygmy pop' Stephen Feld examines the music of Deep Forest (whose dance remixes featuring samples from a range of African 'native' sources sold millions around the world) and he is particularly critical of the marketing strategies that they have adopted:

> Deep Forest's liner notes, publicity, video, art packaging (childlike scrawls, forest symbols) and audio design are a treasure textbook of every essentializing, romanticizing, exoticizing trope available. (2001: 272)

15. In *Natural Born Killers* (directed by Oliver Stone, 1994) Nusrat's music appeared over a hallucinatory riot scene in a prison; in *Dead Man Walking* (directed by Tim Robbins, 1995) it accompanied Sean Penn's final moments on death row and in *The Last Temptation of Christ* (directed by Martin Scorsese, 1988) he added his vocals to Peter Gabriel's soundtrack which constructed a world music orchestra, fusing styles and musicians located throughout the Third World.
16. Each band included written tributes to the great qawwali maestro, praising his role in inspiring their own contemporary musical styles which have, in turn, been used to radically reinterpret a selection of his work on the album. Imran Khan, journalist and editor of *2nd Generation* magazine, sums up the mood of the contributors by writing in the album's liner notes:

> Nusrat Fateh Ali Khan is one of the world's leading voices. Listening to him always takes me back to my childhood and listening to my father's tapes. Now the thought of some of Britain's best young Asian artists collaborating with him gives me such a great buzz. This is our generation's way of saying 'respect due'. (Realworld 1997)

17. This is not limited to the experiences of bhangra musicians, as reflected by the appearance of bands like Fun^Da^Mental and Asian Dub Foundation at several WOMAD events and festivals. The aligning of such contemporary bands alongside more traditional world music(s) could be seen to emphasize again notions of difference and incompatibility with more Western and mainstream norms; that is ethnic = world = difference.
18. During the course of my research I have often found that many people assume that since I am writing a book about Asian music then actually I must be writing a book about bhangra.
19. Early in 2003 the track 'Mundian to bach ke' (Instant Karma) by Panjabi MC entered the singles chart at number five, becoming the first Top 10 bhangra record in the UK. Whether this is the long-awaited breakthrough for bhangra or simply a one-off remains to be seen.
20. Dave Simpson wrote in *Melody Maker*: 'Apache Indian is in the charts and on TV. Cornershop and Fun^Da^Mental are in the press. Suddenly music made by Asians is big news' (13 February 1993: 42).
21. Mistri has self-deprecatingly described himself as a 'porky Asian guy' (Williams 1997: 15).
22. Although both bands enjoyed a degree of success with sales of their debut LPs released on the back of their hit singles, subsequent releases have failed to make much of an impact and have failed to enter the Top 20 of the national singles chart.
23. 'Fat bottomed girls', written by guitarist Brian May, was released as a double A-side (with 'Bicycle race') in 1978, reaching number 11 in the UK chart and features such avowedly heterosexual lyrics such as:

> Heap big woman you made a bad boy out of me
> Oh you gonna take me home tonight (please)
> Oh down beside that red fire light
> Oh you gonna let it all hang out
> Fat bottomed girls you make the rocking world go round

24. Although on a fan-based website his origins are used to evoke the originality and exoticism of Mercury's unique persona, stating that: 'From the day he was born, Freddie Mercury was never far from a unique and exotic lifestyle.' (www.freddiemercury.net, accessed 2002)
25. In 1998 Cornershop were nominated for *When I was born for the 7th time* and Asian Dub Foundation for *Rafi's revenge*. In 1999, when Talvin Singh triumphed with *OK*, Black Star Liner were also nominated for *Bengali bantam youth experience* and in 2000 Nitin Sawhney's *Beyond skin* made the shortlist.

Chapter 5

Marketing the exotic: Asian bands and the novelty effect

The emergence of Asian bands on the national music scene in the UK during the 1990s inevitably drew a great deal of interest and attention from within the industry and associated media. The previous lack of a significant public profile for Asian musicians in Britain was such that a certain focus of this interest inevitably centred on the political and cultural elements of these emergent artists. Within the context of such a notoriously unstable industry and fickle public, the importance of novelty and difference is a key factor in the reporting and marketing of new bands and artists. In the case of many Asian bands, however, the novelty effect, while undoubtedly helping to raise profiles, could also be claimed to draw upon a number of reductive ethnic and racial stereotypes. So while the emergence of Asian artists resulted in the articulation – within the music press at least – of a new, fashionable and hip identity known as 'Asian Kool' (Simpson 1993), a curious mix of political radicalism and mystical exoticism was also apparent in a range of reporting and media interest. Not only did these impressions tend to lump together a range of diverse musicians who had little in common – but for the fact that some or all of their members came from an Asian background of some sort – they did so in a way that confirmed many existing stereotypes of black and Asian people, and often at the cost of ignoring the actual musical output of such artists.

Although certain stereotypical readings of Asian music and culture have been prevalent in much of the media coverage of these bands, it would be a mistake to perceive the nature of such coverage as part of any great conspiracy. It is certainly the case that many of these bands, particularly those who are still functioning after some period of time, have had to fight very hard to make themselves heard in a way that fully recognizes their artistry; but we also have to consider in a more pragmatic way the vagaries of the music industry within which *all* bands have to function. Many of the Asian bands during this initial period were certainly subject to stereotyping and generalization, but it is also fair to say that their profiles were raised and nurtured partly because of the 'unusual' fact of their Asianness, however this was portrayed. Since the music industry is dependent on the new and unusual, the sudden emergence of a number of Asian bands provided the industry with another new scene to promote. Although many of these bands did not necessarily seek out such attention, we need to consider the possible ways in which they could use their Asianness to promote themselves. The wisdom of cashing in on any kind of novelty effect seems a somewhat dubious strategy and would seem to imply a short-lived period of appeal and limited career potential. As we shall see, the musicians interviewed for this study put great emphasis on the integrity of their music above all else and have tended to avoid promoting themselves as some kind of exotic novelty. Despite this the bands in question have not been able to ignore the issue, since how bands are portrayed in the media is often out of their control and bands constantly have to manoeuvre and mediate their identities in order to counter some of the stereotypes thrown up by the industry.

In this chapter I shall focus on the complex negotiations at the heart of the struggle for Asian bands and musicians to be heard on their own terms and to be recognized primarily as artists, rather than as representatives of some exotic and imagined community. First, the initial reaction of the UK music press towards Asian bands will be examined, especially the emphasis placed on the importance of anti-racist political perspectives by music writers and journalists. Second, I shall consider the importance of novelty and difference in popular musical reportage and examine attempts by the music press to exploit and promote the manifestation of the 'new' phenomenon of Asian bands. Third, the potential benefits of self-promotion in terms of novelty based on either exotic mysticism or political radicalism will be discussed by considering issues of pragmatism and artistic integrity. Finally, I will discuss the various techniques that Asian bands have adopted in order to transgress stereotypical readings of their work to enable themselves to survive and flourish as part of the national music scene.

'Angry young Asians': initial press reactions

When Fun^Da^Mental and Cornershop first appeared on the UK music scene they drew a large amount of press coverage which, in retrospect, seemed out of all proportion with the initial size of the bands' audiences and record sales. The two groups had little in common musically or lyrically; both bands used elements of Asian music but in starkly different ways. Fun^Da^Mental used samples of a variety of Asian instruments, fusing them with hard hip-hop beats and uncompromising lyrics provided by dual rappers Goldfinger and Sha-Lallaman. Cornershop, in marked contrast, used actual Asian instruments (sitar and dholki in particular) in their repertoire, although these were usually subsumed behind a wall of sound provided by a three-guitar line-up. Lyrically Cornershop were much more ambiguous in their approach, even when they encouraged people to 'Fight the Power!'[1] they remained rather vague and non-specific about what this actually entailed. This phrase was seized upon eagerly by the national music press, which subsequently portrayed Cornershop as an 'angry' band with a radical political agenda. This image was certainly encouraged by the actions of the band themselves when they burned a photograph of indie-veteran Morrissey outside the office of his record label in London as a protest against the singer's flirtation with nationalist and allegedly fascist imagery. Whether or not this marked Cornershop as a band with an explicitly political agenda is open to debate, but *New Musical Express* and *Melody Maker* certainly portrayed them in this way.

Both of these publications are staffed by writers who have their roots in the punk generation and many of them have a musical background. There is an openly acknowledged anti-racist tone adopted by both publications which is grounded in the specific historical context of the Rock Against Racism movement, as founded and organized by the Anti-Nazi League in 1976 and involving many major punk and new-wave bands, including The Clash and Elvis Costello (Frith and Street 1992). In 1993 the reconstituted Anti-Nazi League set out to emulate the popular anti-racist politics of the late 1970s in response to a number of highly publicized racist attacks and the disturbing (although ultimately limited) increase in the electoral activity of the right-wing British National Party (BNP). Part of this process included harnessing the support of a range of bands and musicians very much emulating the earlier Rock Against Racism movement which had proved such an important rallying cry. The summer of 1993 witnessed a number of anti-racist events such as festivals, carnivals and demonstrations, the most notable being the 50 000-strong march in protest at increased BNP activity near the party's headquarters in Welling, Kent.

The revival of organized and popular anti-racist expression was embraced wholeheartedly by the staff of *NME* and *Melody Maker*, who often evoked the spirit of Rock Against Racism in promoting the events of the summer. Against this backdrop an avowedly political and anti-racist band like Fun^Da^Mental were almost certain to draw attention. In May of that year both publications featured stories on Fun^Da^Mental, who were at that time part of the United Colours of Frustration tour with rapper Blade and ska-punk band Blaggers ITA. This tour was put together by the three acts in order to raise awareness of the everyday racism experienced by black and Asian people in the UK and was an attempt to encourage young people to take an active role in anti-racist politics. The tour was used by the *NME* to run a special edition with a Rock of Rages theme (1 May 1993), which was intended to reflect the existence of a new radicalism on the UK music scene. As the article on the United Colours of Frustration tour shows, the desire to promote this new radicalism was clearly inspired by the glories of a Rock Against Racism past. The header for the article read:

> The 70s had Rock Against Racism, the 80s Red Wedge, and now, for the 90s comes The United Colours of Frustration, a triple header of the most politicised anti-fascist new acts in Britain. (Cigarettes 1993: 17)

The desire to lump together a range of disparate musicians and present them as a seemingly unified and discrete scene is undoubtedly a common journalistic technique within the music press, and the coverage of Asian bands throughout the 1990s was no exception. The fact that several Asian bands emerged during the same period meant that it was perhaps inevitable that they would all be grouped together, despite any real lack of musical similarity between them. Voodoo Queens found themselves associated with two different scenes current in the music press of the early 1990s. They were either associated with the emergent Riot Grrrl scene or with other Asian bands, even to the extent of earning the label of 'the female Cornershop' (Dalton 1993: 17). Lead singer/songwriter Anjali felt that such associations were focused on to the extent that the press coverage that Voodoo Queens enjoyed tended to ignore their actual musical output:

> The whole thing with Voodoo Queens was that people never really concentrated on the music. It was more about that whole scene ... it was like everything to do with the scene rather than the musical content. (Personal interview 2003)

This is evidenced in the way that the band almost automatically would be asked questions about issues such as racism, apparently simply because the band contained a number of Asian members. Anjali also felt that, having raised such issues, the press did not necessarily represent their responses fairly and had misrepresented her views on issues such as racism.[2]

There is no doubting that Fun^Da^Mental were one of the most politicized anti-racist acts in Britain and at the time of the 'National Confront' piece in *NME*'s Rock of Rages issue they had recently released their first single, the provocatively entitled 'Wrath of the Blackman' – which had been declared single of the week by both *Melody Maker* and *NME* – and made no bones about their uncompromising political stance.[3] This is exemplified by their release of 'Dog tribe' in 1994, a track that advocated self-defence in response to racist attacks and began with a recorded threat from the far-right terrorist group Combat 18 that had been left on the answerphone of Nation Records in London.[4] The accompanying video graphically depicted not only the victim of a racist beating but subsequent vigilante action against the attackers. The controversy that followed, including the refusal of a number of daytime television programmes such as ITV's *The Chart Show* to air the video, was typical of the kind of attention that Fun^Da^Mental attracted and perhaps courted in the early 1990s.

Despite the degree of press coverage that Fun^Da^Mental attracted, largely due to the radical political nature of their lyrics, the band themselves were unhappy with their press coverage. Band members Aki Nawaz and Dave Watts both felt that the band had been misrepresented by journalists and that, rather than expressing the true views of the band, the interpretation of the band's political agenda amounted to little more than a token gesture. Aki and Dave felt that their politics were not represented in any depth and presented in a way that simply reflected the journalists' desire to stress their anti-racist credentials by associating themselves with the 'authenticity' of Fun^Da^Mental's radical political views. Dave Watts told me:

> A lot of times when we do press, when we go away with journalists or whatever, what comes out in the final print is ... what you hear is *their* views coming out. (Personal interview 1996)

This criticism was one that I discussed with David Stubbs (staff writer at *Melody Maker*) who explained that restraints on column space meant that the editing of interviews often resulted in an uneven analysis that inevitably reflected the perspective of the writer or the editorial policy of the magazine in question:

> Sometimes the only power you have as a writer is you might talk about an hour and you only get to use about 10–15 minutes even in a large piece, you have to cut out quite a lot and it may be that journalists reflect their own biases by putting down what they want to hear and some of the stuff you can ignore. That's always potential distortion that you get in interviews. (Personal interview 1996)

It is perhaps inevitable that journalists will focus on the novel aspects of any new musical trend or genre; and since political radicalism and authenticity can be a marketable commodity within the music industry, deliberately provocative issues and opinions represented by Fun^Da^Mental certainly lend themselves to this kind of attention. Aki Nawaz and Dave Watts felt, however, that such a focus only amounted to part of the problem and that their misrepresentation in the press had more to do with journalists' inability to adapt to and understand different cultural perspectives. They cited as extreme examples of this occasions when journalists from both of the weekly music papers had accompanied the band to Pakistan: Stephen Sweet from *Melody Maker* in 1993 and *NME*'s Steven Wells in 1995. On both occasions the attendant journalists focused mainly on the deprivations of a Third World setting, Stephen Sweet stating that he'd been experiencing 'every horror that the Third World has to offer' (1993: 8); while Steven Wells dedicated a large part of his four-page piece to details of his stomach upset and his search for 'English' food among the squalor of contemporary Pakistan. This kind of behaviour has led Aki to claim that the white liberal press 'don't know what we're on about' and that, despite their commitment to anti-racist politics, journalists had no real idea about the lived experiences of black and Asian people and no understanding of the realities of the contemporary Third World. In Aki's own words:

> The British and Europeans claim to be so intellectually wise, full of wisdom and understanding, I think they analyse from here because they haven't had first-hand experience of the Third World. That was the whole point of taking these journalists over there and I think it served its purpose brilliantly, for, whatever anyone thinks, it exposed them, it exposed even the most liberal thinking; even the most politically correct journalist does not understand and he does not know how to adapt. (Personal interview 1996)

He felt that this reflected a more general malaise whereby self-appointed white 'experts' study and dissect non-white cultures of which they actually have very little knowledge. As Aki put it, 'people of colour are always having fingers pointed at them' and having their cultures analysed by white, liberal intellectuals who are seemingly unable to look at themselves and talk about their own shortcomings. Aki put this at the heart of the inability of the national music press to get to grips with Fun^Da^Mental; he felt that the Asian press in the UK was far better equipped to analyse the band since Asian journalists had common points of reference based on shared and lived experiences. At times Aki does appear to be retreating towards the 'dubious comfort of ethnic particularity' (Gilroy 1993a) discussed in Chapter 2 and seems to be suggesting that his music can only be fully understood by non-white listeners. This somewhat absolutist stance is not based on spurious notions of biology, however, but centres around notions of difference based on experience. The importance of lived experiences of prejudice and racism was at the heart of Aki's criticism of the music press and white intellectuals in general:

> I have discussions with white intellectuals, they've read so many books but they haven't interacted with people so they don't understand. The best books written about black people are written by black people, with white intellectuals ... it all exists just in that book; it doesn't exist outside.

This rejection of the views of 'white intellectuals' when it comes to issues of race and racism reflects Aki's commitment to unmediated self-expression by black and Asian people and is certainly informed by his experiences within the music industry over a period spanning three decades.

The problem of misrepresentation by the music press was perhaps more pronounced in the case of Cornershop who, despite having a more ambiguous political aspect, were featured in the same *NME* issue as Fun^Da^Mental under the banner Rock of Rages. Despite attempts to link the band to the 'radical scene' and portray them as the 'voice of disaffected Asian youth' the members of the group tended to distance themselves from such a role and guitarist Avtar actually states 'We're not political' (Wells 1993: 13). This is not to suggest that Cornershop did not express any political ideas but was an attempt to challenge the notion that the band were nothing without their politics. As Muggleton has suggested in his study of post-subcultural style, individuals often seek to distance themselves from any notion of an organized political agenda since this is felt to detract from their individuality:

> It is not that they do not hold any political opinions that can be construed as 'political'; rather, they are declaring their indifference to or lack of sympathy for overt political agendas and organised political groups. (2000: 149)

Despite this the band were constantly being portrayed as a group with a radical agenda, in fact this impression resulted in an extremely high media profile even to the extent that founder member Ben Ayres reflected that the band 'got far too much press' during this period. Cornershop's association with the UK Riot Grrrl scene[5] was often used to suggest the band's radical credentials, but it was the exotic politics of a band seen as angry young Asians that plagued much of their press coverage. This label above all has been a constant thorn in the band's side, and still has some currency, despite the fact that in 2003 Cornershop currently had only one Asian member; in the early 1990s two out of four members were Asian but, as Ben explains, this fact was often ignored by the press:

> I think the misreporting was the thing that really annoyed us a lot, when it was, like, 'Four angry young Asian lads', it was like 'Hang on a minute!' You haven't even done your research.' People want to overemphasize anything and to a certain extent if they had said that it was Asian lads *and* white guys together, then it's almost stronger isn't it? (Personal interview 1996)

The portrayal of Cornershop as a radical and authentic Asian band by the music press clearly reflects the workings of an exotic politics which seeks to define non-whites one-dimensionally in terms only of their politics, in particular the struggle against racism. This has the effect (as shown in the use of the Rock of Rages banner) of ignoring the subtleties and ambiguities at work within Asian bands, which are all lumped together in order to represent a political agenda that exists outside the bands (and may or may not exist within them) and finally has the effect of minimizing the importance of, or ignoring entirely, the musical output itself. This initial experience with the national press was a sobering and sometimes bitter one and a reminder of the limited power that emerging musicians have over their own representation. As Tjinder Singh told me in 1996:

> When we first started getting all these interviews, that was just like, ridiculous, we didn't think anything like that was going to happen and we're really, really happy that it stopped.

It is certainly the case that all the band members I spoke to were somewhat wary of the music press in particular and the media in general. While they certainly acknowledged that they had received a good deal of attention from the music press in the early days, they were not always happy with their portrayal. Of course these experiences are not exclusive to Asian musicians and it is clear that emergent bands are vulnerable to misrepresentation or even manipulation by the press, the distress of which is magnified by inexperience and perhaps by unrealistic expectations. After working in the music industry for a number of years most of the musicians I interviewed had adopted a much more pragmatic attitude towards the press. Looking back on her days in Voodoo Queens, Anjali commented that:

> I can understand in a way that that's what happens when you're brought up within this whole *machine* and then you get spat out very quickly. You know, so it's like a learning experience. (Personal interview 2003)

Writing the weeklies: seeking out the new

While it is certainly the case that most of the musicians discussed here have regarded the music press with suspicion and occasional anger, their experiences have undoubtedly increased their understanding of the workings of the industry as a whole. The commercial imperatives of selling both records and magazines mean that the relationship between the artist and the press is a necessary, if at times uncomfortable, one. The pressure for journalists and magazine editors to produce exciting and up-to-the-minute coverage of an ever-shifting music scene is such that the room for misunderstanding and misrepresentation is evident. In the UK in particular, with its long history of innovation in pop and rock and where coverage is geared towards the weekly, these pressures are acutely pronounced. In order to reflect on this further I also spoke to a number of individuals representing two of the most important 'gatekeepers' of the industry, namely journalists and the owners of record labels (Negus 1992).

On the issue of the degree of press coverage assigned to Asian bands during the early 1990s, there was a clear consensus that some had received a large amount of coverage that was not necessarily in proportion to their commercial success. For example Caroline Sullivan, music critic at *The Guardian*, felt that Fun^Da^Mental had received more press coverage than 'they musically deserved' (personal interview 1996) and David Stubbs of *Melody Maker* also thought that Cornershop 'got more press than other bands of say, similar mediocrity' (personal interview 1995). Despite this, both journalists felt that the coverage of these bands was justifiable in terms of what might be defined as their unique or novel position on the UK music scene. The seemingly sudden emergence of Asian bands during the early 1990s[6] was picked up by sections of the music press where, in David Stubbs's words, 'coverage is weighted towards the new' and, even if a band like Cornershop were not perceived as musically innovative, then 'from the journalistic point of view, their existence is more interesting'.

The tendency for press interest to be fleeting and to treat bands in what could be considered a throwaway fashion may well be influenced by the weekly structure of the UK music press. During the mid-1990s Cornershop were gaining much attention in the USA through the success of *Woman's gotta have it* and felt that they had received a more considered press coverage because the emphasis there was on monthly rather than weekly publications. In such an environment bands arguably have longer to establish themselves and particular releases also have a far longer shelf life, as Wiiija boss Gary Walker explained:

> It's swings and roundabouts, do you know what I mean? We've got loads of attention in America, we've got a page in *Rolling Stone*, so you don't get too upset about a shift in interest in the weeklies over here [in the UK]. Also there's a very different kind of emotional set-up over here, for example with 'Jullander Shere', a lot of journalists say. well, 'Jullander Shere' is a track which is nearly a year old now,[7] whereas in America you can flog one album for a year and a half. If Cornershop spend the next six to eight months touring America, again everyone over here will say 'Oh, Cornershop have disappeared without a trace.' (Personal interview 1996)

The weekly frequency of publication in the UK appears to encourage a novelty effect which creates a high turnover of controversial and sensational stories, whereas more leisurely monthly publishing in the USA tends to allow a more considered approach, as Ben Ayres explained:

> Over here, *Melody Maker* and *New Musical Express* ... they create things to be gobbled up by people on a weekly basis. That basis means that they have to keep changing it, keep trying to make it, I suppose in their eyes, seem interesting to people. In the States they write about music on a more monthly basis and therefore they write more about instruments and music and wherever they're coming from musically. (Personal interview 1996)

Although there was some interest in what Gary Walker called the 'background of the band and where they fit, in terms of the social, political context within the UK' all of the bands I spoke to seem to agree that they received a much more considered and open-minded press coverage outside the UK, in either the USA or Europe.[8]

Caroline Sullivan expanded this point further when interviewed in 1996 by reflecting that a lot of the initial coverage 'had a lot to do with novelty' and that her own personal interest in Asian music during this period was inspired by curiosity and that she had approached the subject 'quite voyeuristically' at first. This curiosity was stimulated by the previous lack of Asian bands (or at least Asian bands with a high profile) and by what she saw as a discrepancy between Asian culture and music cultures such as hip-hop and rock. Aside from the personal level of curiosity and interest, she also felt that the media had acted in a supportive manner towards Asian bands of this period:

> I would say that in the beginning when they first came along, say three or four years ago [that is 1992–3], I would say the music press quite sincerely wanted to give them [Asian bands] a helping hand and they realized that there had never been any real coverage of Asian music, they realized that it was a situation which had to be redressed. I think the press gave them a lot of time and space, relatively, a lot of space, to prove themselves.

Sullivan also felt that the relatively small number of Asian bands around at this time inevitably meant that those that did exist would attract a large degree of interest and curiosity. Although several years later the novelty of Asian bands had subsided somewhat ,[9] she felt that there was still a significant curiosity effect to be accounted for because 'when an Asian person makes rock or rap music they are virtually in a field of one'.

Novelty and marketability: exploiting ethnicity or challenging stereotypes?

As we have seen, the music industry thrives on the novel; difference can be marketed and sold like any other commodity (Harker 1980; Lull 1987; Negus 1992), and the emergence of Asian bands during the early 1990s unearthed much potential for marketing in terms of difference. Whether or not intended by the bands themselves, two attendant and stereotypical modes of difference emerged which could be used to promote the bands and help establish a high public profile. The stereotypes of 'angry young Asians' and 'mystical Indians' were paramount in this reckoning and often combined to project an exotic and idealized image for Asian bands. For any emergent band it is important to use any unique characteristics that exist in order to raise profiles and garner attention. Therefore we need to consider the extent to which these bands knowingly or subconsciously used the novelty potential of their Asianness to promote themselves and increase their audience. First, I want to consider the self-publicizing marketing potential inherent in the media's interpretation of Asian bands as radical and subversive, as an authentic political vanguard of the left during the 1990s.

Selling politics

Fun^Da^Mental, as one of the most overtly political acts in the UK, are a good place to begin since they have the most potential to sell themselves in this way and, undoubtedly, the band's politics has gained them a lot of attention in the music press and in the broadsheets. I asked Aki Nawaz whether or not the band had ever made a conscious effort to play up the image of the angry young Asian and he told me that it simply was not necessary since they were routinely asked 'pathetic questions' by the press and portrayed in a one-dimensional manner. Although the focus on the radical political agenda of the band undoubtedly raised Fun^Da^Mental's public image, the single-mindedness of this profile has proved to be a double-edged sword, as Dave Watts told me in 1996:

> Well you see, basically you're in a no-win situation because when we did the instrumental album [10] it was like, 'Ah well, yeah, that's not really an album,' it's just like 'Where's the politics?'.

Both Watts and Nawaz feel that Fun^Da^Mental have been represented in the press simply as a token example of political radicalism; articles on the band seem to focus on anti-racist politics rather than on music. In response to this, attempting to confound press expectations has become part of the band's political and musical agenda; and was certainly part of the reasoning behind releasing an instrumental LP. This understanding of the perceptions and expectations of the national music press has become intertwined with the basic processes of musical expression within Fun^Da^Mental, as Aki Nawaz explained:

> It's like, I was sat down the other day thinking, we're trying to put down the next Fun^Da^Mental album. I know what the press are going to be doing, how we're going to be treated; I want to outmanoeuvre them absolutely and I was thinking about, well, can I talk about racism again? (Personal interview 1996)

Fun^Da^Mental's method of dealing with what they consider to be one-dimensional press coverage is then not to play up to stereotypes but to attempt to confound them; to disrupt and wrong-foot journalists who will hopefully expose their own inadequacies – as reflected by the national media's reaction to the release of the band's instrumental album, exemplified by David Bennun's review in *Melody Maker* (see Chapter 3) which reflects the tendency by many journalists to use the work of authentic Asian bands as an excuse to indulge in radical-seeming polemics.[11]

If Fun^Da^Mental have set out to confound the stereotypes traded within the media, then what are we to make of Cornershop's use of political issues? Was the latter's ceremonial burning of Morrissey's photograph in 1993 a cynical ploy to attract the attention of the media or a genuine and heartfelt statement? The context of this highly public display of disapproval was a period of several months when Morrissey flirted with nationalist and, some would say, fascistic imagery which included the singer wrapping himself in the Union Jack during performances, indulging in 'skinhead chic' and recording the song 'National front disco'[12] which included the refrain 'England for the English' and understandably was perceived by many as racist.[13] When I talked to founder members of Cornershop they explained that the symbolic burning of Morrissey's picture was not a self-publicity move but a reaction against both the artist himself and the music press, which the band felt were sitting on the fence. Tjinder Singh felt that any press coverage of the incident was justified because the burning was done with 'complete integrity' and when I asked him if there was any element of self-publicity in the move, he replied:

> No, not at all. It was a move because the papers were fucking around, pussyfooting around the issue and using it to sell papers and putting his picture on the front page and leaving it at that. I don't think you can do that. (Personal interview 1996)

Ben Ayres felt that the protest was a spontaneous move that the band decided to do when they happened to be in London and was not a planned publicity stunt but more a personal expression of frustration:

Fig. 5.1 Tjinder Singh (left) and Ben Ayres – the partnership at the heart of Cornershop and Clinton

> Well there had been all this ambiguity about Morrissey's lyrics and stuff and we had been fans of his – Avtar in particular was a massive fan – and we felt really pissed off that he hadn't said anything to justify where he was coming from; and that the fact that he hadn't said anything almost pointed to the fact that accusations were perhaps right and so, on that basis, we decided to stand up and say that it was wrong that he was being so ambiguous. (Personal interview 1996)

It does seem that the band carried out their protest as a spontaneous expression of their anger at Morrissey, but it would be naïve to suggest that they were not aware that the possible by-product of such a provocative and public act could result in at least some interest among the politically conscious music weeklies. There was clearly a desire by the band in their early years to be deliberately provocative and, as we have seen, the expression of alternative or radical views within popular music can comfortably co-exist with marketability and commerce. By proudly taking a name associated with one of the many conservative stereotypes of Asians in Britain – the anti-rock and roll image of the Asian shopkeeper – the band immediately seemed to indicate the presence of some sort of political agenda, as David Stubbs of *Melody Maker* pointed out when he thought that 'there's an attitude with that name which ... there's something to address there'. Gary Walker of Wiiija Records agreed that the band undoubtedly wanted to make a political point and suggested that they may have 'played it up themselves as well in the early days' but that this was something that they just had to 'get out of their system' (personal interview 1996).

Although Ben Ayres recognized that the name Cornershop was political and was taken up (replacing the band's initial name of General Havoc) 'with a view to stirring up a bit of a reaction' he felt that this represented a non-specific brand of personal politics which did not represent the existence of some preconceived, radical agenda. That this meant that the band's music was often ignored in favour of their press image as angry Asians continues to be a major source of irritation for all still involved with the band. Tjinder, while also recognizing the existence of personal politics (see Chapter 6) is particularly resentful of any suggestion of playing up a radical political stance:

> A lot of people say 'Why did you call yourself Cornershop?' Fuck off; if I'd really wanted to make mileage out of it I could have called myself Paki-Shop and I could have really gone for the fucking jugular but ... I think that ... a lot of people say 'You didn't deserve that press' and I think that's a load of bollocks and I've gone through everything I've said in interviews and I think that the integrity that we've shown has given us ... these people, we wash our hands of them – they're talking out of their arse. (Personal interview 1996)

Even in Cornershop's more recent laid-back funk/dance incarnation and their association with the ultra-chic 'New Asian Underground', the explicitly political angry young Asians label still has some currency, much to the annoyance of the band's members and record label. Ben Ayres told me:

> It always crops up. I remember last year when it was almost a comeback for us after nearly splitting up and coming back with the acoustic, Asian-angle music and supporting *Woman's gotta have it* and even *The Guardian*'s guide, when we did a gig it was still like 'Angry Asian polemicists!' (Personal interview 1996)

Marketing mysticism

We have already seen how resilient the notion of a mythic India has been in the interpretation of Eastern forms by musicians in the West – as personified by the work of The Beatles and their acolytes during the late 1960s – and there is undoubtedly a great deal of expectation that Asian bands will conform to this stereotype, especially when Indian instruments are being played. For those Asian bands that use non-Western sounds and instrumentation, the stereotype of the mystical East is one that has to be negotiated and challenged constantly. Of course not all Asian bands use exclusively traditional instruments (from the subcontinent or elsewhere), which confounds the stereotype of Asian music as acoustic, spiritually enlightening and invariably involving the sound of the sitar. Clare Wadd, former co-owner of the independent Sarah Records label suggested that the expectation that Asian bands will inevitably include the sitar in their music was ridiculous and thought that '[T]here is something about it that's almost like expecting a Scottish band to have bagpipes as part of their sound' (personal interview 1995). Nevertheless all of the musicians I have spoken to have, at some point, used Indian instruments as part of their sound; and have found that this has exposed them to some deep-seated stereotypes that have far more to do with the mystical Orientalism of the late 1960s than with any actual knowledge of Indian music and culture from any period. Cornershop have always used a range of different instruments in their repertoire; the sitar, dholki and tanpura have become increasingly prominent in the band's constantly evolving sound and the band are acutely aware of the existing stereotypes that this brings them into contact with. Tjinder suggested that the use of the sitar in a Western setting was often 'doomed, a lot of it to do with that hippy shit and the way the hippies saw the East' regardless of how the instrument might actually sound (personal interview 1996). Gary Walker agreed:

> I think there is a lot of that about and it's a cliché unfortunately; if you're Indian then there's something mystical about you, whereas I guess Wolverhampton is not the same as, I don't know, Bombay or something.[14] (Personal interview 1996)

Of course there are many elements of the esoteric and spiritual in the cultural history of the subcontinent (although whether more so than any other culture or location is debatable) and these are certainly an available resource for Asian bands in the UK. The difficulty in using these influences in such a setting is that they can bolster stereotypes of Asian people that are incompatible with the contemporary realities of life in multi-ethnic Britain. As Anjali Bhatia of Voodoo Queens told me:

> I think everyone's spiritual to a certain extent. Like, a white person can be more spiritual than an Asian person; but I think it's just our culture and where you come from and, like, if you do look back at your roots and the whole history of India and

> Ghandi and all that there's nothing wrong with that, but it's what you do with the sound that's important. (Personal interview 1996)

Voodoo Queens rarely used any type of traditional Indian instruments or influences,[15] preferring to employ electric guitars, keyboards and drum kits. But, as she embarked on a solo career, Anjali found herself using them more frequently and felt that this brought her into contact with the legacy of the 1960s, reflecting that 'When people hear the sitar, they think of George Harrison'. This legacy is one which was revitalized to spectacular effect during the late 1990s by the phenomenal success of Kula Shaker, who were deeply indebted not only to George Harrison but also to the nostalgic memory of the entire hippy era. What Kula Shaker showed is that the imagery and sounds of the mystical East still have currency today; a currency that is an extremely marketable commodity but bears little relation to the contemporary realities of Asians living in the UK, or, for that matter, in India. The success of Kula Shaker's use of Eastern mythology has caused much consternation among Asian musicians in the UK attempting to break away from such stereotypes. Choque Hosein, frontman with Black Star Liner, told me:

> … it really pisses me off … every Asian guy that I meet now, there's a lot of young Asian people coming out and saying 'We're just normal, we've lived here for long enough, we were born here, we know what it's like, there's nothing different' and to me, it's just like, fuck it, let's rock and roll and let's kick some ass. We're not allowed to, I think that's half the problem and stuff like Kula Shaker really pisses me off because … they're fucking living out the '60s dream basically. When you read interviews with them you think 'Hang on a minute, who's talking here? Is it some sort of ridiculous fucking hippy from the '60s?' You know, I'm surprised they didn't decide to put some fucking sari on. (Personal interview 1996)

All the featured bands agreed that there was a much wider musical scope for the use of instruments like the sitar, and part of the project of their music was the desire to explore new ways of using Indian instruments, often by incorporating or fusing them with Western rock or dance styles. By using these instruments in new ways and in different contexts the musicians felt that they could begin to dismantle some of the stereotypes associated with Asian music, as Anjali Bhatia explained:

> You can use sitar and tablas in a million different ways; you know, just because someone else is using it doesn't mean that they've got freehold over it, or that, you know, it's their sound. I mean, especially if you do music, you want to reinvent yourself and do something different, I mean, it's a natural thing. (Personal interview 1996)

There is no doubt that the use of such instruments is still relatively novel in British popular music and will inevitably draw comparisons with the heritage of 1960s Orientalism. While such exotic instruments tend to appeal to simplistic notions of novelty and difference it is important to recognize how their use operates in the context of young Asians born and bred in the UK who are finding new modes of musical expression that reflect the cross-cultural realities of their everyday lives. Musical styles drawn from the subcontinent are part of a wide array of cultural influences that Asian musicians have at their disposal and is not perceived by the artists themselves as unusual or novel. Anjali Bhatia acknowledged that such sounds and instruments were still relatively uncommon in mainstream popular music and would inevitably be considered by some as a novelty, but felt that her use of them went beyond such short-term fashions:

> There's always a problem with that but I don't mind that because I've always used sounds like that. In that way of being Asian – of being completely connected to those sounds – you feel like you've always got an entitlement to it in a way. So when I tire of it all, that's fine; it's part of you, it's part of your culture, you've got a right to use those sounds so it will never be a fashion thing for me. (Personal interview 2003)

The new and innovative sounds created by most Asian bands is far removed from the imagined mysticism so often associated with the East and seeks to challenge, rather than exploit, such deep-rooted stereotypes, as Tjinder told me:

> I don't give a fuck about spiritualism, I just think people should get on with their lives and not worry too much about these things ... Some people think, when you teach the sitar, it's two years before you even sit down with the sitar but I'm not into that, I'm more into the attitude of let's sit down and do it now – why have we got to wait 'til tomorrow? And that's what the attitude of the whole group was. (Personal interview 1996)

Most of the bands I spoke to wished to distance themselves from mystical stereotypes associated with the East but not to the extent where they set aside Indian instruments completely. The use of such instruments in contemporary settings has created innovative music that reflects the diversity of the present-day soundscapes of the UK with its vast array of cultural influences and origins. The fusing of sitars, electric rock guitar and rumbling dub bass lines by Black Star Liner on tracks like 'Khatoon'[16] for example reflects an overall sound that is able not only to merge and give new meanings to traditional sounds of the East but also to create new styles and sounds in a contemporary Western setting.

Despite this, many Asian bands feel that they have had to fight against regressive stereotyping of their music, and attempt to challenge the preconceived notions of Asian culture and to be heard on their own terms, which expresses the shifting realities of their ongoing cultural histories. This represents a long and arduous task as young Asian bands are constantly confronted with reductive and patronizing stereotypes of Asian culture, even by appreciative elements of their audience. The Glastonbury Festival of 1993 witnessed a seminal live performance by Fun^Da^Mental which exposed the band to a national audience and reflected the struggle by Asian bands against these preconceptions. Aki Nawaz saw such a high-profile performance as an opportunity to challenge – from the confines of the world music stage – established stereotypes of Asian music. He regards the performance with some affection, describing his best memory of the festival as:

> Being on stage scaring the shit out of the liberals. They expected to see a nice, passive, romantic, stereotypical, Asian love performance. It destroyed all of their illusions ... Thank god! (*New Musical Express* 22 June 1997: 15)

Fun^Da^Mental's full-on hip-hop approach is certainly one way to displace stereotypical notions of the exotic, but it is not the only way. The music of Voodoo Queens, characterized by screaming vocals and snarling guitars, similarly challenged conventional ideas of Asian culture; but as a solo artist Anjali has chosen to work certain elements of the exotic into her music. As well as using instruments such as the sitar and tablas, she also makes use of much of the imagery and atmosphere of the exotic East.[17] Anjali's interest in such sounds and imagery is drawn in part from the somewhat kitsch tradition of 1960s exotica, when artists such as Martin Denny, Les Baxter and Ananda Shankar combined a range of exotic elements with more contemporary 'hip' sounds.[18] Rather than avoiding elements of the exotic, Anjali has chosen to embrace, it but very much on her own terms:

> I love the word exotica; I think it's a fantastic word. I love being exotic and I love exotica. It really is descriptive of what my music is like; there are some sitars in it, there are a few tablas and I find it quite ... you know ... intoxicating and exotic and like those words that I like to describe my music. (Personal interview 2003)

These elements had played an important part in her musical and cultural development and she had no desire to distance herself from such terms simply because they had often been associated with negative stereotypes of Asian people and culture. When I suggested in the same interview that she might be helping to perpetuate certain stereotypes of Asian music and culture by embracing terms like exotic, she countered 'I don't want to have to get political about using a word that I like. I know that it can be political but then why not reclaim it? Maybe it's time for that.' It is clear that Anjali's music does not simply slavishly reproduce elements of Indian mysticism as filtered through 1960s exotica but reconfigures it in a way that represents a multi-accented and contemporary soundscape. The sitars and tablas that feature in her work are set against diverse musical backdrops that take in the beats and rhythms of soul and funk, juxtaposed against tremelo guitars and slick bass lines and intertwined with sections of brass and strings. Such a rich palette of sounds ensures that for Anjali, and indeed for many of the other musicians discussed here, the music she produces is hard to fit into any neat category and is able to reconfigure and redefine musical and cultural meanings.

Fig. 5.2 Anjali Bhatia

Asian Kool: selling ethnicity?

Since the initial emergence of a number of high-profile Asian bands in the UK, there has been a significant amount of national media coverage that has attempted to make sense of the array of contemporary Asian musical expression by constructing the notion of a discrete Asian scene. The variety of musical and political approaches of the bands in this study shows how tenuous this idea might be. Nevertheless the music press has continued to promote such a concept; in the early 1990s we had 'Asian Kool' (Morris 1993) and towards the end of the decade the sound of 'New Asian underground' (Simpson 1997; Mir 1998). The reporting of these scenes (and others) in the national music press, however tenuously based on reality, nevertheless undoubtedly adds to the potential for Asian bands to raise their profiles and perhaps come to the attention of a wider audience. As *The Guardian*'s Caroline Sullivan reflected, any association with political or social issues could be 'used as a means towards an end', that end being the establishment of a prominent profile and, as we have seen, the very fact of a musician's Asianness is often enough to draw such attention. The example that she used was Sonya Madan,[19] lead singer with guitar-pop band Echobelly, who became the centre of a great deal of press coverage, much of it focusing on Sonya as an Asian woman fronting a rock band. As Sullivan commented, although these issues (of race and gender) had played a prominent part in establishing Echobelly's media profile, she felt that Sonya eventually reached a sufficiently strong position to resist having the band (and her role in it) portrayed simply in terms of those issues:

> I rather suspect that maybe the reason she didn't mind talking about it in the past is that she was so grateful to get interviewed at all. So she was willing to talk about whatever those hacks wanted to hear, but now I think she wants to move on to where it's not an issue and, funnily enough, I've actually read some pieces recently when her race wasn't mentioned.[20] (Personal interview 1996)

Since then this process has reached the stage where issues of race or ethnicity are seldom mentioned in press coverage of the band and, if they are mentioned, it is only in passing (Mueller 1997). In fact Sonya has since employed a policy of declining to discuss issues of Asian identity with regard to Echobelly and, as a result, turned down the request to be interviewed for this book.[21] Sonya may have been able to successfully negotiate and perhaps manipulate issues of ethnicity and race to her band's advantage in the early days despite the apparent lack of Asian influences on Echobelly's music; perhaps reflected in the anglicized nature of Sonya's upbringing (more of which later) which arguably made the band relatively more accessible to a white audience. Echobelly, for all the interest in Sonya's ethnicity, were more often associated with the (almost exclusively white) Britpop scene rather than with any of the less prominent Asian scenes.

There was an overall consensus among the bands in this study that the portrayal of such scenes did not represent an accurate account of musical developments, but were in fact spurious media constructs (Asian Kool for example had, according to Tjinder Singh, 'only ever existed in two people's heads') and that attempts to associate a wide range of Asian bands under a generalized banner sold the bands short and tended to ignore the sheer diversity of musical innovations at work. The short attention span of media-constructed scenes and the associated tendency to seek out gimmicks and novelty were seen to be extremely negative and something to be avoided. All the musicians felt that associating with any press-constructed scene or playing up any novelty aspect of the bands was, in the long run, a mistake. I asked Tjinder whether or not Cornershop had ever tried to make mileage out of their Asianness or associate with any kind of Asian scene, to which he replied:

> No, I don't think we've tried to jump on any kind of bandwagon. Anything that's been pushed our way we've always shoved it because we considered ourselves with a bit more integrity than something like the rebirth of Asian Kool or Britpop or whatever; it's best just to leave them to it. I think that's why we've survived, that's why we've carried on. (Personal interview 1996)

Most of the bands had received a certain amount of attention from Asian media sources such as the BBC2 magazine programme *Network East* and journals and newspapers such as *Asian Times* and *Second Generation*; but this was not something that the bands actively sought out themselves as Gary Walker, head of Anjali Bhatia's current record label Wiiija, explains:

> I don't think that Anjali ever used that, she probably could have done if she'd wanted to but never really did. Naturally they [Voodoo Queens] got a lot of interest from those sources because of their colour and everything but I don't think she ever set out to exploit that. (Personal interview 1996)

Nevertheless it is unavoidable to conclude that, despite their disdain for the reporting of what were seen to be media-constructed scenes, many Asian bands certainly profited from such attention. While the music press certainly is eager to discover and build up new music scenes and genres, its interest also reflects a genuine attempt to make sense of the growth of Asian involvement in popular music in the UK. Nobody likes to be lumped together and packaged as a part of some discrete scene – particularly when this scene is based primarily on notions of ethnicity – but it is also the case that the functioning of such scenes and genres is a vital element in the promotion and marketing of a great deal of popular music (Negus 1992; Frith 1996a).

All of the bands felt that they had actively avoided promoting a marketable Asian identity, focusing primarily on their musical output or, as Anjali put it, 'the music comes first'. Part of this assertion is certainly influenced by notions of authenticity and credibility and, as we shall see later, ideologies of musical and political independence are central to their musical expression. Much criticism was aimed at certain other Asian artists who were felt to have exploited their Asian background to a greater extent; in particular ragga star Apache Indian and Levi's-sponsored Jaz Mann of Babylon Zoo. The criticisms raised of these internationally successful stars was that they had manipulated their Asian backgrounds as a novelty, enforcing existing stereotypes and selling short other Asian musicians; as Tjinder Singh commented of Jaz Mann, 'He's making a lot of mileage on the fact that he's Indian ... those sort of gimmicks are going to push people back' (personal interview 1996). Apache Indian was a particular target for much vitriol, since he was seen to have marketed his Asianness to establish himself as a star in a cynical manner that served to bolster existing stereotypes of Asian people. My focus bands felt that such strategies were an inevitable part of the more mainstream popular music market, which was reflected in their commitment to the independent sector where a greater emphasis is placed upon the integrity of the music rather than on the marketability of image. Aki Nawaz had this to say on the issue:

> The commercial scene, I'm not interested in – it's crap, it almost, like, enforces the stereotypes and to me it's like Asian people bending to market pressures, bending to stereotypes ... like Apache Indian and the 'Arranged marriage' thing.[22] I mean the whole reason why that happened is a lot of white people perceived it as an attack against arranged marriages; it's like '*He* sings about it' so everybody must be feeling that, and that's not what it's about. (Personal interview 1996)

Tjinder felt much the same way but was more succinct and merely stated that as far as he was concerned Apache Indian had 'sold out to the man'.

The bands placed their emphasis on the artistic integrity of the music and, although financial self-sufficiency was a desirable objective, they were extremely uncomfortable with the idea of using their Asianness to promote themselves, even if this resulted in reaching a wider audience. There seemed to be an agreement among all the interviewees, (musicians, journalists and record company owners) that exploiting any novelty element associated with Asianness was ultimately unwise and that any success engendered by such a practice would be short-lived. Furthermore, the bands felt that using their ethnicity in a cynical way to promote themselves as marketable commodities would have a negative effect in influencing the way that Asians were viewed by wider society in the UK. This indicates that, despite the reluctance of these musicians to act as representatives of a young Asian constituency, they are acutely aware of the 'burden of representation' (Hall 1988; Julien and Mercer 1996) that their relatively high public profiles expose them to and, as the following chapter will show, this is an issue which they must constantly negotiate and contend with throughout their everyday lives.

The featured musicians were acutely aware of the dangers of representation and were wary of being portrayed and categorized in any way that might help conform to negative stereotypes of Asian identity. Choque Hosein of Black Star Liner suggested for example that the post-war success of Afro-Caribbean music was tempered by the perpetuation of certain racial stereotypes:

> I don't think that black West Indians have managed to come through because I still think that the cliché going on is still your all-singing, all-dancing black man. (Personal interview 1996)

Many of the musicians felt that such stereotypes would be harder to avoid if they were working with major record labels where the focus is on marketability and maximizing sales, and thus their desire to have more control over their own images was a key part of their commitment to the independent sector. Despite this, many of the bands have dealt with major record labels, as evidenced by the licensing of Cornershop's American releases to Luaka Bop in the late 1990s. This label is run by former Talking Heads founder David Byrne but distributed by Warner Brothers, and could be seen to compromise the independence and integrity of Cornershop's music. Furthermore, Byrne's reputation as something of an Orientalist collector of ethnic musical styles and forms raised certain questions about his motives and aspirations for the band (Lipsitz 1994). When interviewing Caroline Sullivan in 1996 I mentioned the deal to her; she responded by saying:

> Luaka Bop? No kidding? Well actually I think that's quite tokenistic of David Byrne; he loves going out picking up 'ethnic' – as he sees it – music. The great white explorer … you know David Byrne, the missionary amongst the savages.[23]

Whatever the shortcomings of David Byrne's motives, the band and their UK label Wiiija felt that their media profile in the USA was more carefully considered and, although there is some interest in the band's Asian background, their image across the Atlantic is associated more with their links to a number of high-profile American bands. Speaking to me in 1996 Tjinder was optimistic that the relationship with Luaka Bop would avoid some of the problematic stereotypes that had plagued much of his band's press coverage in the UK:

> I don't think they will market us on the ethnic thing, they'll be marketing us however we want to do it. Everything we've written down, like our connections with Sonic Youth, connections with the Beastie Boys; that is how they will market us, not on an 'East meets West' thing; it will be the way *we* want to be put forward.

In fact the relationship between Cornershop and Luaka Bop was subsequently felt to have been a fruitful one which had contributed markedly to the success of both *Woman's gotta have it* and *When I was born for the 7th time* in the USA. Although the deal between Luaka Bop and Wiiija lapsed in 1999, Tjinder still regards the relationship with some warmth and remains in touch with those running the label. As we shall see, the handling of Cornershop's 2002 album, *Handcream for a generation* by Beggars Banquet America was not as successful and resulted directly in the band parting company with Wiiija in 2003.

Conclusion: negotiating stereotypes

The common desire of the focus bands, was to resist appealing to any kind of novelty effect, particularly those based on stereotypical notions of Asian culture and identity. This was supported in all cases by a desire to retain as much control over their artistic output as possible. Only by having a large degree of involvement in the production and marketing of their images and musical outputs did these bands feel that any appeal to spurious notions of exoticism or political authenticity could be minimized and, as we shall see in the following chapter, they have adopted various approaches in order to achieve this. In considering the views and experiences of the bands interviewed for this study it became clear that issues of novelty and difference are significant points of negotiation within the music industry. Although the musicians are wary about exploiting novel aspects of their ethnicity that may lead to stereotyping, it is also the case that such factors have played a significant role in establishing the public profile of their bands. The high level of attention and press coverage based around either notions of political radicalism or exotic otherness undoubtedly helped raise the profiles of emergent Asian bands, but the nature of this attention – particularly the reliance on reductive and stereotypical readings of Asian culture – clearly had negative as well as positive effects for the musicians involved. Although the band's public profiles were certainly raised by the media's fascination with stereotypical notions of Asianness, the musicians themselves felt that the prurient nature of such attention was extremely negative and potentially restrictive to the aspirations of Asian musicians within the industry. The bands felt that it was important to base their success on musical achievements rather than on novelty appeal, in order to survive and to nurture successful and long-term careers. As a result of this they sought either to avoid or ignore, or purposefully set out to confound and disrupt, the stereotypes that attracted such attention.

The interest shown by bands such as Fun^Da^Mental, Cornershop and Voodoo Queens in a range of political issues perhaps inevitably appealed to certain elements of a national music press which is fascinated both with sensational stories and with what it regards to be politically radical. In this way we can see that there is certainly a degree of active participation by the bands as well as the media, and it is clear that Fun^Da^Mental at least directly set out to challenge and provoke certain elements of the music press. It is perhaps ironic that, in doing so, a band like Fun^Da^Mental live up to their press billing and perpetuate their image as radical rabble rousers. The more subtle approach of Black Star Liner, who steer clear of explicitly political issues in their music, undoubtedly helps to avoid such attention; although this does not mean that they have escaped other kinds of stereotyping within the media.

The use of Asian instruments within the context of contemporary rock and pop music has also helped to stimulate the fleeting interest of a notoriously fickle music press, which has focused on them as unusual and exotic rather than as components of an overall, contemporary sound. The use of such stereotypes taps into a long history of musical and cultural appropriation which has exploited certain archetypes of the East for the benefit of musicians in the West. For the bands involved here, however, these elements make up only a part of their overall artistic expressions that are based on a range of musical influences and are not seen as viable means for self-promotion. There is undoubtedly a certain legitimacy in the interest that such sounds and instruments stimulate within the music press, and the broadening of the musical palette that this represents for British popular music should be cautiously but critically welcomed. Again the emphasis needs be placed on the ways that meaning is negotiated around these sounds, and the syncretic fusion of exotic instruments with contemporary rock and pop forms increasingly acts as a counterweight to the stereotypical notions of an ancient and mythical culture of the East. Consequently, rather than invoking any novelty appeal based on Asianness in order to court attention and favour, the musicians in these bands can be seen to disrupt and subvert existing expectations by producing music that is difficult to categorize and by asserting cultural identities that do not conform to existing stereotypes and conventions. This process is not without its difficulties, however, and, as the next chapter will show, in a country where race, ethnicity and representation are such potent issues – and faced with the economic realities and pressures of functioning within the highly commercialized music industry – this is a position which is extremely difficult to negotiate and maintain.

Notes

1. From 'England's dreaming' on the *Lock, stock and double barrel* (Wiiija 1992).
2. Speaking in 1996 Anjali still felt unhappy with much of the coverage that Voodoo Queens had received some years earlier and told me: 'I'd be really happy not to talk to *Melody Maker* again, they really misquoted me about a lot of things I said about racism.'
3. In the *National Confront* piece Aki Nawaz (interviewed here as his alter-ego PropaGhandi) talks of the response to racism by saying: 'Asian people aren't scared – they're going to fight back, whether through riots, gangs or a united anti-fascist movement. By any means necessary' (Cigarettes 1993: 17).
4. The chilling message, which thankfully was never acted upon, went as follows:

   > The BNP's got your card marked, you bastards. We're gonna burn your building down, you fuckheads. Combat 18 is watching you, you communists; nigger-loving, Paki cunts. Fucking dickheads, we're gonna hang you for burning the British flag. You'll hang from every flagpole in Britain.

5. This association between Cornershop and the Riot Grrrl scene was one that pleased Tjinder, even a decade later. Speaking in 2003 he told me:

   > Well I think it was a very good thing, it was the only thing that I would say that we've been happy with. It was the only thing that we were stuck with which was brilliant because we were all male on the Riot Grrrl scene and we were the only all-male English group in the Riot Grrrl scene and

> again it was the attitude in terms of music; we were there and also the politics as well. I thought it was a brilliant scene, a very tidy scene.

6. Not everyone would agree that this emergence was as sudden as it may have appeared; Tjinder Singh told me:

   > I think it was significant in that more Asian bands were being recognized but it wasn't significant in that there were more Asian bands around; it was just that they hadn't [previously] been credited for what they were doing. I used to go to Birmingham a lot and there were always Asian bands playing there. (Personal interview 1996)

7. Jullander shere was the first single released from *Woman's gotta have it* (1995). The interview with Gary Walker was conducted a year later during the spring of 1996.
8. Press coverage in the rest of Europe was singled out by many as the most open and thorough. Aki Nawaz told me that 'Europe seems much more open to new things' and Anjali Bhatia felt that the coverage she had received in France (as a solo artist), where journalists seemed to focus more on the music itself, contrasted favourably with her experiences in the UK as a member of Voodoo Queens.
9. In Caroline Sullivan's words:

   > … in fact it [interest in Asian bands] became quite faddish for a while … it seems to have settled down and become fairly underground again. Or certainly, it's not the flavour of the month that it was a few years ago. (Personal interview 1996)

10. The 1995 album *With intent to pervert the cause of injustice* (see Chapter 3).
11. 'Letter of the Week' writer Marcello Carlin (1995) wrote an impassioned response to Bennun's review of the album and thought that it reflected 'the fatalistic liberal approach' whereby a journalist could review a Fun^Da^Mental LP and feel that they had 'done their bit' for anti-racism but effectively '… provides plenty of reasonable and well-argued excuses for sitting on one's arse and doing nothing'.
12. On the 1992 LP *Your arsenal* released by Parlophone.
13. As a fan of The Smiths (Morrissey's previous band) during her teenage years, Anjali Bhatia was also appalled by the singer's behaviour and told me 'I think he should be wrapped in a British flag and burnt at the stake; I hate that man and that I can't forgive.'
14. Although Tjinder's parents are from India, he was born and raised in Wolverhampton, West Midlands.
15. The only 'Indian' reference being a sample from a Bollywood soundtrack on the song Indian filmstar from Voodoo Queens' 1994 debut LP *Chocolate revenge*.
16. From the 1999 album *Bengali bantam youth experience*.
17. As evidenced on the track 'Arabian Queen' from her eponymous album of 2000:

   > Cocooned in silken shrouds
   > And jasmine scented clouds
   > She's the queen of the harem
   > You know who wears the crown
   > She teases and she sleazes
   > You know it never ceases
   > When she does her voodoo

18. Ananda Shankar's version of The Rolling Stones' 'Jumpin' Jack flash' (where the lead vocals are replaced by his decidedly funky sitar) from his eponymous album of 1970 is a particularly fine example of this.
19. Whom she once described as 'on her way to becoming the first Asian pop star' (*The Guardian* 16 December 1994).
20. In 1995 Sonya told journalist Liz Evans:

> I don't want to make an issue out of my gender and I never even thought about Asian culture until I started being interviewed but all of these things are really rising to the surface now. (1995: 64)

21. In response to my request she replied that she 'was no longer interested in talking about those things' (personal correspondence 2002).
22. 'Arranged marriage' was Apache Indian's first UK Top 20 hit in 1995.
23. Prior to Cornershop's signing Luaka Bop's catalogue consisted almost entirely of world music compilations, mainly from Latin America, a particular source of inspiration for David Byrne. Nevertheless Byrne's appearance on the BBC music programme *Later with Jools Holland* during the summer of 1997 saw him accompanied by musicians from the London-based band Morcheeba playing sitar and tablas.

Chapter 6

Politics or pleasure? Asianness and the burden of representation

As the previous chapter has shown, the emergence of a number of Asian bands on the UK music scene has been accompanied by a large amount of interest in the politics of race, ethnicity and identity. The context of a society where race and racism has had, and continues to have, a profound effect on the lives of the UK's diverse non-white populations – often resulting in deprivation and exclusion from many of the country's institutions – has meant that the performing arts have often been a vital source of expression for black cultures, as Stuart Hall has reflected, 'repertoires of black popular culture which since we were excluded from the cultural mainstream were often the only performative spaces we had left' (1992a: 27). The importance of these repertoires takes on huge significance when the aspirations of minority groups are stifled by the mainstream and, although such spaces are sought out in pursuit of pleasure and emotional release, they also take on an important political role because of the relative lack of other expressive and creative outlets. Music has always been at the forefront of cultural expression and for minority groups throughout history has often been the only way to articulate individual and collective expressions of both pleasure and frustration. Apart from this, music also represents a highly prominent and dynamic space where cultural identities are negotiated and transformed, a process that takes on particular significance for migrant groups adapting to the circumstances of a new country of settlement.

These factors are all present in the recent history of South Asian settlement in the UK, and the wave of young bands and musicians reflected in this study represent the range of responses and expressions of culture and identity that are manifested in a multi-ethnic environment. The relative lack of a mainstream profile for Asian youth, particularly in music prior to the early 1990s, has meant that perhaps an inordinate amount of attention has been bestowed upon the activities of relatively few emergent Asian bands on the contemporary music scene. Inevitably these bands have had to shoulder a heavy burden of representation and are seen to reflect and express the political and cultural voice of Asian youth in the UK. While undoubtedly these bands reflect and articulate the contemporary realities of their own lives, we need to consider the validity of their ability to represent a unified cultural community in any meaningful or definitive way. As we have seen, the question of politics has never been far away from the representation of these bands; but to what extent does this reflect the true intentions and practices of the musicians involved?

This chapter will examine both the political agendas of the musicians in question and also their reaction to the burden of representation that is often foisted upon them by others in an attempt to reflect the complexity of cultural and political responses. By doing so I will focus on the tension manifested between artistic and political agendas and also consider the effectiveness of the latter when expressed within the context of the highly commercialized music scene. Moreover, the context within which these musicians operate has political implications since it brings them into contact with the workings of organized capital, which creates certain pressures and tensions that have to be negotiated constantly. Only by considering the range of responses from the bands themselves can we understand the complexity of political perspectives at work that refutes the claims of essentializing and totalizing narratives of ethnic and cultural identity.

Political perspectives

We have already seen how, during the early 1990s, much of the press interest focused on the perceived political significance of emergent Asian bands. Rather than answering questions about their music or their rock and roll lifestyles, most Asian groups found themselves responding to such issues as racism, nationalism and identity. The increased profile of extremist far-right politics at the time, as evidenced by the limited electoral success of the British National Party and the subsequent revival of the Anti-Nazi League, certainly played an important part in shaping initial press agendas towards Asian bands. There is no doubt that such issues helped raise the profile of a number of British Asian bands who responded vigorously to the questions put to them. While acknowledging that this type of press attention can be encouraged or even manipulated by bands in order to raise their profiles, it is nevertheless apparent that political issues are certainly an important part of the expressive arsenal of the Asian musicians interviewed for this study. So just how political are these bands and how do these politics manifest themselves? It is clear that, although issues such as anti-racism are broadly supported by all of the bands in question, it is important to recognize the range of political approaches that exist and that the expression of political issues varies from group to group.

In the case of Fun^Da^Mental clearly politics is a major focus and was a significant factor in the creation of the group in 1991. For founder member Aki Nawaz, Fun^Da^Mental came into being as a direct result of increasing political awareness which was 'sparked off' by a visit to New York combined with reading key black texts such as those written by Malcolm X (1966) and Eldridge Cleaver

(1968). Fun^Da^Mental have since produced vibrant and provocative music which has incorporated angry critiques of global capitalism, racism and colonialism. As Aki told me in 1996, the political aspect of the band continues to take on a significant role:

> If tomorrow it [Fun^Da^Mental] lost its politics I won't be there. I'm into it because of the human kind of ... creating a few bridges and trying to open people's perceptions ... to give people a bit of understanding if they need the political element ... it changes in different situations.

Dave Watts, who joined in 1993 and describes the band as a 'political folk group', also felt that politics was central to their purpose and was committed to expressing often radical and controversial issues. Although there was clearly a desire to raise people's awareness of certain issues such as the politics of race or colonialism, Dave is realistic about the ability of music to effect social or political change:

> I don't think that when somebody hears a record, that they are going to go out and do something because the record told them to, because of something within that record. Yeah, you've got people who are, like, more open-minded musically who might just think 'Well, I've never really thought about this before ...' It depends on the person that hears something and they're moved by it and they ... it's something to aid them on a journey and you don't know where it's going to end. It's like Fun^Da^Mental have a platform and we're able to introduce ideas and sounds ... and for the people who buy our records, it's like getting a taste. (Personal interview 1996)

For Cornershop, politics is also an important factor in the band's character but is less of a driving force in the trajectory of their music. In fact their emergence as a band was not because of a desire to raise a radical political agenda but was more to do with boredom and musical experimentation; as Tjinder Singh explained to me in 1996, 'The main impetus for us to get started was boredom and a lack of music going around at the time.' Despite this, politics was always a part of Cornershop's repertoire but not in any systematic way, limited primarily to an uncompromising attitude and the occasional exhortation to 'Fight the homophobic, racist, sexist powers that be!'[1] As Ben Ayres explained of the band's early years:

> We were very political but it was a kind of personal politics, we knew what we felt was right and we knew what we felt was wrong and we didn't think there was anything wrong with saying it loudly. (Personal interview 1996)

Voodoo Queens similarly expressed a personalized form of politics and shared an aggressive attitude towards their music and lyrics that led the British music press to label them as a political act. Although Voodoo Queens supported anti-racist causes (such as the Anti-Nazi League), their main political focus was very much the issue of gender and they were often associated with the UK's nascent Riot

Grrrl scene. Songs such as 'I'm not bitter (I just want to kill you)' and the band's motto 'Who needs boys when you've got guitars?' – which was printed on all early releases – undoubtedly helped to maintain the Riot Grrrl tag which was established with the release of their first single 'Supermodel, superficial' in 1993. This song was highly critical of the media and the fashion industry's perpetuation of thinness as the prerequisite of female beauty (as embodied by the ultra-thin figure of the supermodel) and of the damaging consequences of such images for teenage girls and young women.[2] Lead singer and lyricist Anjali Bhatia herself had suffered from an eating disorder as a teenager and, as well as writing 'Supermodel, superficial', exhibited an art installation entitled *Doll bathroom* at the Institute for Contemporary Arts in London in the winter of 1994 that raised many of the issues reflected in the song.[3] Her rejection of this beauty myth expressed so vehemently in the single is also reflected in the band's celebration of chocolate confectionery, culminating in the naming of their first album *Chocolate revenge* (Too Pure 1994).[4]

The notoriety of 'Supermodel, superficial' ensured that the band were subsequently labelled as explicitly 'political' and undoubtedly helped the press to dub them the 'female Cornershop' (Dalton 1993) much to their annoyance. I asked Anjali whether or not Voodoo Queens were a essentially a political band and she replied:

> Yeah, [we were] political to a certain extent … I mean definitely the 'Supermodel' stage. I know that riled a lot of people and I quite enjoy that, I mean I was speaking to one of the journalists at the *New Musical Express* and a lot of rock journalists like that were quite scared because one, you're Asian and two, you're a woman … you're like … out there on your own in a way – I'm not talking musically but the whole thing was quite different. (Personal interview 1996)

Despite the somewhat aggressive and controversial lyrics of 'Supermodel, superficial' and the band's regular performances at Anti-Nazi League benefit concerts, Voodoo Queens were not simply a collective of over-earnest politicos and much of the band's output, both live and on record, is memorable not for its politics but for its humour and its enthusiasm. As a solo artist Anjali has reinvented herself somewhat: not only does the music she has produced since sound radically different, it also does not appear to be as overtly poltical as the output of Voodoo Queens.[5] I asked her in 2003 whether or not the music she produced as a solo artist could be considered to be at all political she responded by saying:

> Well if you want to think that a woman producer twiddling knobs behind machines is political, then in that way it's political. You know because there's not many female producers that are doing that kind of stuff. I programme the stuff, I write the stuff, I arrange it and I know how to use the sampler. In that sense, that's probably the most political I get right now. So it's political but not in an obvious way.

The very fact that Anjali is working within a part of the music industry where both women and Asians are traditionally under-represented can be considered to be a political statement in itself since it challenges established stereotypes of who does and does not make popular music.

This is also reflected in the music of Black Star Liner as masterminded by frontman Choque Hosein; he was the only musician in any of the featured bands who avoided any explicit political content in his musical output. This does not reflect a lack of interest or awareness in political issues but is based on a desire to create music that is primarily meant to excite and entertain. As he told me in 1996, 'I am interested in politics but I'm not interested in introducing it into my music because it would just become a bore.' Choque felt that his political views were not relevant to the musical output of Black Star Liner and personally felt turned off by bands that used their music to put across a political message, preferring a more subtle approach:

> The political element behind it, I'm not really into going round and pointing fingers because I don't think anyone's really interested in this country; the struggle [against racism] is bad enough as it is. I'm sympathetic towards it and I've got my beliefs but I will not stand up on stage and say 'Look here!' I remember when I was young, growing up and I used to go out and see bands and some arsehole would come on the stage ranting and I just used to turn off because I'm there to be entertained primarily and then after, if there's something following it underneath, then something will come out of it.

Although Choque rejected any notion of a political agenda in the music of Black Star Liner, in general conversation it is apparent that he possesses a number of strongly held views and opinions on a range of political issues. In the same interview I suggested that Black Star Liner could be seen by some as a band making a political statement simply because of the way they fused musical sources from a range of cultural sources. Choque replied:

> Yeah but I don't see that as a political statement, the fact that it's mixed together because, to be honest with you, what gets me really excited is the fact where the two things clash and it's like, 'Wow – that's really fucking exciting!' I don't think 'Well is this politically correct?'

Despite this, it is clear that politics are never far from the surface in the output of Black Star Liner, as reflected in titles such as 'Ottoman empire strikes back'[6] and 'Intifada powder line'.[7] Choque feels strongly that humour is a vital component in any successful musical endeavour and it is often through the use of humour that political issues and ideas are raised. This is particularly pronounced in the band's live performances, which are quite distinct from their recorded output. In the studio the lyrics usually take a minimal role and are often recorded in an improvisational manner by guest musicians and singers, whose voices are treated almost as additional instruments. During live performances Choque takes on the role of vocalist but does not function in the same way that a more traditional singer might act and inserts into the music playful and improvised soundbites and comments. Choque delights in reshaping various elements of popular music by injecting lyrical snippets of artists as diverse as Pulp, Queen and Elvis Presley. At the opening of their set at the BBC's *India Five-O* live broadcast (15 August 1997) Choque began by intoning the lyrics to the theme tune of *It Ain't Half Hot Mum* ('Meet the gang 'cos the boys are here, the boys to entertain you!') before going on to borrow lyrics from Queen ('Bohemian rhapsody'), Pulp ('Common people') and Oasis ('Roll with it'). Since this event was organized partly to celebrate the 50th anniversary of Indian and Pakistani independence, this type of playful and ironic statement on the nature of multi-ethnic Britain is a good example of how humour and politics are combined in the work of Black Star Liner.

As the members of relatively few, high-profile Asian bands, the musicians in question are clearly acutely aware of the issue of politics in the production and performance of their music. There was certainly a broad agreement on a range of issues and the bands all shared a general distaste for issues of inequality related to race, sexuality or gender. All of the groups and individuals chose to deal with this in different ways, some preferring to push a political agenda to the forefront while others were content to let such issues lie beneath the surface. Despite this range of perspectives and responses the bands did however suffer from being painted with the same brush, as highly politicized, anti-racist representatives of Asian youth in contemporary Britain. It was clear that, whatever their political views or aspirations, the bands did not wish such issues to detract from their music. Whether or not the bands wanted a political role for themselves was an issue that would not go away and one that needs constant reappraisal and negotiation.

5.2: Representation and community: representing whom?

The very lack of Asian bands with any kind of national profile in the past has meant, that from the very beginning, the musicians in this study have had to shoulder what Stuart Hall calls the 'burden of representation' (1988). Whether they liked it or not the pioneering Asian bands have been forced into a spotlight where they have been analysed and identified as the representatives of a youthful Asian constituency. This mode of representation puts extra pressure on the musicians since attention is focused not just on their musical output but also on their supposed role as representatives of a 'community'. As we have already seen, this pressure can result in some frustration among musicians such as Sonya Madan, who has pointed out that similar questions are seldom asked of white bands of equivalent stature and profile:

> Why do I get asked such in-depth questions? Do Oasis get asked all these questions? People are trying to take bits of me all the time and yet I know, talking to other bands, they don't get asked the same questions. (Fadele 1994: 20)

It is clear that the position of role model is generally not one which is actively sought out by artists, but nevertheless is hard to avoid. Paul Cox (head of Too Pure, former label of Voodoo Queens) felt that:

> … it's thrust upon them almost by default and sometimes it will be rejected by the artist because it's not what they set out to do and other times I think they will be quite happy to do so and take up that mantle and be quite happy to do so and it will vary from person to person. (Personal interview 1996)

Despite the fact that none of the bands that I spoke to felt comfortable taking on a representative role, there is no denying that they have played an important part in presenting diverse and positive images of Asianness that have affected both the self-perception of young British Asians and also the way in which Asians are viewed by society in general. David Stubbs of *Melody Maker* felt that the initial wave of Asian bands (Fun^Da^Mental in particular) had been particularly significant in asserting a positive influence on images of contemporary Asianness:

> Yeah it has been very important, especially when you are culturally disenfranchised. As a white person, role models is something I can take for granted, something I don't even have to think about, although you do get it with the North, I think that a lot of people from the North like to see northern people doing well, like Oasis, so the role model thing has been extremely important. (Personal interview 1996)

When speaking to the bands it became clear that the Asian members were acutely aware of the pressures of representation but generally sought to distance themselves from being seen as role models as they felt ill-equipped to speak for any collective identity. Cornershop's Tjinder Singh felt no obligation to act as a role model for the 'Asian community' and thought that such a role was inappropriate for any individual to take on, although he did recognize the difficulties of avoiding such issues: 'I don't think it's possible to separate music from politics; especially if you're an Asian person, especially if you're in these times where there's not a lot of Asian bands full stop.' This relative lack of Asian bands inevitably raises the profile of those that do exist, creating certain expectations for bands like Cornershop to reflect and express the views of a generalized Asian constituency. At the same time I asked Tjinder whether he had experienced external pressure for him to adopt a representative role and he responded by saying:

> Yeah. The thing is, how can a person who's … we're just talking about an individual and how they live … how can they have any responsibility to a wider community when all they're talking about is themselves? If other people can associate with that then that's all well and fine.

Despite Tjinder's reluctance to take on the mantle of role model it is clear that merely by being one of only a few Asian musicians in the public eye it is a position that is inevitably evoked by others and has to be carefully negotiated. To this extent, Gary Walker at Wiiija felt that Tjinder had adapted to certain expectations and did function as a role model within the industry: 'I think he does and I think he's very good in his interviews in terms of what is said and politically I think he's very aware of that.' Although Tjinder was conscious of the pressure to act as a role model and the tendency to be presented as such – particularly by the media – he often counters this by stressing that his views are simply his own rather than being representative of a diverse community with which he clearly has an ambiguous relationship. When I asked him whether people ever suggested that he might have some sort of responsibility to present himself as a positive role model he replied:

> Yeah and I tell them that I don't. I have a responsibility just to reiterating what I feel as an individual and that's why it's politics with a small 'p'. You see there are things within the Asian community that I don't like, so how can I have responsibility to elements of things that I don't like?

Aki Nawaz from Fun^Da^Mental also preferred to speak as an individual rather than a role model but more readily accepted responsibility for an Asian constituency. He felt conscious that, as an Asian artist in the public eye, it was necessary to defend Asian 'culture' in an environment where that culture was under constant attack and critical appraisal:

> Personally I feel there's a lot of pathetic analysis of our culture and I'll stick up for things I don't agree with within our culture, that I don't really, personally, necessarily believe in but I understand why it exists and I understand that it might not be good for *me* but it doesn't mean that *my* opinion matters; it's somebody else's life. I mean, the whole perception of arranged marriages, some people it works, some people it doesn't. (Personal interview 1996)

For Aki, an essential part of Fun^Da^Mental's project is the religion of Islam, which comes across in the band's lyrics, sounds and samples.[8] He seeks to use his position as a musician with a reasonably high profile to educate non-Muslims about Islam which is often perceived in an extremely negative manner in the West (Said 1978; Kabbani 1986; Modood 1997). In this context Aki clearly sees himself as a cultural intermediary and uses his band's music to alter people's perceptions of Islam. He told me:

> I think that the way I can put it across to certain people who are non-Muslims, probably some of them understand it better; 'Oh, I've never thought about it like that' and I think Islam and religion generally, it gets attacked in the same way black people get attacked, the same prejudices, the same stereotypes, you know, understanding. People take the negative elements out and use them as generalizing that religion, it happens day in and day out with me.

As Aki explained, the Islamic 'project' that manifests itself within Fun^Da^Mental's music is very much a personal one and is central to his involvement with the band. Since the band has collaborated with a range of non-Muslim musicians throughout its existence I wondered whether the religious aspect had become a source of tension. I put this question to Dave Watts who forms the other half of a partnership with Aki that represents the core of Fun^Da^Mental. Dave comes from an Afro-Caribbean background and is not a Muslim himself, but nevertheless feels that the Islamic element of the band is important. He believes that many of the issues surrounding Islam that are articulated in much of the band's music have a wider bearing on a range of political concerns such as racial and colonial oppression which form Fun^Da^Mental's broader political agenda; as he explained:

> OK, let's take something like the Gulf War [of 1991] and here we are being fed all this stuff about how Saddam Hussein was like the devil basically and you had the forces of good being George Bush, the Americans, the United Nations and so forth. If you look at the situation and try to read between the lines, you *know* that it was just a complete scam; no-one gave a fuck about Kuwait, the invasion of Kuwait has nothing to do with the situation whatsoever. So you check that situation and say, well they've found themselves a new devil because communism is dead ... you have got to have some justification, have something to justify military expenditure, maintaining the status quo and that new enemy, that new devil, that new evil was Islam. Like I said, I'm not a Muslim but you don't have to be a Muslim to see that, so from there it's wrong. So I understand ... being amongst Muslims as well, that helped me understand even more so, what the situation was about; you see where people are coming from, you get to know how people feel so, yeah, it was a period of enlightenment, you know, every day is a period of enlightenment for me ... it's like what they're doing to Muslims they've done to black people, do you know what I mean? It's done to anybody that stands outside of the white, male power structure. (Personal interview 1996)

Although Fun^Da^Mental use their music to critique a range of controversial political issues, the band also assert that this amounts only to a personal expression and represents the politics of individuals rather than of any wider community. Both Dave and Aki felt that their own experiences and political views were shared by a significant number of people who identified with Fun^Da^Mental, but that this again was based on individual experience rather than on a fixed ethnic or racial marker such as blackness or Asianness. For this reason Aki felt unable and unwilling to speak as any kind of cultural or political representative and rejected the notion that he should act as a role model for Asian youth, or anyone at all. I asked him if he had ever acted as a spokesperson for the Asian community and he replied:

> No ... people say it but I think it would be wrong for me to do this, honestly I can't stand up and say I represent anybody, all I can do is represent a lot of issues in my life and realities which I know, which I know in my heart of hearts that a lot of

Fig. 6.1 Aki Nawaz (top) and Dave Watts, the longest-serving members of Fun^Da^Mental

> people are going through as well. So I think that is why certain people respected me for saying what I feel because there is a lot of people who have gone through the same thing and they could be in my position; I don't monopolize the position.

Despite this, the fact that Fun^Da^Mental *have* spoken out so loudly and provocatively on a range of contentious issues – and often in such a high-profile way – has meant that people often turn to the band expecting them to express a representative voice in times of crisis, as when Aki appeared on a number of news reports in the wake of the Bradford disturbances of 1991,[9] and he continues to be a regular contributor on the BBC's Radio 5 Live station. This puts a great deal of pressure on the band who have to deal with the general expectation that whatever they do will be controversial and deeply political, hence much of the confusion in the media over the band's 1994 instrumental LP. As Dave Watts told me when interviewed, it is extremely problematic putting musicians into this position where they are granted the role of experts and representatives of a community rather than a group of individuals expressing their own frustrations and sense of injustice through music:

> Who do we have to please? I mean the only people we have to please is ourselves, we're not representing anybody, we're not coming out and saying 'We are the voice of Asian or black youth' – we're not. People kind of ask you for answers for questions that ... like economics, that economists should be asked or major-league politicians should be asked. I'm no different, no more special than anybody, I don't have ... I'm not university educated or whatever; it's just, we are emotion basically, that's our goal.

As we have seen, one of the most significant problems faced by a band like Fun^Da^Mental is that, because of the highly politicized nature of much of their music, they often are portrayed and interpreted in a rather simplistic manner both in the national media and also in academic studies (Sharma, Hutnyk and Sharma 1996; Hutnyk 2000). Fun^Da^Mental's radical political agenda, in conjunction with their diverse ethnic make-up, serves to encourage 'exotic politics' whereby the band are taken to represent an idealized and authentic political vanguard of the oppressed. I do not wish to minimize the importance of political issues in their music, but we need to step back and look at other motives behind the band – lest we forget that music is at heart a *pleasurable* endeavour – and we need to recognize that even a band like Fun^Da^Mental indulge in the more corporeal pleasures of life. Ironically the very name Fun^Da^Mental, with all of its connotations of radical Islam, was chosen to represent the duality of the band's identity: 'Mental' was intended to express the band's radical, political stance and 'Fun' to stand for the more sensual side; the beats and rhythms of the music are not intended to stimulate political debate but to make people dance. As Dave Watts pointed out, if Fun^Da^Mental were as unremittingly serious and political as the press made out, the burden on the individuals in the band would be intolerable:

> There's got to be a point where you've got to step back because this shit gets heavy and you kind of wonder and question what your role is: 'What is my function?' Am I just a normal Joe, what does that entail? Or a community activist? A spokesman? A lot of people come up and say 'Does Fun^Da^Mental actually have any fun with it?' Hell yeah, because if there wasn't that, that would be it, do you know what I mean? Something just to counter-balance this serious shit, to counter-balance the everyday display of oppression, sexism ... whatever, you just, you know, you need some time out from that.

For bands with a less overt political agenda than Fun^Da^Mental the expectation to represent and reflect a political or cultural perspective is nevertheless still present, as reflected by the experiences of both Voodoo Queens and Black Star Liner; although these bands have dealt with this tension in different ways. For Voodoo Queens the band's constitution of all-female and partly Asian (three of the original line-up were from an Asian background), combined with the high profile attained from the release of 'Supermodel, superficial', attracted a great deal of press attention that sought to portray the band as highly politicized. Although the band often critiqued gender politics in their lyrics and played a number of benefit performances for anti-racist groups, politics was not at the forefront of their philosophy. From the very outset, however, the band found themselves subjected to intense media interest which invariably focused on issues of race and gender, with little space given to the music. As lead singer and lyricist, Anjali Bhatia found herself carrying out the role of band spokesperson and, as we have seen, eventually became so disillusioned with the media that she became wary of any contact with journalists or music publications. Following her experiences with Voodoo Queens Anjali had developed a somewhat cautious approach to the media, which she felt had put unnecessary pressures on Asian musicians; as she explained to me in 1996: 'Everything's questioned, like when it's an Asian person doing it, everything becomes, like, magnified.' In 2003, now as a solo artist with over a decade's experience in the industry, Anjali still felt ambiguous about having to answer questions pertaining to her Asianness:

> In a way it would be easier if you didn't have to ask these questions, if I didn't have to sit here and answer these questions, it would be easier if I didn't have to sit here and explain about who I am ... you know, I'm an Asian person making music. Like, 'You're an Asian person: can you explain it please?' It would be a lot easier not to focus on that. (Personal interview 2003)

Ultimately, however, such misgivings have not driven Anjali to totally reject such questions – as in the case of Echobelly's Sonya Madan (see Chapter 5) – and she recognizes that ethnicity and cultural heritage are important factors in shaping her musical identity. She felt that such issues are only relevant to a certain extent, however, and should not be used in a way that threatened her individuality either as an artist or an individual:

I think that it shouldn't take away from the fact that I'm a musician and a producer and songwriter; but it is part of me and a part of me that goes into the music, it's fairly integral but what is more integral is the music and the sounds that I'm producing and I think that subjects like this have a danger of becoming quite staid and just polemics for the sake of polemics really.

There seems to be a consensus among the musicians I interviewed that issues of representation and ethnicity are important and relevant subjects for them to talk about but that they should not detract from their primary role as musical artists. This is certainly the case with Choque Hosein, who has not felt the pressure to act as a representative voice to the same extent as the other featured Asian musicians. The relative lack of pressure put on (or perceived by) Choque may well be due to the fact that Black Star Liner emerged on the UK scene a little after the initial breakthrough of Asian bands, when perhaps the novelty of such acts had receded somewhat, or may be a reflection of the lack of explicit political content in his band's music. Despite this, it is clear that Choque has at times acted as a somewhat strident voice, speaking out about issues of cultural ownership and stereotyping. Choque's virulent criticism of Kula Shaker in the national music press for example (see Chapter 4), was an uncompromising attack on elements of the music industry that adopt an exploitative and Orientalist attitude towards Asian music and culture; and he has often been scathing towards the attitude of both white record bosses and audiences whom he feels perceive Black Star Liner as little more than an exotic novelty act. When I suggested that I had witnessed large numbers of 'liberal white clubbers' in the audience at live performances by bands such as Fun^Da^Mental and Black Star Liner, Choque's frustration surfaced to the extent where he suggested that perhaps his band *did* have a political role to play, insomuch that the musicians in question were in a position to disrupt existing stereotypes of Asian music and culture. Of this element of his audience he said:

I tell them they're all wankers; I mean I hate all them fucking cunts. I don't care if they buy me fucking records, I just think they're so ... I don't know ... I want them to carry away something with them, I want to put the fear of God into them. I think that's really important. (Personal interview 1996)

Although none of the bands were particularly concerned with the ethnic make-up of their audiences, there was a certain amount of debate within the music press about what they felt was a high proportion of white rather than Asian patrons at live performances.[10] As David Stubbs of *Melody Maker* commented:

Whenever I've seen Fun^Da^Mental play, the audience seemed to be mainly white; they didn't seem to be galvanizing that kind of restless youth from the streets of Bradford. I suspect that they weren't listening to people like Fun^Da^Mental, the kind of people listening to Fun^Da^Mental would be people like me, you know, maybe slightly guilty whites or people with quite eclectic tastes, who listen to indie-

> rock but have crossed over to hip-hop, people a bit like that. (Personal interview 1996)

There seemed to be an implication that by playing to largely white audiences the 'authentic' nature of such bands was open to question, suggesting that Asian bands should play to primarily Asian audiences is rather reductive. Both Dave Watts and Aki Nawaz acknowledged the fact that their audience in the UK was largely white, but felt that this was the ideal audience for Fun^Da^Mental to put across their radical political message. Aki told me in 1996:

> Well we usually play to white audiences, I don't really care; they need it. People say we're preaching to the converted, the white press say we've always played to the converted – no we haven't, white liberals; they're not the converted, they don't even know what we're on about, they don't understand a thing we're on about. Would I like to see more Asians at gigs? That's like asking would I like to see more black people at anti-racist demonstrations, I don't give a fuck because it's the white man's problem.

Although the perceived lack of Asians at live performances was often used to question the cultural authenticity of these bands, the musicians involved were not greatly concerned with this issue. Indeed, the eclectic audiences can be seen to support the Asian musicians' rejection of a representative role, since none of the bands has an agenda to target a specifically Asian constituency. In 1996 I asked Tjinder Singh how he felt about criticisms that 'not enough' Asians attended his band's performances:

> See, a lot of people ... again with the reliance on the Asian community, well a lot of people say 'Well how can you say these things, when there's not even Asians at your gigs?' There *is* Asians at the gigs and there's more in gigs than before but the thing is, we don't say to Asians 'Come to our gigs' ... You see, the thing is, I'm really happy about the representation of people at our gigs, different ages and colours, that'll do me, that'll do me for a start. I couldn't think of a better audience.

Independent and solvent: the politics of the music industry

For all of the musicians I spoke to, political issues were clearly an important part of their lives and there seemed to be a broad consensus on issues of inequality such as racism, sexism and homophobia. These political views were not always articulated through their music, although, more often than not, they were discussed during press interviews. That such issues were raised, however, had perhaps more to do with the preconceptions of journalists conducting the interviews rather than the personal agendas of the bands. When political views were expressed, whether through music or interviews, the bands felt that they were reflecting their own views based on their own personal experiences. The musicians were acutely aware of the burden of representation that was often placed upon them and, despite a general reluctance, some inevitably shouldered some of this load. The expression of individual politics and identities can be understood as an integral part of the dynamic process of musical self-expression for many artists working within the music industry. When these ideas are disseminated into the public sphere where they can be discussed and dissected by audiences and critics alike, artists are forced to negotiate between their personal self-images and those projected on to them from an array of sources. In such an environment where commercial imperatives are paramount, such artists must constantly struggle to assert their own sensibilities and identities and attempt to retain control over their own public images. The desire to keep their destiny in their own hands has been tempered by the financial realities of survival within a highly commodified industry, and the rest of this chapter will look at various ways in which these Asian bands have attempted this survival on their own artistic and political terms.

Of paramount importance for these musicians then is the desire to retain as much control as possible over their music and releases, but this is mediated by the financial and commercial imperatives of working within the music industry. Although the bands discussed here started on small independent labels and, with the exception of Black Star Liner, continue to do so, they have adopted various strategies and relationships which reflect the pragmatic realities of working within the commercial music industry. As we have already seen, all of the bands in this study place a great deal of importance on the artistic integrity of their music, which they feel comes before any financial or commercial concerns. Nevertheless, the desire to be heard and reach an audience that is at the heart of music-making means that it is inevitable that any musician must come to terms with the realities of the marketplace. In order to produce, promote and distribute recorded music in a manner that reaches a significant audience any band or musician must take into account both the need for financial investment and adequate expertise of the music market itself. Needless to say, both of these elements are in abundant supply within major record companies, but for both practical and ideological reasons these are usually beyond the grasp of new bands and musicians; so it is more often than not that they turn to the smaller-scale operation of the independent record labels.

Indeed, all of the bands focused on here released their first records on independent labels that enabled them to establish their initial audience and public profiles. Although almost all of them have continued to release records on such labels, however, their subsequent careers have eventually brought them all into some kind of contact with major record companies attached to global corporations. The inter-relationship between minor and major record labels that characterizes much of the contemporary music industry is such that it is increasingly hard to distinguish a standard pattern or career path for any band or musician; and this is certainly reflected in the experiences of the artists in this study. The range of contacts and affiliations that characterize the bands' experiences reflects the complex inter-relationships between musicians and record labels of varying size and status. What the bands in this study reflect is a range of strategies that have sought to maximize their own potential on terms that guarantee their own artistic and political independence while simultaneously reaching a national and international audience. The remainder of this chapter will examine the various strategies that have been adopted in order to achieve these goals and consider some of the problems that bands have had to overcome with small, as well as with larger, record companies.

Independent beginnings: doing it for yourself

For any new band seeking an audience the desire to release records is paramount and raises a number of practical and ideological issues. The practical realities of finding the means to produce, release and distribute recordings is counter-balanced by the desire to retain control over the artistic expression of the music itself. These two complementary needs are such that it is often through small, independent labels that new bands are able to create and release their first recordings (Kelly 1987; Hesmondhalgh 1998). In this way all of the bands focused on here released their first records on independent labels and, although this was certainly born of necessity, it also allowed them to retain control over their artistic and musical integrity. The independent record sector in the UK has a long tradition stretching back to the punk era in the late 1970s when the DIY ethic reigned supreme, through to the pinnacle of the independent movement in the 1980s with the success of a number of regionally based labels such as Rough Trade in London, Rhino in Leeds and Warp in Sheffield. During the heyday of the independents in the mid-1980s these small but successful labels co-operated with each other to form national distribution networks, as represented by Revolver and The Cartel. One of the driving forces behind the development of independent labels was an ideological position which sought to create a nurturing environment for uncompromising and innovative bands away from what was regarded as the crass commercialism and corrupting influences of the corporate mega-giant record labels (Kelly 1987; Hesmondhalgh 1998).

This environment created a space for dissident voices where various political and musical statements could be allowed to flourish without the constraints of overtly commercial concerns. Within such labels deals could be based more around personal relationships rather than contracts and it was certainly often the case that independent labels were set up and run by individuals who were primarily fans of the music that they sought to release. Although the independent scene fragmented somewhat in the 1990s with the collapse of most of the principal labels of the 1980s[11] and the co-option of an 'indie ethic' by some of the major record labels – with their practices of signing established indie acts and the setting up of 'bogus' (Negus 1992) independent labels – there is still a significant independent sector functioning in the UK, giving many new bands their first access to a national audience.

Cornershop began to release records in 1992 on Wiiija Records, a label that embodied many of the ethics and business practices that so characterized smaller labels throughout the 1980s. The label was set up by music fan Gary Walker who, in typical independent style, ran the business from his bedroom for a number of years before Wiiija moved to bigger premises in 1996 after merging with the larger Beggars Banquet group. As is often the case with smaller independents, the personal relationship between the band and the label owner is vital to the success of what amounts to a joint venture. From the very beginning of the relationship between Cornershop and Wiiija there was a strong partnership at work whereby the label – as embodied by Gary Walker – allowed the band the freedom to develop on its own terms; an arrangement which ultimately has been beneficial for both parties. As Tjinder explained to me in 1996, the relationship cut both ways:

> We have control over the whole lot. Everything that they gave us was controlled by us, everything we want to do is controlled by us. It's a mutual thing really, I mean Wiiija Records wouldn't be here if it wasn't for us.

This refers to a period in the mid-1990s when Wiiija Records had contracted to the degree that Cornershop were the only band still signed to the label. The subsequent success of the band's second LP *Woman's gotta have it* not only ensured that the label continued as a going concern but that it was able to expand and sign further upcoming artists. The reliance during this period exclusively on Cornershop's output reflects the interdependence that can exist between musicians and the management of a small record label and is also a reflection of the large degree of artistic and commercial control for the bands involved.

Such associations do not necessarily continue indefinitely, however, and neither are they guaranteed to run smoothly at all times; any business built upon close personal relationships and bound by such tenuous factors as musical taste and style is vulnerable to change and disruption. That this degree of co-operation and like-mindedness is not always present in the relationship between artists and independent record labels is shown by the experience of Voodoo Queens with their original label Too Pure. The band were signed to Too Pure in 1993 with a similar arrangement to that which Cornershop enjoyed with Wiiija; Voodoo Queens were given a large degree of control of their output, from production and artwork to press releases and publicity. However, this relationship faltered in 1994 when the label became unhappy with the musical direction that the band were taking and Voodoo Queens parted company with Too Pure, setting up their own Voodoo label later that year through which the band's final single 'Eat the germs' was released. As Anjali Bhatia told me in 1996, this short-lived label (the single was the last record produced by Voodoo Queens before they disbanded) was set up and financed by the band primarily for the practical purpose of releasing their own material which their previous label had rejected:

> We did a demo tape and they [Too Pure] didn't like it at all. Plus we were not really happy being on the label because, well, we were struggling financially as well and I think it came to a natural end and they didn't like what we were doing and we'd sort of had enough of being on the label as well and obviously we wanted to put stuff out so we needed a label to put records out.

Aside from these practical considerations, however, it is clear that the thinking behind the label was also committed to promoting many of the ideological concerns that characterize many independent companies. Both the physical nature of the actual single and its packaging suggest a close adherence to many of the indie ethics that have shaped the business practices of many small labels. The single was released only as a limited edition vinyl 7-inch and packaged in hand-painted record sleeves, thereby avoiding many of the conventions of design and packaging. (It is common practice for major labels to mass produce singles in a number of different formats including two-part CDs and cassettes.) This shows a subtle but clear commitment to the ideological imperatives of independence and this is borne out somewhat more forcefully when viewing the message 'Fuck the corporate!' which is scratched onto the inner ring of the vinyl.

It is clear that, despite these tell-tale signs of the more ideological aspects of independence, the primary drive behind creating the label was always the fundamental desire to release records but, as I have suggested, these two factors are not necessarily incompatible. If we look at the case of Fun^Da^Mental and Nation Records we can see how these two elements have managed to be combined success-fully enough for the label to function and thrive for over a decade. Fun^Da^Mental have released all of their records through Nation, which was set up in the early 1990s by Aki Nawaz and Kath Canonville.[12] For Aki the setting up of Nation Records was partly an ideological move to provide a supportive outlet for 'world music fused together with street sounds'. He is quite clearly influenced by the punk DIY ethic that has become central to the ideology of the independent sector and this has played an important part in the development of Nation Records, as evidenced in the label's logo which contains the slogan 'Uncompromising, Creative, Innovative'. It is also significant that these ideological and idealistic impera-tives are supplemented by the knowledge that Aki has gathered from his experiences in the music industry since the early 1980s; in particular his role as drummer with post-punk band Southern Death Cult. Aki has sought to shape these experiences into sound business practice by creating an open and non-exploitative environment at Nation Records where new bands can be nurtured and supported by somebody who already knows the ropes:

Fig. 6.2 'Eat the Germs': the 7-inch single released by short-lived Voodoo Records in 1995

> I've been around a long time, I'm a bit of an old fart and I'm not shit at business, I'm quite good at it. I've been in situations where I've been in bands that have done better than Fun^Da^Mental, The Cult, things like that and I sort of look at that time and think what we got out of it and what people were offering and how people treated us; and with the Fun^Da^Mental thing, it's like we've got more press out of Fun^Da^Mental and we've done more gigs – I've put the experience to good use. I can read a record contract inside out; I've only got three O levels, I'm not well read, it's just that I can do that. (Personal interview 1996)

Aki stressed that it was vital for all the bands at Nation Records to have control over their musical output, all the way from production through to distribution and sales, as he explained to me, 'Yeah we've all got control, it's stipulated in our contracts.' Aki's dual role as the head of Nation Records and as a member of

Fig. 6.3 An early (1993) example of the Nation Records logo

Fun^Da^Mental has ensured that his often controversial music has continued to develop artistically as well as reaching a significant audience. As head of his own record label he has subsequently come into contact with elements of the corporate sector of the music industry where he has had to negotiate between his independent ideals and the everyday practicalities of producing and distributing recorded music.

It is certainly the case that the accumulation over time of experience within the music industry helps develop a more pragmatic attitude among many musicians, as in the case of those discussed here. Choque Hosein had worked within the industry for a number of years before founding Black Star Liner, having released a number of records in several other bands as well as working as a professional songwriter. Black Star Liner began by releasing records on their own Soundclash Sound label and for Choque the purpose was solely practical, although once again the influence of the DIY ethic acted as a source of inspiration and encouragement, as he told me in 2003:

> It's more fun making your own records and it always has been since the punk times. Musically I like the whole thing about making your own records and having worked in a record shop and seen people carry on doing that for 10 years even well after it; you could put out your own records.

Despite his obvious enthusiasm for DIY record labels, Soundclash Sound acted as a calling card for the band within the industry and subsequently led to the band being signed by EXP Records, a much larger independent label which released their debut album *Yemen Cutta connection* in 1996. The move to a larger label meant that the band had access to greater marketing and distribution resources able to cope better with the growing success of Black Star Liner. For Choque the size and status of a record label was not an issue as long as the band were able to retain as much control over their music as possible. Eventually, in 1997, following the financial collapse of EXP, Black Star Liner signed to a major record label in the guise of Warner Brothers, moving the band out of the independent sector for the first time. Again issues of musical integrity and control were paramount to the band, who continued to produce innovative and critically acclaimed records seemingly unhindered by the corporate concerns of their parent label. The association between Black Star Liner and a major label is one instance of an increasingly interconnected music industry where bands come into contact with a range of business practices and alliances that incorporate the interests of both small and large companies. Although none of the other bands has followed suit, many of them have come into contact with major labels, sometimes to their benefit, and all have developed strategies of pragmatism and practicality which have allowed their musical careers to survive and flourish.

Pragmatism and pop: making the most of making music

The ideology of independence which has developed since the late 1970s was certainly an important factor for most of the musicians I spoke to although, as we shall see, the functioning of this ideology is far more pragmatic than the somewhat romanticized and uncompromising model that dominated the 1980s (Kelly 1987; Hesmondhalgh 1998). This pragmatic approach is based largely on the financial imperative of survival, with labels and bands alike recognizing the need to remain financially stable in order to endure and flourish within the industry. This financial pragmatism does not necessarily result in the compromising of the band's musical and political objectives, however; it is merely a more realistic understanding of working within an industry which is essentially commodity led (Harker 1980; Lull 1987). What the experiences of the various musicians show is that the combined issues of financial reward and artistic control are paramount whatever the size or status of the record label and that negotiating a satisfactory relationship with the company owners is the key to the long-term survival and success of any musical endeavour.

If we look at the case of Anjali Bhatia we can see how she has been able not only to survive and prosper within the industry but also to redefine her musical direction. Following the break-up of Voodoo Queens, Anjali went through something of a musical reinvention, eschewing the punk rock approach and developing a more laid-back sound based on a wide range of musical styles, beats and samples.[13] In 1996 she signed for Wiiija Records, who were able to provide a degree of financial security that allowed her the time and space to write, record and produce material from her own bedroom studio. For Anjali the freedom and control that she is able to maintain over her music is the most important factor in her relationship with her record label and it may well be the case that only an independent label such as Wiiija would be willing to support a new artist in this way. Nevertheless Anjali does not place a great deal of importance on the status of her record label and would work quite happily with a major company as long as she could make the music she wants and have that music reach an audience. When in 1996 I asked her whether notions of ideological independence would prevent her from working with a major record label she responded:

> Not particularly, no. I just want to … I'd just like to sell records really. I want to make music that I like – I don't think about the business side of it that much – music really comes first, however corny that sounds.

The more idealistic notions of independence and the DIY culture that characterized the work of Voodoo Queens were balanced out by the stark financial realities of attempting to become a full-time musician, and the shortcomings that Anjali experienced during the early 1990s had played a significant role in developing a more pragmatic and practical approach to music-making:

> I think when you start off you're very naïve about, 'Oh yeah we can live, we can do this and be really punk about it,' but then you think, 'Well hang on a minute, I can't afford to live.' At first it's like, 'Yeah – punk rock' which it, like … is; then you come to a point where if you want to do something with your career, you realize that you do need, like, basic necessities like a proper record deal, just some money to live on or money for equipment. We never had any money to buy guitars or pedals or stuff like that … getting things fixed … it always had to come out of our own money and I was just sick of that.

By signing to Wiiija Records Anjali was joining a label which had strong associations with the ideologies of independence that had been so influential during the 1980s. This influence was undoubtedly a crucial factor in the creation and running of the label, and the relationship between artist and owner in such a setting is key to a successful outcome for both parties. Although the indie ethic had undoubtedly played a part in the creation and maintenance of Wiiija Records, in 1996 owner Gary Walker felt that this was counterbalanced by the practical needs of running a stable business:

> There is a certain ideology that goes with the territory. I think there's a certain stage where it goes beyond ideology in that you can own a successful business without having to have a political motivation behind it.

This practical approach has enabled the label to function successfully for over a decade and part of this longevity is due to flexible working practices that have allowed it to work in partnership with other, larger labels. In 1995 Wiiija merged with the larger Beggars Banquet,[14] which, since its conception in the early 1980s, has become one of the UK's most successful independent labels. This relationship was negotiated to provide Wiiija with a much-needed injection of cash but not at the cost of the integrity of the smaller label, which retained total control over its own musical output. I asked Gary in the interview whether Beggars Banquet had any say in the artistic direction of Wiiija:

> No, not at all. At first it was very much like somebody who will leave you alone but the more we work together, the closer I want to get because of the support they can give me, the marketing, distribution, their experience and resources. Eventually we will be moving in with them, in their offices so that we can have closer contact.[15]

Such practices were supported fully by members of Cornershop who clearly feel, after being in the band for several years, that finance is central to the continued existence of the band. As Ben Ayres told me:

> Well, we've been going for a long time now and we felt basically we wouldn't exist as a band if it wasn't for someone at some stage giving us some money. I mean Wiiija itself would have folded about a year ago if it wasn't for Beggars Banquet having faith in it and saying, 'Look, we'll come in and co-own the label and give you complete freedom.' (Personal interview 1996)

During the mid- to late 1990s, as well as making music with Cornershop, Ben was working for Beggars Banquet – which reflects the some of the stark financial pressures placed upon members of even relatively successful bands. Even with the critical success of their third LP *When I was born for the 7th time* the band were still unable to generate enough income for all the members to dedicate themselves to music on a full-time basis, as reflected by Tjinder Singh in an interview for *The Independent*:

> We've been doing this for five years and we've still got no money. I'm the band's only full-time member – the others have all got jobs. Saffs [sitar player] works with old people and Ben [Ayres] works for the record company and can't get time off so we have to tour Europe without him. (Thompson 1997: 20)

The success of Cornershop in the United States has led to a further collaboration between Wiiija and a larger record label, this time one of the major global corporations. In 1996 the band negotiated a deal with the Luaka Bop label to distribute their second album *Woman's gotta have it* and subsequent US releases. The fact that Luaka Bop is distributed by Warner Brothers could be interpreted as compromising the band's independence but, as Tjinder has stated, the ultimately successful deal was forged with the understanding that Cornershop retained control over the artistic output and image projection of the band (see Chapter 5). As Gary Walker explained, dealing with a subsidiary such as Luaka Bop allowed Wiiija to benefit from the resources of a major corporation while retaining artistic control over the musical product and ensuring flexible and personalized day-to-day working practices:

> We, as a record label, have the worldwide rights for Cornershop and we have licensed our recordings of this album [*Woman's gotta have it*] to Luaka Bop, basically. Luaka Bop, in turn, have a licensing deal with Warner Brothers so basically Warner Brothers are doing all the marketing, the manufacturing, promotion and everything, they got most of the support money and Luaka Bop are just co-ordinating it. It's nice because you actually deal with a small label, based in their own offices in New York and you've got the backing of Warner Brothers.

As already outlined in Chapter 3, such business practices are symptomatic of the interlinked structure of the contemporary international music industry. As we have seen, doing deals with major corporations is regarded with great suspicion by many within the independent sector, and to engage in such practices is to expose oneself to accusations of selling out. The notion that any kind of alternative musical or political expression will be stifled or watered down by the pressures of corporate capital is central to such concerns but, as I have already suggested, such processes are neither inevitable nor desirable. Major labels have come to realize that it is beneficial to allow smaller subsidiaries to function relatively unhindered in order to retain the aura of distinction and independence that made the minor labels successful in the first place (Negus 1992; Hesmondhalgh 1998). Marketing deals and injections of capital into smaller labels allow major labels to profit from the unique skills of the independent sector without threatening the 'authentic' status of their junior partners. For the smaller labels, access to greater resources allows them to reach a larger audience while retaining their integrity of independence. The blurring of the boundaries between large and small labels that has become characteristic is such that some have questioned the relevance and liability of traditional notions of independence (Negus 1992). Music journalist David Stubbs suggested that the idealism of independence that had emerged in the wake of punk had since given way to more grounded practices that reflected the everyday realities of running a successful business of any size:

> I think it was just an initial thing with indie labels, it was kind of some collective set-up existing outside of the whole corporate machinery but that's clearly not the case any more. As far as I'm concerned they're all small businesses, they're all organized capital, all registered as businesses – they're just small businesses as opposed to big businesses. (Personal interview 1996)

Despite the increasing interdependency between large and small record companies, it is clear that the philosophy of anti-corporate independence is a still powerful influence on numerous people working within the industry. For many, the idea of working with a major record label is seen to represent a betrayal of principles. In his 1996 interview I asked Paul Cox, co-owner of Too Pure Records, whether he felt that making deals with major labels compromised the integrity of his smaller label. He replied:

> I don't consider we're doing deals. Licensing to a major label is different from being owned by a major label. I don't know, some indie labels – indie ways of thinking – people would turn their backs on even releasing a record thorough a major. Like at the moment in America, all our records come out on Too Pure Records but they are released through the Warner Brothers system. Yeah, that to all intents and purposes is us working with a major label but what we are doing is licensing our bands to them so I consider that different from, like, setting up your label with outside money from a major label because with none of these licensing deals that we have, like PJ Harvey to Island or Faith Healers to Elecktra, they don't have any say over company policy.

Even for a defiantly non-conformist and dissident label like Nation Records there is room for flexible working practices in order to ensure that its bands reach their full potential and that the label remains financially solvent. Aki Nawaz combines his role as musician with that of businessman to help create an environment for musicians which is both financially stable and artistically open. Despite the overtly political and often confrontational approach of much of its musical output, Nation Records has to function like any other business and has had to adopt a pragmatic and flexible outlook in order to survive. Nation has also turned to Beggars Banquet for extra funds in order to expand and, as with Wiiija, the smaller label retains total artistic control, although Nation has sacrificed a lesser share of the company than Wiiija. I asked Aki about this relationship and he explained that:

> The Beggars Banquet link is that Nation Records at one time, a long time ago when we really needed more finances, we were getting the profile but weren't getting enough sales – we never really have done brilliantly with sales anyway – we needed the money and we were going round and saying, well 'We came to you first and you said "No" and now we've gone away and done it, we've given ourselves a profile, we've given ourselves respect, now just give us some money.' It was just in order to grow and they said 'Yes, we should help you out' and came in and bought up a share in Nation; just a quarter of the company. (Personal interview 1996)

The relationship between Nation Records and Beggars Banquet would appear to be a purely financial one and does not seem compromise the integrity of the smaller label or the bands on it, as Dave Watts (who also works at Nation Records) outlined with regard to Fun^Da^Mental:

> We do what we want to do, we're with Nation Records, we're allowed to do what we want to do. We're licensed to Beggars Banquet but still we do what we want to do, so there isn't anybody, kind of, dictating; there is no external dictatorship of where we're going or what we should be like. (Personal interview 1996)

The flexible and open approach of Beggars Banquet in supporting smaller labels like Nation and Wiiija reflects the ideology of owner Martin Mills, who formed the label in the 1980s. The success and growth of Beggars Banquet as an independent label has allowed Mills to support and nurture a number of smaller labels financially and his dedication to the indie ethic has meant that he has been quite happy to allow them to retain total control over their output. Even with the international success of bands like The Prodigy and The Charlatans, Beggars Banquet has continued to adhere to many of the principles of independence, as Ben Ayres explained to me in 1996:

> I really like their ethics, I don't know if you saw the office back where I work but it's all open plan and Martin Mills, who owns Beggars Banquet and loads of other things like RTM distribution and God knows what else, he's just across the way and you can hear everything he says to all his business people – he's totally open. Everyone seems to be an equal, which is really quite remarkable. It's basically one of only two big independent record companies; us and Mute. Beggars do have dealings with major record companies – they have an agreement with Warner Brothers to distribute their bigger acts like The Prodigy – but they are fiercely independent, one of his absolutely sworn statements is that he'll never, ever, sell to a major; he could make millions.

Mainstream success experienced by bands on smaller labels can actually threaten the continued existence of an independent company, since this success attracts the attention of major labels who often buy out the owners, thus swallowing up and incorporating minor labels (Negus 1992). Beggars Banquet have resisted this by establishing a sound financial base over a long period and also by forging more flexible deals with major labels (such as distribution), which allows them to retain control over and for their artists. Such deals are necessitated by the national and international success of individual acts who, because of their mainstream chart success, need access to greater resources in order to reach an expanded audience.

Although Nation Records is a relatively a small label with modest sales – so much so that a 1997 compilation album was ironically entitled *...And still no hits – Nation Records – the story so far*[16] – it has experienced a certain degree of chart success, most particularly with the world dance fusion band TransGlobal Underground during the early and mid-1990s. The crossover success of a band such as TransGlobal Underground, whose first two LPs featured in the Top 40 of the UK album charts,[17] puts a great deal of pressure on a small label with limited resources which can often struggle to meet greatly increased demand. In order to ensure that TransGlobal Underground were able to better reach their expanded audience, Nation Records negotiated deals with major record companies, initially BMG and later with Sony; two of the giants of the global music industry. I suggested to Aki that this was a surprising partnership, given that his own band often criticize the corrupting and exploitative influence of global capital. His reply reflects the pragmatic approach that many independent labels in the 1990s have adopted in order to survive and flourish:

> Well, I have to wear different hats for different situations and for someone like TransGlobal, they came to Nation first and we put out a record, 'Templehead', and as soon as that record was put out they got signed to BMG – licensed through us – like a massive deal and they spent some time there and it didn't work out with the big record company so they came back to Nation and we started working with them again and they started doing really well; and then Sony came in and they wanted to do a deal and we did a deal where outside the UK we released on, like, Sony in different countries and then they got pissed off with Sony as well, and then they came back here and now they're signed here again properly. (Personal interview 1996)

Aki did not feel that either he or the band had compromised their independence since, throughout the entire period of this somewhat convoluted saga, TransGlobal Underground had retained complete artistic control over their actual musical output while simultaneously taking advantage of the greater distribution and marketing resources made available by a larger label.

Making music work: majors or minors?

Any significant degree of success for an artist working on an independent label increases the likelihood that they will come into contact with one of the larger record companies. As we have seen, such a relationship grants access to wider resources for the band which, in return, helps generate profits for both parties. The licensing to a major label of a band signed to an independent is one method of establishing such a relationship; one that allows both the artists and the smaller label to retain a certain degree of autonomy. Of course a band that has demonstrated its potential appeal and marketability on the independent scene may simply choose to sign directly to a major record company, which is exactly what Black Star Liner did in 1996 following the financial collapse of their previous label EXP. The decision to sign to Warner Brothers was taken in order to benefit from the same economies of scale that result from licensing deals between small and large labels without the middleman of the independent company. For those more idealistic artists and workers in the industry such a decision is viewed as selling-out, the implication being that a band signing to a major has placed financial and commercial concerns ahead of artistic integrity. This criticism is rejected by Choque Hosein, whose wide experience has led him to question the validity of the independent ethic in the workings of most minor labels. He felt that the need for financial stability to ensure that a record label is able to enjoy any degree of success or longevity is such that the working practices of small labels differ only in terms of scale when compared to larger companies:

> They are small businesses and Warners are a big business and they have to work in the same way. They've got product and they've got this to promote ... they've got the same machinery, only they've got less money to do with it. So the ideology is nothing. The only way you can make it work is if you work with someone like Daniel Miller on Mute and you do a handshake with him and split 50-50 down the middle but that's an exceptional case. (Personal interview 2003)

Although Choque recognized that they were some exceptions, he felt that most record companies functioned essentially in the same manner, and the decision to sign a three-album deal with Warner Brothers was based on the label's promotional and distribution resources and the understanding that there would be no interference in the band's musical direction. The fact that Black Star Liner record and produce their music from a studio at Choque's home meant that they retained complete autonomy over their day-to-day working practices.

At first this relationship appeared to work well, as evidenced by the critical acclaim that accompanied the 1999 album *Bengali bantam youth experience*.[18] Appearances can be deceptive, however, and behind the scenes the relationship between band and record label was deteriorating badly and the subsequent fall-out resulted in Black Star Liner's complete absence from the British music scene for several years. The apparent unwillingness of the record label to provide adequate resources to support *Bengali bantam youth experience* was at the heart of these difficulties and this was perhaps precipitated by a number of structural changes at Warner Music UK. The US parent company's decision to downsize its UK division resulted in a number of bands and employees having their contracts terminated. This reduction in the size and ambition of the label was compounded by the arrival of Roger Aimes as chairman in place of Rob Dickens – at whose behest the band had been signed originally in 1997. Thus the album was released on a label that was going through a process of contraction and without Black Star Liner's original patron. According to Choque the label appeared to have low expectations for the album, which was reflected in the relatively small amount of copies initially pressed and distributed. Even following the positive critical response and a number of high-profile endorsements – including not just the Mercury Music Prize nomination but also the use of the track 'Low BMW' in a Nike television advert – the label failed to provide adequate support for the album, as Choque explained:

> We had loads of coverage that year and lots of press and basically they just couldn't meet the demand and it just kind of fell on its arse because they couldn't get their shit together; Warners couldn't get their shit together. We were still doing gigs but the thing was, Warners at this stage were, like, crumbling and so basically we were playing gigs in Switzerland, France – wherever we could – we had a credible name and we were doing all that and yet ... the same old story: 'Your album isn't available here' and we were on a major label! (Personal interview 2003)

Ultimately, this lack of support from Warner Music UK created irreconcilable differences between the two parties with Black Star Liner unwilling to produce further records for the label. The band subsequently spent 18 months trying to extricate themselves from their contract, a process that involved a great deal of legal wrangling at great financial and artistic cost. Black Star Liner eventually facilitated the termination of their contract by producing an album's worth of deliberately uncommercial and almost unlistenable material.[19] By the time Black Star Liner parted company with Warner Music UK in 2001 they had not released a record for over two years and the financial and emotional strain was so great that drummer Tom Salmon and guitarist/sitarist Chris Harrop decided to call it a day and left the group, leaving Choque Hosein as the sole full-time member.

Black Star Liner's problems with Warner could be seen to confirm all of the suspicions and criticisms that characterize traditional ideologies of independence; having sold their souls to the machinations of international capitalism what else could they have expected? There is no doubt that the relationship was extremely damaging for the group, but it does not mean that the problems Black Star Liner experienced are specific to the working practices found within major labels. In the early part of 2003, after some 10 years of working together, Cornershop parted ways with Wiiija Records following a similar period of dissatisfaction and recrimination. Although Black Star Liner and Cornershop were making music at opposite ends of the major–independent spectrum, their experiences and grievances are remarkably similar.

As in the case of Black Star Liner, problems emerged for Cornershop as the result of a change of personnel at the head of the company when Gary Walker left Wiiija Records in the autumn of 2000. I have already indicated that the close level of co-operation between Cornershop and Walker was the key to their mutual long-term success. The subsequent relationship between Cornershop and Walker's successor Chris Sharp ultimately proved problematic and the band were extremely unhappy with the promotion of their fourth album *Handcream for a generation* (2002). Once again the album was a huge critical success[20] and once again the band felt that that their record company had failed to back it with the promotional tools at their disposal. Tjinder Singh certainly felt this, as evidenced in the 'disastrous' organization of their American tour (now under the aegis of Beggars Banquet's US wing) and the fact that Cornershop had to personally fund their own UK live shows. The lack of support and communication between Cornershop and Wiiija Records during this period was felt to be in stark contrast to the years when Gary Walker ran the label, so much so that Tjinder told me in 2003:

> Inadvertently – and it wasn't our fault – inadvertently we'd got involved with a label that was the anathema of everything that we thought about. It was everything we didn't want in a label when we started out.

Although Tjinder was clearly dissatisfied with the way that the label was being run under new management, this was undoubtedly exasperated by a certain lack of personal understanding and of shared vision between himself and Chris Sharp. In fact, when discussing the deterioration of the relationship between the two parties, Tjinder found it difficult to separate these two factors. When I asked him whether the difficulties in the relationship were based on personal differences rather than on the way the label was run, he responded by saying:

> It was totally to with the way the label was run because Gary was the label. We shouldn't have to put up with shit like that, we should be with people like Gary and that should be it.

The breakdown of the working relationship between Cornershop and Wiiija in the wake of *Handcream for a generation* proved to be irretrievable and, despite the band having played a large part in the label's longevity, early in 2003, after 11 years of successful co-existence, Cornershop were dropped by Wiiija.

The similar experiences that both Cornershop and Black Star Liner found themselves having to negotiate serve to illustrate further that the workings of independent and major record labels are hard to separate. Although it is certainly the case that the more formalized nature of Warner Music UK resulted in a more drawn-out and costly separation period, in both cases the success or failure of the business relationship was based largely on the personal rapport between the band and the head of the respective record label. For both bands, the replacement of the head of the company ultimately proved costly, since it was the personal relationship between this individual and the members of each band that underpinned the business agreement with the label. In this sense, it is clear that such personal relationships are vital to the success of any potential liason between musicians and record labels of all sizes, and the ability to achieve this can be much more significant than the terms of any contract.

Some years on from the deal with Warner Music UK, Choque Hosein certainly does not bear any grudge against major record companies in particular, preferring to accept that the problems experienced by both Cornershop and Black Star Liner are an inevitable consequence of working in the music industry and that one must be equipped to deal with such circumstances in order to survive and prosper:

> If you're not prepared – that's why people get burnt out in the industry because no matter how many times a mistake is made by a major label or an independent label or a manager or a band, they're always the same mistakes; continually. But it's not a cynical attitude, it's just basically if you want to get through the music industry, you've got to be prepared for all these things and you've got to know what's going to happen. (Personal interview 2003)

The primary concern for all of the bands discussed here was to maximize their potential to produce music in an environment that was open and afforded them a large degree of artistic freedom; but they also recognized the need for financial security in order to maintain careers that have in all cases spanned at least 10 years. Although the desire to retain artistic and political integrity undoubtedly draws upon some of the ideological influences of the post-punk independent ethic, this is counterbalanced by the more practical and pragmatic realities of functioning as a professional musician. The flexibility that these two needs entail throws up a variety of working practices and allegiances which have been reflected in the latter part of this chapter and are apparent in the future careers of bands such as Black Star Liner and Cornershop. In the spring of 2003, when my final interviews for this book took place, both bands were poised to sign new record deals to replace those that had ended in disappointment. Choque Hosein, with a large body of unreleased work at his disposal, had decided for a second time to sign with a major record company where, once again, the head of the label happens to be a big Black Star Liner fan. Tjinder Singh, on the other hand, was writing material for a new album and Cornershop were about to sign to another London-based independent label and looking forward to the future with some optimism.[21]

Conclusion: pragmatism, politics and pleasure

The mere fact that, until the 1990s, Asian musicians had been noted only by their absence on the UK music scene has ensured that, for a young generation of Asian bands emerging in the 1990s, issues of politics and representation have been ever present and highly visible. There has been a great deal of expectation from various quarters, from the national music press and from the Asian community in particular, who have looked to these bands to present the nation with a definitive understanding of the realities of being Asian in contemporary Britain. For many of the current wave of Asian bands and musicians working in the UK, political issues form an important part of the way they function, both within the music industry and in their everyday lives. They also, however, reject any direct notion of representation, asserting instead an individual expression of personal views that may very well be grounded in the condition of British Asianness but are not intended to be representative of the overall Asian community. Despite this, as we have seen, being in the public eye means that, almost by default, the individuals and bands in question are interpreted, at least by others, as representatives of a youthful, Asian constituency. The pressure felt by these bands may well be a contributory factor in the desire to retain musical and political integrity; Asian bands suffer insomuch that they are portrayed and interpreted in a way that often reduces their role as musical artists.

Although the bands that I spoke to clearly had different approaches to the interaction of politics and music, the need to retain total artistic control over their outputs was universal and a number of strategies were adopted. This meant that the bands had to function in a flexible and pragmatic way which allowed them to express themselves both musically and politically on their own terms while ensuring that they had sufficient resources to be able to reach their audiences and remain financially viable. Although the bands are clearly influenced by the legacy of independence and the DIY ethic drawn from the punk era, they have no romantic notions about the nature of producing music within a highly competitive and commercialized industry. This has led the bands to adopt a number of ways of releasing records: by setting up their own fledgling labels; by working with established independent companies; and even by signing to major record corporations. This reflects a pragmatic understanding of the need for any artist to reach an audience but, as the experiences of the musicians discussed here have shown, the desire to retain a sense of musical integrity has been central to their relationships with record labels of all sizes.

The ways in which the various bands and individuals negotiate their personal and political beliefs in the realm of the contemporary music industry tells us much about the contingent and contextual workings of self-identity and damages totalizing rationales of ethnic essentialism. It also reflects the conflicts and negotiations between how individuals view themselves and how they are viewed by others; the interaction between these two interpretative modes is an important factor in the emergence of new modes of ethnicity and identity. By examining the complex and varied processes at work in the everyday experiences of even this small sample we can begin to present a more rounded picture of young Asians living in contemporary Britain; where they represent not a simplified and fixed community but a dynamic and shifting model of ever-changing ethnic identity.

Notes

1. 'England's dreaming' from the *Lock, stock and double barrel* EP, released on Wiiija in 1992.
2. The lyrics to 'Supermodel, superficial' include the lines:

   Whose role models do you think you really are?
   Young girls that make themselves sick
   Feel guilty for being size 14
   Living in their self-hate.

3. In an article for *FAD* magazine, Anjali explained the ideas behind her installation:

   As a teenager, I spent half my life in the bathroom, desperately trying to beautify myself. There was a universal image of female beauty that was equated with being thin and flawless. I didn't fit into this category (I was a size 14/16 and 5'3" tall) and saw myself as being a fat, ugly lump of lard with bad teenage skin. The Barbie Doll image constantly haunted me. If I wasn't smearing L20 mud packs on my face, then I was either puking my chocolate cake guts out or was permanently glued onto the weighing scales in tears. I wanted to become a size 8 stick insect.

I was determined to try anything. I became compulsive and would steal any product with the words diet or lose weight fast written on them (I could never afford to pay). Needless to say, they never worked and were a complete rip-off. I was making myself ill. It took years to get over my disorder.

I'd wasted so much time bullying myself, because I didn't live up to the images that were forced into my psyche, vacuous images of so-called female perfection.

My bathroom installation is partly based on these experiences. The actual bathroom look is sterile, Candy pink latex moulds of Barbie dolls, dissected and whole, are fixed onto latex shower curtains, weighing scales and toilet seat covers. The bathroom cabinet is filled with laxatives and the dustbin near the door is laden with empty chocolate wrappers.

There's enough pressures on people of either sex without the supermodel empire being forced down our throats. It is sad, but not surprising to read desperate letters in teeny mags from thirteen-year old girls wanting to kill themselves, because they don't have the Kate Moss rickets look. The whole fashion, beauty, diet, supermodel industry is based on big money – superficial and sucks! Be proud of what you are, remember, you are beautiful and they are freaks. (Rowden 1994)

4. This celebration of guilt-free consumption of chocolate is reflected by an incident that I witnessed at a live concert in Bristol in 1994 when a female member of the audience threw on to the stage a popular branded chocolate bar which Anjali gratefully unwrapped and ate.
5. The punk- and rock-influenced sound of Voodoo Queens is in marked contrast to the laid-back grooves of her solo output. As Anjali told me in 2003:

   I felt that I'd screamed as much as I could and then I went back to writing more kind of … panoramic soundscapes, hence the new kind of stuff I'm doing now.'

6. From the album *Yemen Cutta connection*, released on EXP in 1996.
7. From the album *Bengali bantam youth experience*, released on WEA in 1999.
8. Samples used by the band range from the sound of the muezzin calling the faithful to prayer to the provocative speeches of Malcolm X, and lyrically the band often draw from much of the imagery of Islam:

   You go for yours 'cos I'm in Jihad
   Allahusamad
   There is no other way but Islam
   Lamiah allidh, wu lamiah ullahd
   Fool don't bother me wid no immortality
   Walalmiah qullahu kufhuan ahad
   There is no other way brother, Allah uh akbar.
   'President propaganda' from *Seize the time* (1994)

9. An attack on an Asian wedding party by a number of white skinheads provoked a violent response from young Asian men that escalated into pitched battles with the local police.
10. This was certainly the case at most of the gigs that I attended featuring the bands focused on here, although the musicians felt that the ethnic mix varied considerably depending on the venue and geographic location.
11. With the exception of Beggars Banquet, 4AD, Mute and One Little Indian, who continue to maintain a significant profile in the UK and internationally.
12. Kath Canonville left the label in 1999, leaving Aki Nawaz as the sole owner.
13. As she explained to me in 2003 (see n. 5 above), this reflected both a shift in her musical interests – away from a guitar-based rock format and towards more technology-based techniques such as sequencers and samplers – and also the feeling that she had achieved all she had set out to do with Voodoo Queens.
14. Under the terms of the deal Beggars Banquet initially had a 50 per cent stake in Wiiija Records.
15. The move took place in 1997, although in the autumn of 2000 Walker decided to move on from the record business and left the label so that Wiiija became solely a subsidiary of the Beggars Banquet empire.
16. An advert for the LP printed in *New Musical Express* (23 August 1997) went as follows:

    Do not read the following ad as it may cause offence.
    It doesn't matter what we do,
    We're not allowed to have hit records.
    To celebrate this fact, Nation Records presents:
    … And still no hits.
    Nation
    If you don't buy it, no-one will.

17. *Dream of 100 nations* was released in 1993 and *International times* in 1994.
18. The *Evening Standard* newspaper heralded *Bengali bantam youth experience* as 'The future of Rock and Roll' (24 July 1999) and *Time Out* described it as 'A truly wondrous record' (12 August 1999).
19. This was achieved much in the tradition of Lou Reed's notorious *Metal music machine* album that the artist produced in order to grudgingly fulfill his contractual obligations with RCA records in 1975. As Choque explained to me, this was very much a last attempt to free Black Star Liner from their contract with a label that they felt was not willing to support them adequately:

    > To get ourselves dropped we made an album of complete crap and put it together and I went through the Warner's back catalogue and named every track after Warner's songs without them realising. I went to Neil Young and Sisters of Mercy and loads of different artists that they had and picked a track off all their albums and named all the tracks after them and we just put lots of crap on there. We basically just put lots of backwards crap on and fucked it all up and just sent it to them and mercifully they said this isn't obviously good enough, we want to drop you and it was like, good. (Personal interview 2003)

20. *Q* magazine called *Handcream for a generation* 'a meaty, substantial, truly multi-dimensional project' (March 2002), *The Guardian* made it their album of the week

(29 March 2002) and in *The Independent*'s album of the year list Andy Gill wrote: 'Unaccountably ignored by the Mercury Prize nominations Cornershop's *Handcream for a generation* is a marvellous album, a life-affirming celebration of music as both a pleasurable listening experience and a cultural force' (20 December 2002).

21. Since neither band had completed the actual signing of their respective deals at the time that I interviewed them, they preferred me not to name the record companies involved, although by the time this book is printed their identities should be common knowledge.

Chapter 7

Old and new identities: music, ethnicity and syncretism

As we have already seen, the notion of a fixed and unified Asian community in the UK is extremely problematic because of the varying historical, religious, regional and linguistic identities apparent in the backgrounds of people from South Asian origins (Jackson 1989; Mitchell 1996). The bands that I have focused on in this study reflect the diversity of the Asian population in the UK and, although often associated with each other, do not reflect a unified constituency of Asian youth. Furthermore, these bands reflect the processes of syncretism that are at the heart of the functioning of a multi-ethnic society and the music they produce draws on a wide range of cultural sources which is restricted neither by the boundaries of some imagined Asian community nor the constraints of the nation state. Even though the featured bands are invariably defined – by the media at least – as Asian, all of them in fact display a multi-ethnic character, and include members from a range of ethnic (both non-white and white) backgrounds. This means that the music produced by these bands is more than a simple expression of Asian culture; it is also a reflection of the increasingly syncretic nature of contemporary British society. The processes of global communication and interaction have an important influence as well, giving these musicians access not only to their own cultural heritages but also to cultures previously isolated by time and distance.

The increasing flexibility and permeability of cultural interaction does not necessarily herald the emergence of a free-flowing and equal exchange of cultural forms, however, since the world is still subject to inequalities based on regional and ethnic differences. The specific local and historical conditions of living in the UK in the latter part of the 20th century, particularly the perpetuation of inequalities based around notions of race and difference, continue to have a significant influence on the Asian bands in this study. The inequalities present in contemporary British society that have seen Asian culture stereotyped and under-represented have had a profound effect on both the music of these bands and the self-identities of their members.

This chapter will examine the articulation of a flexible and dynamic sense of Asian identity within a framework of cultural syncretism and change that reflects the contemporary realities of a multi-ethnic society by focusing on the specific experiences of the musicians interviewed for this study. First, I will consider what are perceived to be the underlying factors that facilitated the emergence of Asian bands in the 1990s in contrast to those that perhaps hampered earlier involvement in the popular music scene. Following this, the range of cultural influences that combine to make up the contemporary musical practices of Asian bands will be examined. As well as highlighting the importance of 'traditional' forms of Asian music, I shall also focus on the influence of both global styles and more localized 'white' popular musical genres which have all played a significant role in the articulation of syncretic musical forms by young Asian bands. Finally, I will consider how these individuals negotiate and balance a range of cultural inputs in order to express flexible and multi-accented articulations of self that reflect the syncretic dynamics of a contemporary multi-ethnic environment.

Out of the cornershop and into the charts

The emergence of Asian bands onto the national music scene has been a relatively recent phenomenon and, prior to the 1990s, Asian bands and musicians were noted only by their absence. This is in marked contrast to the influence and involvement of the UK's Afro-Caribbean population, who have had a significant influence on the development of popular music and youth culture in the post-war period. Since both broadly defined groups settled in the UK during the same period it is worth begging the question 'Why has it taken so long for Asians to be involved and noticed in popular music?' Popular consensus outside the Asian community has invariably focused on what is seen as the restrictive and inherently conservative nature of 'Asian culture' which has been perceived as a barrier to young Asians entering the music business. This notion of a restrictive culture has been bolstered by stereotypes of Asians as hard-working and industrious, concerned primarily with educational and business success, with little time or significance placed on leisure pursuits such as music (Modood 1988). It is certainly the case that the traditional role of musician is one that is not always afforded a great deal of status in countries such as Pakistan and India. Although more contemporary musical performances such as those on display in almost every Bollywood movie are incredibly popular throughout the subcontinent, the industry is also seen to represent suspect morality and is often associated with dubious sexuality, the free consumption of alcohol and has even been linked to organized crime. As Aki Nawaz suggested to me in 1996, many of the older generation of Asian settlers in the UK had a very negative perception of the music industry, which was not viewed as a legitimate or desirable occupation:

> I think some of the older generation have kind of a prejudice and negative thinking of what a musician represents. Obviously, in India and Pakistan, all over … in a lot of other countries in the world as well, they see musicians essentially as a low-caste thing or not a career and that's understandable especially from our parents' point of

> view; that's what they've been brought up with and that's what they've been told. I understand parents not wanting kids to get into the music business. I think there's a big difference in the music business of especially India and Pakistan and the music business over here. Over here it's a lot more promiscuous and drug related … it's almost like idol worship and egos, it's not based on feeling humble and modest.[1]

Although there has been a certain degree of suspicion towards the music industry in the UK from some older Asian settlers, it would be a mistake to ignore the role of music in the expressive culture of Asians in Britain prior to the 1990s. Music has always been a central element in the lived culture of Asians in the UK but has largely been confined within the boundaries of the Asian community and has not crossed over into the mainstream to any great extent. As we have seen, the enjoyment and consumption of Asian music by Asians themselves, from Bollywood soundtracks to the growth of bhangra, has taken place within a system of manufacturing and distribution that has existed independently of the mainstream music industry in the UK. These musical forms have their origins in the Indian subcontinent, which has continued to exert a great deal of influence on the cultural lives of Asians in the UK. Cornershop's Tjinder Singh felt that this 'looking back' to the country of origin had played a significant role in stifling Asian involvement in the mainstream music culture of the country of settlement:

> Asians want music to put them on a sort of plane of escapism, or maybe escapism isn't the right word; but whether it's Punjabi folk music that has turned to bhangra or whether it's religious music, they want people that will take them away from whatever hardships that there are in their lives. So they don't want anyone to talk about anything else other than love or God. As for Hindi musicals, it's as if they're still being controlled by the government in India and they're still getting that control over in England just because of the traditions they've brought over with them. For some people to go out and sing about things that aren't about love – things like whatever tensions they've got in their lives – then Asians aren't going to give a shit are they? They're just going to listen to it and say, 'Oh well, I don't like this, I want to have a chat, have a beer and get out of my head and I want to relax and not think about having to go to work tomorrow.' That's on the one side, on the musical side to do with it. I think also the development side of it, in terms of when Asians came here, they came here to make money and go away and obviously it wasn't easy for them to do that so they stuck at it for longer, whereas the African-Caribbean community, they came over here and they didn't think about going home, they just thought, 'This is our life here.' So they had integration into the whites … it was a lot easier and Asians have only just started thinking in those same terms. (Personal interview 1996)

The effect of the so-called 'myth of return' (Watson 1977; Anwar 1979) – at least for the older generation of Asian migrants – may have contributed to the relatively low profile of Asian musicians on the mainstream scene which has only recently increased now that younger generations have been born and raised in the UK without the expectation of a return 'home'. Choque Hosein of Black Star

Liner certainly felt that the 1990s emergence of Asian bands and musicians was part of the recognition that the UK was a permanent home, however much links to their (or their parents') country of origin were maintained. When I asked him in 1996 why he felt that things had begun to change in the 1990s he replied:

> Well because we've been here for 25 years. It's because there's people like you, people like me and it's great now. I can go out to a club now and I can see Asian girls out having a beer – 10 years ago, 15 years ago – that weren't happening.

Undoubtedly the effect of long-term settlement has influenced the expectations of second and third generations of young Asians who increasingly have become able to break away from the more conservative outlook of many of their parents. Although the cultural traditions and expectations of the older generation of settlers undoubtedly had a stifling effect on the involvement of Asians in the mainstream of the UK music industry, it would be a mistake to place all the emphasis on the Asian community at the expense of ignoring the role played by the host society. As I have already stated, music has always played a significant role in the cultural lives of Asians living in the UK but has never really crossed over into the mainstream, or, to put it another way, the mainstream industry has never shown much of an interest in Asian-based musical forms. The stereotypes associated with Asians in the UK, particularly those of conservatism and self-containment, have all contributed to the failure, until recently, of Asian music to be accepted as part of British cultural life. In the past, Asian culture and Asian music could be perceived as 'alien' and incompatible with British cultural life, whereby Asian music was perceived by the music industry as having no great potential for cross-over appeal. Development brought about through generational change therefore may have more to do with the perceptions of those *outside* the Asian community than within it. On the relatively late emergence of Asian musicians into the mainstream Caroline Sullivan of *The Guardian* told me:

> There's never been Asian music that white audiences could relate to, as racist as that might sound. I think it's taken this long for Asians in general … for Asians to become settled in Britain. I mean this is the second or third generation and only now are kids who were born in Britain, who were brought up here – Asian kids – a lot of their cultural references are British now, rather than Asian, Indian, Pakistani, whatever. And so they're making music in the style of … in the British style … I think it's the first time Asian kids have had enough of a British identity to be recognized as pop musicians. (Personal interview 1996)

Despite the lack of actual physical involvement of Asian musicians in the mainstream, there is a well-documented history of Asian influence on contemporary popular music in the West as personified by The Beatles (see Chapter 4). Although bands like the Beatles and, more recently, Kula Shaker, make a point of recognizing the origins of the Asian elements in their music, much has gone unacknowledged, reflecting a general lack of appreciation of non-Western influences on contemporary music in the West. Aki felt that:

> The problem with quite a lot of white musicians is the whole philosophy of being in a band and the music business, it's all about *you* and *you* being worshipped and all that sort of thing. When they get their influences, whether it's from India or wherever – Echo and the Bunnymen, when they did that track ... what was it? Anyway, the sample on that track was from India and The Beatles, you know, they did a bit of Indian stuff ... there's loads and loads of tracks out there that have been influenced by Indian music or African music but when you get people, they never talk about where they came from, they don't credit it at all. This is just like a colonial mentality, this is in the music industry as much as in society. (Personal interview 1996)

The issue of recognition by the wider population is an important one since, in order to cross over into the mainstream music industry, Asians have needed to be viewed as a legitimate part of British cultural life, not as members of a closed and separate alien community. So, if Asians are now more 'acceptable' in the eyes of mainstream society, what has changed? Have young Asians become fully assimilated by British culture at the expense of their parents' cultural heritages thus enabling them to move into the mainstream? All the Asian musicians I spoke to were wary of the idea of assimilation, which they saw as a negative and one-sided process that meant giving up certain cultural resources in an ultimately flawed attempt at gaining acceptance in the eyes of the white majority. Unsurprisingly, Aki Nawaz was strongly opposed to the idea of assimilation, preferring to be accepted on his own terms, and saw no need to compromise:

> We come here, which is still a foreign land to us and start assimilating and we apologize, you know, for the smell and our eating habits and like, it's wrong; we shouldn't be doing it, we should just say, 'OK I'm a human being, Pakistani or Indian or Asian or Jewish or Hindu or Christian or whatever' – we have to accept it.

Assimilation was equated with a loss of cultural heritage by many of the musicians I interviewed; and was most apparent in discussions about Sonya Madan from Echobelly. Although Sonya was born in India and has Indian parents, her cultural and musical influences are almost completely British,[2] causing Aki to declare that:

> She's not Asian – she's admitted she's not Asian. I think that at the time there was this, like, interest in the Asian wave in the indie side and she's got gathered in, she's sat on the platform but she couldn't really express and she didn't really feel .... She's admitted to me that she doesn't really understand the whole thing because she hasn't been brought up that way and now she won't talk to the music press about it. I don't think she puts forward that Asian thing at all.

The consensus among the focus musicians was that Sonya had assimilated to such an extent that she had compromised her Asian identity and heritage in favour of greater acceptance within the mainstream music industry. In our 1996 interview Choque Hosein was particularly scathing in his criticism of the singer:

> Oh I hate her. She's everything that I fucking hate about fucking Asian people who fucking integrate. It's the rich fuckers ... there's something about her I don't believe.

Despite this hostility directed at Sonya and her band by other Asian musicians, Echobelly have experienced a great deal of chart success, far more than that enjoyed by the bands that I spoke to – at least until the success of 'Brimful of Asha' for Cornershop early in 1998. Although it is hard to quantify, one of the factors in her success might well be her level of assimilation, which made her a somewhat anodyne and non-threatening figure rather than a representative of an alien culture. Although a band like Echobelly may well help to challenge existing stereotypes of Asian culture by choosing to produce decidedly 'non-Asian' sounding music, they also expose artists to accusations of cultural betrayal and self-denial. Since the music of Voodoo Queens also failed to explicitly draw upon Asian influences, the potential of such criticisms was always apparent to the band's Asian members and in 1996 Anjali told me: 'It's difficult being Asian and doing music, it's easy for ... your own kind can just turn around and call you a coconut, you know what I mean?'[3] The process of assimilation is often associated with the pressure to suppress or deny cultural difference and distinction and is therefore often viewed with particular suspicion by non-white minority groups. As David Stubbs of *Melody Maker* has suggested:

> Sometimes black people may distrust the idea where they are being asked to join the melting pot, when what they're really being asked to do is join a sort of white liberal consensus. I think the kind of people that whites are more comfortable with are people who are basically white in all but colour. (Personal interview 1996)

The combination of expectations from inside and outside the Asian community undoubtedly puts extra pressure on those working within the music industry, but the emergence of a range of bands since the early 1990s represents the articulation of an assertive and youthful sense of Asian identity which is grounded both in the cultural heritage of the 'homeland' (that is, the Indian subcontinent) and the host society in the UK. There is some evidence to suggest that the increasingly high profile of Asians since the 1990s is beginning to break down some of the existing negative stereotypes of Asian youth, replacing them with more positive and contemporary images. These more attractive associations with Asian youth culture are able to move outside the boundaries of the previously rigidly defined community and appeal more generally to all sections of young people in the UK. Caroline Sullivan felt that Asian bands were playing a significant role in redefining Asian identity and culture in a contemporary setting and suggested that:

> They've come up with a whole new set of identities. Before Cornershop you just never thought of an Asian punk group or an Asian low-fi, crappy guitar group rather, and before Fun^Da^Mental people never thought of political, Asian hip-hop groups. People like Sonya from Echobelly and Anjali from Voodoo Queens are offering images, very cool, glamorous images; they're actually providing an image of Asian female glamour that white and black girls can relate to as well, white and Afro-Caribbean girls. They're providing glamorous images that haven't existed before and I think that people will start seeing Asian guys with new eyes, saying, 'Hey – it's kind of cool to be Asian.'

What these new identities and images reflect is neither a pure reflection of traditional Asian culture or a representation of complete assimilation, but a syncretic negotiation of a variety of cultural influences that are at play within the context of a multi-ethnic environment. The expression of music and style in this context is not an either/or situation and neither is it a simple combination of two distinct cultural traditions. The transformation of both British and Asian cultural traditions that is taking place in musical practices is also developing new identities which simultaneously draw on existing cultural patterns and create and develop new and unique modes of self and identity.

Fusion and flux: music as syncretism

It would be a mistake to think of the bands and musicians discussed in this book simply as 'foreign imports', since the music they create is rooted in a dynamic and multi-accented environment. While certainly drawing on the cultural and musical traditions of the Indian subcontinent, these bands are nevertheless firmly rooted in the context of contemporary Britain. Furthermore, these musicians also locate themselves within a global context, where music becomes an international language of cross-cultural dialogue and exchange. In order to appreciate fully the dynamics at work in the music of these musicians we need to take into account the cultural input from three areas: from the point of emigration on the Indian subcontinent, from the influence of global musical forms and from the local conditions and traditions of the contemporary realities of the UK. These three sites of cultural influence should not be examined in a reductive way but identified as elements of an organic whole which represents the processes of syncretism and cultural change.

The sound of the East: maintaining and transforming tradition

All the bands I spoke to in the course of my research have drawn upon the cultural and musical heritage of the Indian subcontinent. This has taken many forms, including the use of samples, instruments and languages drawn from a range of Asian cultural traditions. In doing so these bands have not simply transported traditional sounds from the Indian subcontinent and relocated them to the UK but have adapted and transformed them to form part of the array of cultural influences that are experienced and negotiated in their everyday lives. The fusion of these influences with Western sounds and styles has created new musical developments that reflect and inform the expression of contemporary articulations of ethnicity and identity. In this way, young Asian musicians are maintaining continuity with the cultural traditions of their ancestors; but also transforming them as well as reshaping the contemporary landscape of British society and culture. By using Asian influences in their music, the focus musicians felt that they were drawing on a part of their cultural heritage that not only had links with previous generations but was extremely relevant in their own upbringing in the UK.

Anjali Bhatia felt that the emergence of bands and musicians using Asian influences represented a rediscovery and reassertion of a cultural heritage which, in the realm of popular music, had been previously neglected:

> I've always felt that Asian people and Asian youth in this country, always diverted to black music, like hip-hop or whatever and feel, sort of, affiliated with that music culture, whatever; but I think Asians have got so much culture to pick from. (Personal interview 1996)

The repository of Asian tradition is one of many cultural and musical resources which are drawn upon in order to develop new styles and musical practices. For a band such as Cornershop, Asian instruments and sounds are not used primarily to assert a forceful sense of Asianness but represent a process of utilizing available cultural resources to create new and varied musical textures. Throughout their existence Cornershop have sung a number of songs in Punjabi as well as in English.[4] As Tjinder Singh pointed out to me in 1996, this represented a flexible and open approach to music-making which sought to incorporate a wide range of cultural styles and influences:

> We try to do different songs in different ways, we don't just try to come up with lyrics and then just do them, take it from there; we try to maybe come up with a sample or drumbeat or a bass-line or a vocal line or whatever, so we try to keep it varied and that's one reason why there's Punjabi lyrics and the reason why there's French lyrics.[5] I see it as a sort of sample, another texture, another layer.

Black Star Liner similarly use Asian instruments to create varied and dynamic material, often fusing sitars and tablas with more traditionally rock-based Western instruments such as guitars and drums. All of these instruments and influences were used to create an overall sound that treats all the constitutive parts as equally important, thus resulting in a unique end product. Choque Hosein explained the band's working practices:

> We play all of the instruments ourselves. What we do is put a basic, simple rhythm track together with maybe like a loop, any loop, and jam on it. We jam sitar, we jam tablas on it, we jam everything and then we listen to it, listen to what's good and then we sample it ourselves and we replay over the top again and then we re-create new loops by going over the top and building it up. Some of the things that sounds like Bollywood tablas is actually played down in the basement of my house. (Personal interview 1996)

By creating music in a layered way like this, a range of instruments from different cultural traditions are fused in an almost organic way that reflects the realities of growing up in a multi-ethnic environment which, as Choque has stated, feels like the 'natural' thing to do:

> We're just using what we've got and building on it. Where I live, I can be in the garden listening to some Bollywood album and across the road some students will be blaring out Blur and next door it will be house. It just blends automatically. (Heller 1996: 28)

Choque's exposure to a variety of musical and cultural traditions during his upbringing is central to the music he now writes and produces for Black Star Liner and incorporates all the musical forms he has enjoyed over the years. But it was his rediscovery of his Asian roots that provided the stimulus behind the band's emergence, as he explained:

> What really kicked me off was my old fella had lots of Bollywood records from the '50s and '60s, lots of films and I just stopped listening to them in the '80s and about five years ago I just got back into it again. (Personal interview 1996)

In the case of Fun^Da^Mental, Asian forms and instruments are central to the band's overall sound, but they do not exclude other musical traditions, such as hip-hop which provides many of the beats at the heart of their music. Aki Nawaz felt that, although elements of Asian music were of great importance to the band it was equally important to have a flexible and open-minded approach to other musical traditions:

> You know, I've been influenced by American music, I've been influenced by Norwegian music, I've been influenced by all sorts of music. I don't have any musical barriers, I think that everything is really important. My biggest influence is from Asian music, that's what keeps me ... that's the spirit. (Personal interview 1996)

The use of Asian sounds and instruments as one element in the fusion of several musical forms has left some bands open to criticism by traditionalists who feel that such practices represent an 'inauthentic' use of such cultural resources. Cornershop have been criticized at times for the way that they use Asian instruments in non-traditional ways as Tjinder explained:

> Some motherfucker told us we shouldn't be playing our instruments – Asian instruments – because they're not meant to be amplified and that we should keep it really warm, really, really folk. He thought that you should totally strip raw and have real basic, just wood against wood and that's it and it can't be amplified. What he was talking about was keeping it at a certain level and that's bollocks as far as I'm concerned. (Personal interview 1996)

When bands like Cornershop and Black Star Liner use instruments associated with traditional folk or classical styles the criticisms they attract from cultural purists from all sides is often based on conservative or stereotypical notions of Asian culture. Although their use of instruments such as the sitar is based on primarily on musical factors, there is also a clear intention to provoke and disrupt existing stereotypes of Asian music. According to Tjinder Singh, Cornershop's unconventional use of the sitar set out to challenge not only notions of spiritual antiquity but also to undermine the elitism inherent in the traditional use of the instrument:

> We went out of our way to go against that image of Asians anyway and very much anti-class based instrumentation which the sitar represents as well; it is a class thing, it is a classical instrument and a lot of middle-class Asians like to listen to it in the Asian diaspora which fucks me off as well. (Personal interview 2003)

The innovative use of traditional Asian instrumentation by these bands has to compete with those who continue to evoke more Orientalist notions of the mystic East. Crispian Mills (lead singer with Kula Shaker) is one of the most vocal advocates of this rationale and has often justified his own use of Indian sounds by attempting to tap into this imaginary spiritual authenticity:

> I am touched by the whole culture and the spirituality that permeates it. The danger is the crossover stuff, say a dance track, just uses superficial musical aspects. If you take the spirituality out of Western music there will still be something left. If you take it out of Indian music, there's nothing left. (Datar 1997: 14)

This rather reductive interpretation of Asian music reflects the resilience of certain Orientalist tendencies within popular music in the West and, as we have seen, there is a history of white musicians appropriating carefully selected elements of Asian music and transporting them into a popular Western musical setting. We can see how an artist like Crispian Mills acts like the Western 'expert' that Edward Said talks of, 'discovering' the ancient spirituality of the East, dissecting it, making sense of it and ultimately claiming ownership of it (Said 1978). The often superficial way in which instruments such as the sitar have been used by Western musicians, that evokes a stereotypical notion of the East as exotic and mystical, has engendered a great deal of cynicism and suspicion among many Asians of all generations. Such misgivings mean that it is difficult for many Asians to accept a white musician playing a sitar. Aki Nawaz certainly felt that this was the case:

> It's a spirit isn't it? There's a spirit to sitars, there is a spirit attached to the instrument. Here in the West, instruments are just ... not even a part of you. If you've got, you know, the spirit from India, you have to take your shoes off with the sitars or tablas; they're spiritual instruments and people respect them. When you get a white man playing a sitar – unless he's been brought up in India, whatever, breathes the spirit – he'll never play it as good. And I have seen that, like the Sons of Arqua, they're really into the Indian influence, they know a lot about it, they've tried copying it and they just can't. (Personal interview 1996)

There is clearly a tension here between the desire to create and develop the use of Asian instruments in new contexts and settings and the need to defend and preserve a cultural tradition that has been subject to domination and appropriation in the West. Aki's views on this subject – which seem to advocate a position of ethnic particularlism (that is, only Asian people can play Asian instruments) as well as lending credence to notions of the East as a place of spiritual and mystical enlightenment – are undoubtedly a reaction against the years of appropriation (and, some would say, exploitation) of Asian music by white musicians. If we listen to the music of Fun^Da^Mental, which is made up of a bewildering array of cultural sources that are often fragmented, distorted and reconfigured, we can see how Aki's own use of instruments such as the sitar disrupts notions of ethnic particularity and purity. As Aki himself stated in an interview for the BBC (1997), the music of Fun^Da^Mental 'respects tradition but also destroys tradition'. The question of cultural ownership is a difficult one, as many Asian musicians set out to reconfigure the use of traditional instruments in a contemporary setting but are also understandably defensive of their use by non-Asians. This means that an artist such as Anjali Bhatia (in our 2003 interview) can completely reject the notion that white people should steer clear of the sitar – 'That's like saying that Asians shouldn't be allowed to play the electric guitar!'[6] – but also hint that being able to play such an instrument properly is: 'almost inherent' and based on life-long dedication and study.[7]

As the bands interviewed for this study incorporate musicians from a range of cultural/ethnic backgrounds, in the case of both Cornershop and Black Star Liner this involves white musicians playing 'Indian' instruments such as the sitar or tanpura, which has led some to question the authenticity of their musical output.[8] I asked Cornershop's Ben Ayres, who plays the tanpura, whether or not he felt uncomfortable as a white person playing an Asian instrument:

> Sometimes I have but I really think ... I'm of the school of thought that it doesn't matter what colour you are, whatever instrument you're playing and how you play it. I've never been trained to play tanpura but I don't see that as a problem. (Personal interview 1996)

In fact the whole band adopted flexible and multi-instrumentalist roles, exemplified by Tjinder Singh, who plays a range of instruments in different styles including Western instruments such as guitars and electric bass as well as Eastern ones such as dholki and harmonium. He felt that such an eclectic approach was an important factor in making music and saw white people playing sitars as part of this process:

> I think it's great. Why should anyone stop you from ever doing anything? I think it's great, I think the actual fact that we have a white sitar player, Saffs, on our stuff was pretty good. (Personal interview 1996)

It is notable that the white sitar players in both Black Star Liner and Cornershop are classically trained, although this is not necessarily reflected in the music that they play in each band. It was not deemed particularly important that the sitarists had classical training since the instrument was being used in a different context, although it obviously helps to have a greater understanding of any instrument; but still it was felt that the attitude and quality of the music was of primary importance, as Choque Hosein explained in the case of Black Star Liner:

> It's about passion and rock and roll. Chris [Harrop] can play it; he plays brilliant, really really good but he plays it like a guitarist and he's really good at it and he understands all the … that's what shocked me when he knew all the ragas; 'Fucking hell,' I thought, 'how do you know that?' (Personal interview 1996)

It is clear that all of the musicians featured here were acutely aware of the long history of appropriation and stereotyping of Asian sounds within Western popular music and this was something they sought to challenge and disrupt. Their use of sounds, styles and instruments drawn from their Asian background is an important component of their overall musical output. Undoubtably they were influenced by the music and culture of their Asian backgrounds, but this can only be understood in the specific context of their lived experiences as musicians raised and nurtured in the UK.

The sound of the world: cultural syncretism or global exploitation?

The featured musicians' use of Asian sounds and instruments manifested itself in several ways: the actual physical playing of instruments such as tablas and sitars and also in the use of sampled sounds and instruments. We have already seen how Black Star Liner combined these two methods by sampling instruments that they have played themselves but, generally, sampling involves the use of other people's recorded music. Bollywood film soundtracks and classical Asian music provide the source for a great deal of sampling among many Asian bands in the UK, but they also look to other areas for samples, in the national or international context. In this way Asian bands have access not only to the cultural traditions of their contemporary setting and the heritage of their parents but also to a global network of musical information and interaction. We have already seen how issues of cultural authenticity and ownership have been raised over the use of Asian music by non-Asians. How then do Asian musicians justify their own use of sampled recordings, particularly those taken from sources as far removed as Africa and Australasia?

The stimulus behind the increasing use of samples by the musicians in this study was that it opened up a wider palette of sounds and resources which could be layered and manipulated in a much more flexible way than could be achieved by the playing of live instruments. Again, the emphasis was on the integrity of the musical product, although the use of samples taken from other sources – particularly those from Third World settings such as Africa and Asia – was rationalized in a number of ways. For Cornershop, sampling was seen as another element in creating a dynamic and varied sound and was legitimated in terms of quality rather than in terms of cultural ownership and authenticity. I asked Tjinder in 1996 whether he felt that the sampling of Third World sources was justifiable:

> I think if it's interesting and it adds something, then I think it's a good idea. If I think it's shit, it's the same thing isn't it? If it's shit, I don't see the point, it always comes down to that basic level.

Cornershop have used samples from various sources that usually originate from Western Europe and the USA but occasionally combine these with samples from the Third World. The band's 1997 album *When I was born for the 7th time* made use of a range of samples on tracks such as 'When the light appears boy' which is based around US poet Allen Ginsberg reading his poem of the same name, combined with the singing of religious pilgrims recorded at Dhereh in the Punjab. Gary Walker of Wiiija Records felt that the all-embracing attitude of Cornershop's music-making practices was a positive and non-exploitative one: 'I think that there is something about Cornershop's music which is kind of celebratory in a way that's not, kind of, ripping people off.'

For Anjali Bhatia, the use of samples and computer manipulation of sounds in her solo career was stimulated partly by what she felt were the limitations of playing in a more traditional band like Voodoo Queens. The utilization of sampling technology has allowed Anjali to have greater creative control over her music and has also rekindled her enthusiasm for music-making:

> I feel really confident about what I'm doing now, like, it's different when you've got a sampler and you can layer things. I became really frustrated with Voodoo Queens as well; that you're quite limited in a band form if you want to move on and there's only a certain amount you can do in a band. (Personal interview 1996)

Most of the samples Anjali uses are drawn from Western sources and used to capture the sound of previous musical eras. The fact that such music was recorded on perhaps now defunct equipment and using obsolete techniques means that such sounds are both hard to reproduce and keenly sought out by many contemporary musicians. Despite the advance of digital technology, which has undoubtedly made music-making simpler and more accessible, the 'lost' sounds of valve amps and analogue recordings have their own distinct aesthetics which many contemporary musicians seek to revive. Anjali's use of such samples is out of love of music from the past and also out of necessity, such are the difficulties of reproducing such sounds with more up-to-date equipment:

> As a songwriter and musician, I would rather be able to create a sound myself but considering that a lot of music I adore is from the '60s, '50s and '70s, it's very difficult to reproduce the actual sonic sound and that is mainly why people sample. It is too hard to do; the samples you're using have been recorded through mainly old valve mics, desks, then they're cut onto a record, then cued, then they're mastered and then you're using them again ... more the *sound* that you're using. (Personal interview 2003)

In the case of Fun^Da^Mental, who also sampled material from all around the globe, once again the emphasis was on the quality of the final product; but the band were nevertheless mindful of the potentially exploitative nature of sampling other people's music. They recognized that the sampling of Third World sources from a relatively privileged position in the UK was problematic and that it was important to try to retain the integrity of any borrowed musical elements, as Dave Watts explained in our 1996 interview:

> I suppose that on the one hand you could say, yeah, it's just continuing the tradition of colonialism, taking other people's cultures. I think you should use things, or if you feel something, if you really genuinely feel something and you've got a piece of music going ... you just come across something that, like, knocks you and you say 'Oh man – wow!' I just want to take that and just do a little something and represent it in a different form to people; if you can remain true to the essence of that, then cool; it doesn't matter what colour you are if you genuinely feel it. We try to remain as true to the sound as possible, but a lot of people sample for the sake of sampling.

According to Aki Nawaz, part of the reason for sampling sounds and music from Third World sources was the practical difficulties related to the physical distances between musicians working in the UK and elsewhere. Aki felt that Fun^Da^Mental were putting into action a collaborative project that in an ideal world would be developed on an interpersonal level, but the logistics of the situation were such that sampling was the most practical way of bringing about such a collaboration. This is clearly a sensitive issue and, when I suggested to Aki in 1996 that his band's use of samples from the Third World could be interpreted as cultural imperialism he replied:

> I agree with you, I think it's a very difficult because if you ask a classical musician from India to come to England, he'd jump at the chance – he'd do what you would have sampled in the first place, you ask him what he thinks of it and he thinks 'brilliant'; he'd approve. The music doesn't belong to anybody, I think at least psychologically music belongs to certain groups, in India it's everyone's – it belongs to a spirit – it's yours, it's mine, it's everyone's. Personally I would say it's wrong but then again, the amount of good that is coming that way ...

Although such arguments raise issues of copyright and ownership, it is significant that a policy of global collaboration and exchange has subsequently been developed by Fun^Da^Mental. The music produced by them and by other bands at Nation Records can be seen to represent an international flow of cultural and musical ideas that has been represented in a number of ways, with sampling only one. Over a period of several years Fun^Da^Mental have collaborated with traditional Asian musicians on a number of occasions, performing in London with qawwali maestro Nawazish Ali Khan[9] in 1995 and in 2001 recording and touring with Rizwan Muazzam Qawwal from Pakistan.[10] The collaboration with musicians from Asia in a UK setting reflects the band's attempt to establish an international network of musical and cultural exchange. Following the release of *Seize the time* in 1994, both Aki Nawaz and Dave Watts travelled around the world in order to establish greater links with a range of local musicians. During their extensive travels in Asia, Africa and Australasia, Fun^Da^Mental's two core members often performed with local musicians which in South Africa resulted directly in the signing of rap band Prophets Of Da City to Nation Records. In their contact with geographically diverse communities around the world the band were able to exchange musical ideas – some of which have been incorporated into Fun^Da^Mental's music – as well as cultural and political exchanges which reflected shared experiences based on the realities of racism and oppression of non-white minority groups. In 1996 I asked Dave Watts what impact their travels was going to have on the band's then forthcoming third album *Erotic terrorism* (released in 1998). He replied:

> Well, since the last one there's been ... it's stepped up again. We've come across music from, say, since the last album, come across music from the Ivory Coast, from New Zealand, I've got discussions, interviews from Maoris, like, it's got to go right in there because what they're saying is just fucking right on, it's spot on, do you know what I mean? What they're saying about their situation, the global parallel. We've got something to talk about, we've experienced more, it's our chance to relay those experiences, to pass those experiences on.

The establishment of dialogues with disparate groups around the globe, based on common musical and political experiences, represents what George Lipsitz (1994) has termed 'families of resemblance' and is evidence of the articulation of flows of cross-cultural exchange on a global scale. We must not forget the serious power imbalance that exists between First and Third World sources, but the practices of a band like Fun^Da^Mental and Nation Records suggest that this relationship can benefit all parties and can bring together the most unlikely musical bedfellows. In 1999 Fun^Da^Mental released the provocatively titled *Why America will go to hell* – a phrase attributed to Martin Luther King on the cover; see Figure 7.1) – which included remixes of the track 'Ja sha taan' and collaborations with William and Jim Reid of the Jesus and Mary Chain that resulted in an intoxicating mixture of qawwali, hip-hop and psychedelic indie rock. Such musical alliances have been sought out and developed by Fun^Da^Mental throughout their existence and represent how recording with a range of musicians can be combined with sampling technology to create new and innovative sounds. Increasingly Aki Nawaz has worked with musicians from a variety of backgrounds, writing and recording material with them in partnership. The collaborations with Rizwan Muazzam Qawwal and with Zamo Mhbuto and

Fig. 7.1 The cover artwork for Fun^Da^Mental's *Why America will go to hell*

Comrades from South Africa that feature prominently on the 2001 album *There shall be love!* is further evidence of this. Instead of using samples recorded in the field or bringing musicians to the UK, Aki visited the countries of the local musicians themselves where the music was developed and recorded. As he explained:

> I actually went there and sat down with them and actually worked with people and constructed the whole thing. I sat down with people – I knew people there – sat down and they were actually involved in the construction of it and I learned more off them than they learned off me. We went in studios but they were working with somebody who wasn't testing their knowledge it was somebody who was trying to learn off them – I was just trying to learn off them. So we were collaborating and probably, to be honest, the word collaboration in the best possible way. (Personal interview 2002)

It is important to recognize that all bands function as subjects of an international music industry which is able to transmit all over the world musical and cultural influences that were previously restricted to relatively small locales. The global flow of musical and cultural capital has the potential to expose locally based music to an international audience and plays an important part in the transformation of tradition and the re-articulation of cultural identities. We have identified the importance of south Asian traditions and sounds in the cultural expression of all the bands focused on here and, in the case of Fun^Da^Mental at least, have seen how sources from the Third World have impacted on their musical output. But we also need to recognize the networks which link these bands into the West; into Europe and the USA and of course into the UK itself. So often the exotic practices of non-white minorities living in the West are examined in a reductive and anthropological manner which privileges the effect of cultural traditions related to origin at the expense of the impact of contemporary, multi-accented settings.

The sound of the suburbs: Asian bands and 'white' music

I have already demonstrated how Asian bands draw on the cultural heritage of the Indian subcontinent in the development of their music. But we need to restate the fact that these bands emerged out of the UK music scene and thus draw on the traditions of British popular culture as well. As I have already made clear, these musicians are not simply transporting elements of Asian culture into a British setting, but are forging a syncretic and multi-accented means of cultural expression that reflects the daily experiences of those living in a multi-ethnic environment. There is some evidence then to suggest that the assertive and vibrant attitude of many of the current generation of Asian bands is beginning to be interpreted as a manifestation of British culture rather than as the sound of an exotic or alien interloper. It is important to recognize that, although such bands have drawn extensively on their Asian heritage, they have also emerged as artists in contemporary Britain where what we might think of as distinctly non-Asian influences have played a vital role. The one common influence in this regard was that of punk; both in terms of musical approach and perhaps more significantly in terms of attitude and ideology.

This is most clearly reflected in the career of Aki Nawaz, who was deeply affected by punk as a young man growing up in Bradford during the late 1970s and early 1980s. The profound effect that punk had on both his musical development and his career as the head of Nation Records remains the most significant 'white' influence on Aki, who told me in 1996:

> I think that the only thing that I've been influenced by really is punk music, kind of the music and the attitude. Yeah, yeah, I was into it, you know, the [Sex] Pistols and shit like that and The Clash, at that time it was like, you know ... to me that was like breaking away from the norm. To me it was more of a philosophy, to a lot of the white kids it was just a fashion; they weren't breaking away from anything because they had nothing to break away from because they didn't have any restraints, you know, culturally or religiously. I mean punk was a massive influence on me, the philosophy has just developed from punk which is like, that kind of, you know, music and barriers, all the clichés about 'music speaks'.

Aki found that the cultural space opened up by punk music allowed him to express himself as an individual on his own terms; asserting his own sense of identity away from the usual constraints of both the Asian community and white mainstream society. Not only was punk 'colour blind' in this way, according to Aki it had also allowed him to establish an identity that set apart second- and third-generation Asians from the more conservative aspirations of their parents; as he explained in an interview with *Melody Maker*:

> There was one punk in our school, so I made it two. Then after a few months there were six or seven. We used to hang around in the Manville Arms [pub] in Bradford and go to gigs in Leeds at The F Club. Of course, this didn't go down well in the Asian community. My dad had brought us up to be prime ministers – not doctors and accountants, but prime ministers. To be a doctor was a 'C' [grade], so as punks we were 'Z', off the spectrum! But punk wasn't a fashion to me, it was a philosophy. It was about being different, and it didn't matter that you were 'coloured', cos no-one cared about things like that. Punks were a gathering of tribes, misfits. (1996: 14)

For Aki, punk was an inclusive movement which allowed him the space to express his own individuality in a context that reflected his contemporary surroundings but ultimately did not detract from the importance of his Asian roots. In this way the attitudes and ideas of punk have acted as significant sources of inspiration for all the featured musicians, although not all of them embraced the actual subculture of punk with as much enthusiasm as Aki. It is important to remember that, for all its democratic principles, punk in the late 1970s was primarily a white domain and for many young Asians was perceived as a somewhat threatening and inaccessible subculture. So, although Tjinder Singh had taken on many of punk's ideas and principles, actual involvement in the subculture itself had little appeal for him:

> Punk itself was never an influence to me at the time because when punk came over from New York to London and went over to places like Wolverhampton it wasn't an open-minded attitude that it started off with; it was a right-wing attitude. But, yeah, the ideas behind punk has always been about being quite open. So in terms of being influenced by punk, I didn't really care for punk because it was a very right-wing thing, but in terms of the attitude it was important. (Personal interview 2003)

Despite this, the influence of punk is most apparent in the early work of both Cornershop and Voodoo Queens, as both bands started their careers as noisy guitar–bass–drums combos, epitomizing the DIY 'anyone can play in a band' [11] attitude that had been at the heart of punk in the late 1970s and also had helped spawn much of the UK independent scene in the 1980s (Kelly 1987; Hesmondhalgh 1998). Both bands enthusiastically embraced notions of non-professionalism and self-sufficiency in their early years that had their immediate origins in the punk era, as evidenced by the 'low-fi' or even 'shambolic' [12] quality of their live performances. Cornershop's early gigs were certainly driven by a punk attitude, as Tjinder explained:

> In terms of attitude it was punk and we didn't know how to tune, we did get gigs any way we could and we did get chucked out and we did get personally threatened [laughs] and we couldn't play. So that's the DIY thing.

Although the early sounds of Cornershop and Voodoo Queens exhibit certain elements of punk, there is no doubt that it was the attitude and ideology of the subculture that has had the most significant effect on all the musicians discussed here, as reflected in both their working practices and their choice of small non-corporate companies to release their records. Such influences are most apparent in the setting up of new labels to facilitate the release of commercially unproven material, as in the case of the short-lived Voodoo Records and the longer-term success of Nation Records.

The legacy of punk was a primary motivation in the establishment of both Fun^Da^Mental and their label Nation Records, representing an independent and non-conformist attitude reflected in the energy and vitality of musical performance and production. The focus of Fun^Da^Mental and other Nation bands primarily on the fusion of dance-based musical forms with elements of traditional Third World sounds at first does not seem to reflect the impact of punk to any great degree but, as witnessed on the liner notes of the Nation Records compilation CD ... *And still no hits – Nation Records – the story so far* (see Appendix 2), the philosophy of punk has played (and continues to play) [13] a vital role in the formation and development of the label. In identifying and understanding the impact of a Western music form such as punk on Asian bands and musicians we can begin to assert their role as artists working at the heart of contemporary Britain, rather than as exotic interlopers representing the sound of a foreign culture, as reflected by *NME* journalist Steven Wells back in 1992 when he wrote of Fun^Da^Mental:

> Their whirling dervish mish-mash of hip-hop, North African/Indian rhythms, reggae toasting, heavy metal wig-shaking, Brechtian agit-prop and didgeridoo-wop sums up all that is glorious about OUR music and is – in both form and content – a heavy back-handed slap in the face of puny minded racists.

Over a decade later, this intoxicating mix of cultural and musical influences continues to shape the band's work, as I witnessed at a live performance in Bristol during the spring of 2003. On stage Aki Nawaz and Dave Watts were joined by bass guitarists, rappers and dholki players from England, Zulu singers from South Africa and qawwali vocalist Nawazish Ali Khan from Pakistan, with Aki declaring 'This is our nation, we have no immigration control, no borders – just punk rock!' At the end of what was certainly one of the most exciting live sets that I have seen Fun^Da^Mental perform, the collective on stage launched into one final dissonant number that Aki dedicated to 'the last true British culture' and that was introduced with the sampled vocals of Johnny Rotten sneering the words 'Right ... now!' first heard way back in 1976.[14]

Similarly Black Star Liner mix Eastern and Western instruments in a manner which fuses them at an almost organic level and Choque Hosien is constantly asserting that the music should 'kick ass' and be 'full-on rock and roll' very much in the rock-based tradition of much Western popular music – including punk – in the post-war period. This is very much reflected in the live output of Black Star Liner which, as I have already indicated, differs markedly from the style of their recorded material. The playful improvisations and borrowings from a range of contemporary cultural sources that characterize Choque's live vocal style means that his band's music is able to continue to mutate and develop long after it has been recorded and fixed on record. As broadcaster John Peel has commented, Choque's live persona is inherently reflexive and adaptable:

> It's such a great fusion of stuff, all the things that Choque, the front man, has picked up over the years. So he'll do, like, Elvis Presley impersonations and stuff like that, he works everything he's ever heard in his life into what they do. (BBC 1997)

This adaptation of the group's recorded output has clearly emerged in order to make Black Star Liner more accessible and exciting in a live context but has done so without challenging their musical integrity; in fact it has resulted in a dynamic and creative live act which is both unique and unpredictable. When I asked Choque in 1996 about the differences between the band's live and recorded output he replied:

> We're just doing it that way because it's the only way to make it cut, to be totally honest with you. We tried, when we first started, we tried doing it ... because we were signed we were releasing records and we tried the shows ... doing them as kind of mellow, that kind of vibe but it doesn't work. Now it's really good and we get a lot of press, that's why we do these shows in the way that we do, make them really, like, rock and roll, really full-on.

The reinvention of Black Star Liner in the live environment shows that bands can be adaptive and flexible without affecting the integrity of their music; indeed it reflects the dynamic nature of musical expression. The way that bands like Black Star Liner have combined traditional Asian elements with Western-based rock and dance forms has been an important factor in beginning to challenge some of the deeply ingrained stereotypes of what Asian music is supposed to represent. As *Melody Maker* has often asserted, Black Star Liner 'rock like bastards' and are able to combine instruments and sounds from all over the world as part of an overall sound that is far removed from the mysticism and exoticism perpetrated by bands like Kula Shaker:

> Their [Black Star Liner] understanding of the sitar and tablas is as instruments that sound good not merely as heavy-handed bywords for multi-culturalism or dodgy signifiers of ethnic=exotic. (Simpson 1996: 43)

Locating identity: black, British or Asian?

We have already established that the range of music produced by Asian bands and musicians reflects an environment of cross-cultural dialogue and interchange which is rooted both in the traditions of a South Asian heritage and in the lived realities of contemporary Britain. The manifestations of new musical sounds and fusions performed and produced by Asian bands do not belong exclusively to any specific or fixed cultural heritages, and are as much a part of UK culture as of the Asian diaspora. All the Asian musicians that I spoke to asserted a strong sense of continuity with their heritage combined with an acknowledgement of their contribution to an ever-shifting and increasingly syncretic British music culture. The combination of these two factors is not negotiated easily, however; the historical and contemporary realities of inequalities of power between these points of identification – particularly those focused around issues of race and racism – have a significant impact on developing modes of self-identification and belonging. All the musicians shared a flexible and multi-accented sense of self that enabled them to express their distinct identities as individuals with a range of cultural inputs and affiliations.

There was a general reluctance by all of them to be pinned down to any one mode of cultural or ethnic identity, since they rejected the articulation of totalizing definitions of self. In 1996 I asked Tjinder Singh of Cornershop how he identified himself in terms of ethnicity. He indicated that, although Asianness was an important reference point in terms of the way he perceived himself, it was not something that was rigidly enforced in all contexts: 'It's something that if you ask me unawares I always say Asian, or I say Indian, if they say you're black then I'll say, yeah, well I'm black.'

The identification with a wider 'political' category of black was something that most of the Asian musicians bought into at various times and was linked to particular contexts; there was no sense of contradiction felt by simultaneously inhabiting black and Asian identities. Aki Nawaz felt that 'we're all black' in reference to all non-white people and this is reflected somewhat in the ethnic make-up of Fun^Da^Mental as well as in the band's lyrics.[15] The desire to project a politically unified and inclusive black identity is obviously important for Fun^Da^Mental, although the music writer David Stubbs felt that this was not necessarily reflected in reality:

> What's interesting about Fun^Da^Mental is the fact that you've got two black guys and two Asian guys in the same group. Now, I suspect that, on a street level, there isn't the same kind of mutual ... uh ... jollyness between black and Asian. (Personal interview 1996)

I asked Aki in 1996 whether or not he felt that there was a tension between the articulation of black and Asian identities and he replied by restating the flexible and contextual aspect of self-identification:

> First and foremost you consider yourself as a human being, you know, that's it. Everything else is like little categories, everything else is a debate and an issue and I think that is part of the confusion. It's very, very confusing, it's like how you deal with it. You know there are problems with the Asian and African communities, you know, culture and all that sort of thing, I think it all goes off into different paths but on that issue I'd rather generalize; I think we have more in common than we don't have so when I say about people being black who are like ... white people who are politically in a black situation.

Although both Aki and Tjinder were able to articulate a sense of identity in terms of blackness or Asianness, both of them rejected an affiliation with identities associated with either Englishness or Britishness. They associated these terms with nationalist sentiments which were often linked into notions of racial purity which they saw as excluding non-whites and, although they asserted their position as legitimate citizens in the UK, they had no desire to identify with nationalist modes of identity. For Aki, even the notion of a category denoting a 'British Asian' identity was rejected since it denied individuals the right to articulate themselves as complex and flexible subjects. He told me in 1996:

> I don't want to say I'm 'British Asian' I don't feel 'British Asian'. I'm Asian. I'm black. I'm Muslim; you know, I'm all of these things and people need to understand that.

Tjinder also felt frustrated at totalizing modes of identity that denied individuals their true complexity and failed to reflect the multiplicity of identifications that his experiences had encountered. When I asked him in 1996 if he ever considered himself to be British he replied:

> I don't say that but then again I'm not proper Indian, I'm not proper English and that's why I'm in the middle and that's what songs like 'WOG' are about,[16] being in [the] middle of that and that's about it really, between the two if I'm asked.

This does not reflect the articulation of any kind of 'identity confusion' so much as the inadequacies of discourses of race and ethnicity which fail to provide a suitably complex vocabulary able to express the elaborate processes at work in the negotiation of self-identification. In fact the position inhabited by individuals such as Tjinder represents the development of new modes of identity that are able to incorporate a number of cultural allegiances which are themselves in a process of transformation and also combining to form new multi-accented identifications.

Choque Hosein perhaps best embodies the development of new expressions of identity that are emerging from the interactive and dynamic cross-cultural exchanges at play in contemporary multi-ethnic society. Choque's background encompasses a range of cultural traditions which he has articulated effortlessly in the music of Black Star Liner and also his articulation of self-identification, which is both flexible and all-encompassing. As he explained to me in 1996:

> My old fellah is from Trinidad and when he came over; he's got about 10 brothers but was the only one who came over with some friends of his ... it's quite weird with them being from Trinidad, it's very strange because I've got a lot of black relatives as well, so it's a real mixture so it's really bizarre.

Choque felt that his mixed background provided him and others with a dynamic and vibrant sense of identity that represented and captured the contemporary zeitgeist of multi-ethnic Britain in the late 1990s. The stress Choque placed on the importance of a mixed cultural identity is such that he rejects all broadly based racial or ethnic categories, preferring to express a range of integrated and flexible modes of identification. I asked him whether he considered his identity primarily as Asian or black: 'To be honest with you, I don't. I mean when England play football, I support England.' By identifying himself in this way Choque is not rejecting his Asian identity outright, but asserting his right to express a multi-accented and dynamic sense of self which reflects the range of cultural experiences to which he has been exposed throughout his life. He felt that the expression of a mixed cultural identity was not only reflecting the contemporary realities of multi-ethnic Britain but that it also sought to disrupt stereotypical notions of Asianness. When I informed him that I also came from a mixed background he said:

> Well this is what you want, that makes you perfect. When people see you as Asian, they expect certain things, they expect us to light joss sticks and shit. I like that mixed cultural thing, I think it's really good, I think it really kicks off.

Choque did not feel that his experience and expression of a mixed cultural heritage was at all unusual; in fact he felt that it represented the contemporary realities of Britain in the 1990s and beyond. In his experiences as a member of Black Star Liner Choque identified a growing interest in issues of cultural change which were seeking to deconstruct rigid definitions of ethnic and cultural identity which he felt heralded a period of significant change and dynamism:

> Do you know what? Everywhere I go, I meet people who are doing exactly the same thing, there's a whole fucking generation of people doing it. Well this is what I find really interesting; meeting people who have got the same ideas, who are excited by life. Do you know what? It's a horrible word ... it's synchronicity but it's true. I think Britain is going through a transitional period.

Conclusion: new sounds, new identities

What the varied responses posited by the Asian musicians in this study represent is the multi-accented and flexible articulation of self-identification which represents the processes at work in a contemporary multi-ethnic setting. Although their experiences are grounded in a sense of Asianness that relates both to the importance of cultural tradition and to the significance of functioning as a minority group in a sometimes hostile environment, they are also asserting an ability to incorporate a range of other cultural inputs, most importantly those originating from mainstream society. We need to recognize that such influences are not experienced as distinct and separate entities but as part of living in a dynamic and diverse cultural environment. This then, does not represent a 'culture clash' between Asian and British traditions but the merging of the two in a context where continuity and change are able to co-exist and interact in a dynamic way which allows the transformation of both traditions and the creation and nurturing of new and syncretic modes of identification. The articulation of the new and old modes of identity is not uniform and does not conform to existing rationales of national and ethnic allegiance. In order fully to appreciate and understand the workings of these dynamic processes we need to recognize the ability of individuals to articulate a range of cultural perspectives which, rather than challenging existing forms, enrich and transform them and, in the process, create some that are new and unique. It is in the realm of expressive culture that we are witnessing the clearest manifestations of these transformative processes, and the music being produced by young Asian bands since the beginning of the 1990s is one of the most vibrant of these. Despite the many pressures and expectations placed upon these young people they have been able to produce new and innovative music which is playing an important part in reshaping contemporary British society. Their experiences of music-making and complex articulations of self challenge the expression of reductive notions of discrete and absolute ethnic identity and reflect the dynamic processes at work which point the way towards the continuing transformation of culture and society in these late modern times.

Notes

1. Aki is talking about traditional musicians and not about more contemporary forms such as Bollywood which, as I have suggested, are often associated with the 'sex, drugs and rock 'n' roll' elements that are so familiar in the music industry in the West.
2. In an interview for *NME* in 1994 she told journalist Dele Fadele:

   > I'm so British I don't have any other culture apart from the culture of parents in the house. For me to keep harping on about Asian this, Asian that, makes it a little strange for me.

3. A popular derogatory term used against people of colour who are thought to have sold out their cultural heritage by being completely assimilated into the host culture and are thereby viewed as black or brown on the surface but essentially white inside.
4. As on 'We're in y'r corner' on the 1997 album *When I was born for the 7th time*.
5. This refers to the track 'My dancing days are done' from the band's *Woman's gotta have it* LP (Wiiija 1995).
6. Similarly Gary Walker commented to me in 1996 that if it was inappropriate for whites to play sitars, 'then you could say that Asian people couldn't play electric guitars.'
7. Although on the surface Anjali's views are the opposite of Aki's, her interpretation of what it takes to play a sitar (undoubtedly a tricky thing to get to grips with, although perhaps no more so than a whole range of Western instruments) is remarkably similar:

   > If you really want to play the sitar well, it's something that you have to do all your life; you have to dedicate your life to it. I mean normally it's passed down through families; your father was Ustad Pandit – whatever, and you carry it down the line. I just think that if you want to funk out on a sitar, you have to be able to play it classically as well. (Personal interview 2003)

   Ignoring the technical debate surrounding how difficult it is to play one instrument compared to another, we can see how there is a desire to retain a certain degree of cultural ownership over the sitar, rather than simply allowing it out into the world along with every other instrument.
8. In a review of a live Cornershop gig in 1995 published in *Melody Maker*, Neil Kulkarni reflected that their use of 'Indian' instruments amounted to little more than 'cultural tourism'.
9. Nawazish Ali Khan also features on the CD single 'Ja sha taan' which was released during the spring of 1998.

10. The troupe feature extensively on the 2001 album *There shall be love!* and were only able to tour in the UK after Aki spent some months working to obtain a work permit for them.
11. According to an *NME* interview with Voodoo Queens: 'The band exist on their own terms and describe punk rock as "do it yourself, don't be affected, don't try and be part of any scene. Enjoy yourself, that's what we do" ' (Dalton 1993: 17).
12. Gary Walker at Wiiija described to me in 1996 how he was first made aware of Cornershop prior to signing for his label:

    > A friend of mine who kind of helped manage the band to start off with basically said: 'Gary there's this band that's right up your street. They mix politics with a kind of youthful sound which was punky and a little … shambolic.' No, that's the wrong word perhaps but something that was more enthusiasm over ability.

13. Speaking in 2002, Aki told me: 'I don't think I've sort of matured out of my old punk ways. I've still got this real passion and that kind of vision.'
14. The sample having been taken from the Sex Pistols debut single 'Anarchy in the UK'.
15. For example, the track 'Dog tribe' from Fun^Da^Mental's debut album *Seize the time* which advocates a self-defence agenda for black people in the face of racist attacks includes the line 'Afro-Caribbeans, Asians together is tuff'.
16. 'WOG' features on the *Woman's gotta have it* album, and includes the lyrics:

    First I was a foreigner
    Then suddenly everything was cool forever
    This Western Oriental's going full circle.

Conclusion

Then and now: Asian bands in the 21st century

In hindsight, the arrival of a number of Asian bands on the British music scene during the early 1990s seems as exciting and significant now as it did then. Until this genesis there had been simply no noticeably Asian musicians of any kind making music in the mainstream and suddenly we had radical hip-hop groups, garage/punk bands and devastating fusions of rock and dance forms which drew upon styles and genres from a bewildering range of cultural sources. What was so exhilarating about these musicians was their sheer diversity; they may have emerged at the same time but they did not do so on the back of a clearly delineated genre or single musical tradition. Their ability to incorporate sounds and influences that drew upon a range of elements reflecting the multi-accented nature of their lives in Britain during the latter part of the 20th century betrayed a confidence and, at times, a swagger that simply could not be ignored. That they have managed to survive and flourish within the bounds of the notoriously fickle music industry is a testament to their creativity, enthusiasm and, not least of all, their determination which at times have been sorely tested.

The difficulties and negotiations that these musicians have had to deal with are not specific to the unique environment of the music industry, however; the same processes can be witnessed in all realms of cultural and social life. The experiences of the musicians in question show us how individuals negotiate a sense of self and belonging in an environment where there are no fixed certainties, where reality is shaped by processes of syncretism and cross-cultural interaction. Apart from learning how to be creative artists and musicians, these individuals are constantly reappraising what it means to be who they are in relation to a number of reference points; in this instance what it means to be Asian living in multi-ethnic Britain. For any individual, identity is not a simple and easily defined state of being but a shifting and dynamic process which reflects both continuity and change. Undoubtedly issues of race and ethnicity are central to the identities of these musicians; the existence of inequality, stereotypical images and outright hostility aimed at people of Asian descent means that a sense of Asianness is an extremely important resource in the maintenance of self and identity. The ethnic resource of Asianness is not fixed, however, and neither is it the only source of identification for these individuals; its importance is in fact relative to the needs of specific contexts and settings. The flexibility of what a sense of Asianness means for particular individuals in specific settings undermines any notion of constructing an 'authentic' or unified Asian identity. The experiences of the musicians I spoke to clearly undermine the validity of such a project, while their thoughts and actions represent the living out of multiple modes of Asianness that are undergoing constant development and transformation.

Music, identity and reflexivity

The role of these individuals as artists and musicians is particularly significant as the terrain of popular music represents not only a space where identities are expressed and displayed but also a site where identities are open to different interpretations and meanings which have to be negotiated and contested. The propagation of a series of reductive stereotypes of Asians by elements of the national music media is such that the identities of the musicians I have focused on are, to a certain extent, reflexive and reactive. The relatively sudden emergence of Asian bands and musicians onto a scene previously devoid of them inevitably meant that they came under close scrutiny by representatives of the national media. The notoriously capricious and sensationalistic aspects of popular press coverage meant that Asian bands were often considered not for their music but for their novelty appeal, a focus which is inherently transitory and superficial. Since Asian musicians and Asian influences on popular music previously had a relatively low profile in the West, reference points with which to make sense of these new young bands were few and far between. Those that did exist unfortunately amounted to little more than crude stereotypes which have had a significant effect on both the musical output and the articulations of identity expressed by young Asians throughout the 1990s and beyond. The combined impact of these stereotypes has been felt by all the featured musicians, and their ability to continue to work successfully as creative artists has been affected profoundly by their responses to these limiting archetypes.

First, the fetishization of non-whites as politically radical, particularly in terms of anti-racism within the media and by a number of academics, meant that undue focus was put on what were perceived to be the political agendas of these bands. This focus inevitably led to the devaluing of their music, which was all but ignored in various interviews and written studies that sought to construct agendas that were not necessarily the intention of the musicians involved. Although political ideas and aspirations have played significant roles in the output of many Asian bands, their manifestation has not always conformed to the appropriate stereotypes of Asianness, as in the case for example of the feminist approach of Voodoo Queens. Bands with a more explicitly political agenda, such as Fun^Da^Mental, have continually used their notoriety to question, challenge and confound their somewhat simplistic portrayal within the mass media.

Second, the existence of a stereotype associated with a Western interpretation of the East as mystical and exotic has had a significant effect on the musical output and cultural identities of Asian bands in the UK. The pivotal role that the

1960s has played in the genealogy of Western popular music is such that the mythic Orientalism of bands such as The Beatles continues to exert a significant impact in defining how Asian music is understood and interpreted in the West. The resilience of the notion of the East as exotic and mystical is such that, even in the face of an increasingly eclectic body of Asian musicians, this stereotype continues to enjoy a great deal of currency in the popular imagination; the success of a band such as Kula Shaker is evidence of the continuing marketability of this notion. The fact that this stereotype is grounded in an imaginary location – that of a mythic India – has meant that it has been hard for Asian musicians to be accepted as relevant contemporary artists on a national UK scene, unless they conform to any of these existing and reductive stereotypes.

The interpretation of Asian music as somehow bound up with late 1960s hippy values means that the use of 'Indian' instruments and sounds has become associated with nostalgic notions of psychedelia – another stereotype that Asian musicians have had to counter. This has been done in a number of ways. Some bands (such as Voodoo Queens and Echobelly) have produced music which uses exclusively 'Western' instruments from the pop and rock idiom – guitars, bass and drums. Others, however, have not been discouraged from using instruments that have been colonized by the Orientalist gaze and have taken a range of traditional instruments such as sitars, tablas and tanpura and redeployed them in new and innovative ways. Fun^Da^Mental mix samples of sitars onto their hip-hop beats, Black Star Liner fuse tablas and tambours with heavy dub bass-lines and Cornershop juxtapose a whole panoply of 'Indian' sounds with distorted guitars, funky beats and country rhythms.

Indeed the eclectic approach of a band such as Cornershop continues to confound all expectations and their constantly shifting sound textures make it difficult for them to be categorized in any simplistic way, least of all in terms of existing stereotypes. That the success of these bands is reflected not just in the diversity of their music but also by their longevity is significant: there is some indication that they have become accepted as artists in their own right, rather than as novel and exotic interlopers. All of the musicians felt that 21st-century critical analysis of their output placed more emphasis on their music and had begun to avoid focusing on their Asianness as an 'issue', as evidenced in the glowing reviews that Cornershop and Black Star Liner enjoyed for their most recent albums. Speaking in 2002, *The Guardian* journalist Caroline Sullivan felt that this reflected an inevitable process of familiarization and normalization that has been fostered over time:

> It's become less of a novelty, I mean don't forget, 10 years ago … the expression 'Asian hip-hop band' was an oxymoron – they just didn't exist. I think one of the ways that we've progressed is that Asian bands – the few that seem to be emerging now – aren't immediately labelled 'Asian', they're thought of as … they're actually, I think generically classified. So it wouldn't so much be an Asian band but a punk band or whatever. (Personal interview)

A crucial factor in the long-term success of these musicians has been their desire to retain absolute control over their musical output and they have employed a number of strategies in order to achieve this. Generally this has meant releasing records on independent labels, although most of the musicians have had some dealings with larger record corporations – a fact that reflects not only the increasing interconnectivity of the music industry but also the ability of these individuals to adapt to the practical realities of functioning as professional musicians. These bands are acutely aware of the financial realities that underpin their existence and have adopted pragmatic and flexible strategies in order to survive – while retaining their musical integrity – within a notoriously cut-throat industry. Although these bands generally share an affinity with the ideology of non-conformity and independence that emerged from the punk and post-punk DIY ethic which flourished in the late 1970s and throughout the 1980s, their understanding of this is practical and adaptive rather than romantic and unrealistic. There have certainly been problems along the way, the balance they have sought to achieve is the ability to maintain themselves financially and to reach a national audience, without having to compromise the integrity of their music or undermine the full expression of their cultural identities.

Community, identity and representation

The seemingly quite sudden emergence of Asian bands and musicians on the UK music scene that began in the early 1990s inevitably meant that an inordinate amount of focus and expectation was placed upon a relatively small number of individuals who have had to shoulder a burden of representation and who were expected to act as role models for an entire generation of British Asian youth. This pressure has come from a number of sources, most significantly from the national media and also from those concerned with representing the aspirations of the Asian 'community'. As we have seen, the concept of an all-encompassing 'authentic' Asian identity is extremely problematic and, despite a number of common musical practices and shared political outlooks, the views and experiences of these bands serve to highlight the inherent problems of such a concept. Not only do these young Asian musicians reject the notion of representation by asserting their roles as individuals and artists, they also display a number of different lived modes of Asianness, reflecting the shifting and contingent character of a sense of ethnicity. That a sense of Asianness is a flexible resource (and one that competes and links with other modes of identity) does not detract from the importance of what is still undoubtedly a significant site of identification. It is clear that the cultural heritage derived from an Asian background is an important resource in the musical expressions of these artists, as well as in the articulation of individual and group identities. This resource is not all-encompassing, however, and its importance depends on the desires and needs of individuals in particular temporal and physical locations. The articulation of Asianness by these musicians is shaped by the particular dynamics of what it means to be young and Asian in the multi-ethnic setting of the UK at the turn of the 21st century. For these young people, Asian identity is not something that is fixed and absolute and tied to some unified and 'authentic' community. Instead it is an important element of identity which is constantly revalued and transformed by the daily interactions and adaptations that are representative of a multi-ethnic environment.

The output of these young musicians represents the expression of cultural identities that are the latest instalment of an ongoing process of a sense of Asianness which is undoubtedly tied to historical and diasporic traditions, but which is also rooted in the specific context of multi-ethnic Britain. The importance of the cultural resource of Asianness is not eroded in this setting but is renewed and invigorated by processes of re-evaluation and cross-cultural exchange. The experiences of these musicians suggest a way of thinking about Asian identity which is self-assured and outward looking; a sense of ethnicity which can be articulated with confidence and assertion and is not threatened by interaction and change but strengthened by them. Such a manifestation of ethnic identification is desirable and empowering not just for Asians themselves but also has implications for the successful development of British multi-ethnic society as whole.

I do not wish, however, to suggest that such progress has brought about a wholesale transformation of cultural life in the UK; we do not live in a multicultural paradise and issues of inequality and racism still continue to blight the lives of many. Nevertheless, it is certainly the case that Asians in 2003 have a much higher public profile than they did 10 years earlier, and the musicians who have provided the basis for this study have undoubtedly played an important part in this process. This is apparent across a range of mass media as Asians have become a regular and recognizable part of British mainstream culture – not just in music but also in television, on film and on stage. While recognizing the potential benefits of such progress it is important not to place too much emphasis on the immediate effect of this growing presence. The high-profile cosmopolitan successes of stage musicals such as *Bombay Dreams* (Rahman 2001) or films such as *The Guru* (directed by Daisy von Scherler Mayer 2002) bear little relation to the experiences of, say, an unemployed Asian teenager living in Burnley in Lancashire, or indeed the political aspirations of a first-time voter for the British National Party.[1] The impact of media successes on the actual lives of Asians living in the UK in the short term is questionable, as Choque Hosein of Black Star Liner suggested:

> It's like anything isn't it? It's just a fad isn't it? But the reality of day-to-day living is a whole different ballgame. And being on the front of the *Evening Standard* or *The Times* is all well and fine but it doesn't put money into your pocket if you're poor does it? Being a trendy colour doesn't change anything; is of no use. (Personal interview 2003)

There is a suspicion by some that such trends are simply the latest short-lived fashion, providing little more than a sanitized and exotic distraction for largely white cosmopolitan audiences. Is then the flirtation with the kitsch imagery of Bollywood which has become prevalent at the beginning of the millennium an indication of the UKs increasing multicultural outlook, or simply the latest development in a long history of Orientalist appropriation? Cornershop's Tjinder Singh is clear in his assessment of the situation:

> *Bombay Dreams* and that – fuck it – it's white, it's not brown; it's white. It's white! Look at the bloody posters when you go up the escalators on the tube, you know; for fuck's sake, it's whiter than white. I don't see why people should be pleased with that shit. (Personal interview 2003)

This is a view that was clearly advocated by Aki Nawaz of Fun^Da^Mental, who also felt that such changes were all but cosmetic. He clearly felt that, while Asian culture was becoming more flexible and diverse, white mainstream society still remained bound to deeply ingrained stereotypes:

> I think the time's over when you kind of … for me anyway, the time is over for me to entertain the ignorance or try to build a bridge because all along all they're doing is kind of … .I haven't changed because society hasn't changed. As simple as that. (Personal interview 2002)

Here I must differ with Aki, for while such concerns about the lasting impact of particular cultural fashions are justified, quite clearly something *has* changed and the very presence of Asian artists and cultural workers impacting on the mainstream represents, if nothing else, a real engagement with the growing diversity of multi-ethnic Britain. Undoubtably, offensive and negative stereotypes still exist, but no longer do they do go unchallenged and it is Asians themselves – particularly those in the public eye – who are actively engaged in asserting a range of possible cultural articulations and identities that say as much about the society they are part of as it does of their own sense of self.

Sounding out the syncretic: new music, new ethnicities

The reflexive and multi-accented processes at work in the music of young Asian bands and musicians point the way forward to a new way of thinking about how ethnicity and identity are articulated in multi-ethnic settings in late modernity. The juxtaposition of a range of cultural forms and influences in the artistic expressions of these young musicians and the transformation of identities that this suggests indicates the existence of a reflexive self which is neither bound by cultural tradition nor eroded by processes of change and adaptation. What the dynamic and innovative musical practices of these young Asians suggest is the ability of individuals to balance a number of cultural traditions and influences in a positive and creative way. The manifestation of these syncretic cultural forms indicates the ability of these individuals to resist and subvert the articulation of absolutist discourses of identity and belonging, as well as the stereotypes of Asian culture traded by the highly commercialized music industry. The fusing of traditional Asian instruments with global sounds and Western pop and rock styles shows how these individuals are able to look simultaneously to the past and to the future by creating something of dynamism and vitality out of their lives. As Martin Stokes has suggested:

> Individuals can use music as a cultural 'map of meaning', drawing upon it to locate themselves in different imaginary geographies at one and the same time and to articulate both individual and collective identities. (1994: 214)

The ability to manipulate such a range of cultural traditions is evidence that these individuals are not constrained by limiting and absolutist notions of 'authentic' and uncompromising ethnic identities. Their sense of allegiance and identification with an Asian heritage is not a fragile one and, in spite of the contemporary pressures afforded by the articulation of delimiting stereotypes and outright racism, they are able to nurture and transform this resource in assertive and dynamic ways. What their experiences and artistic endeavours teach us is the ability of groups and individuals to break away from public discourses of inflexible allegiance and exclusivity in order to construct new modes of self and belonging. For these musicians a sense of Asianness is an important resource which plays a significant part in their articulations of self, but it does not represent a fixed essence which is dominant in all contexts and settings. Being Asian does not determine any unified characteristics or behaviour but is one of a diverse range of inputs and modes of identity that combine to make up a sense of self; and this is true of people from all ethnic backgrounds. It is important not make the mistake of limiting our understanding of processes of cultural transformation and syncretism merely to the experiences of non-white minorities within the UK, for these processes affect everyone and are shaping what it means to be British as much as what it means to be Asian. The syncretic manifestations of a dynamic and shifting sense of Asianness are not taking place within the confines of some discrete and separate community but rather are impacting on the entire cultural life of the 'nation'. The expression of complex and shifting identities maintained by these young Asian musicians points the way to a future understanding of multi-ethnic society which is able to both recognize the importance of cultural heritage and tradition, and celebrate the emergence of syncretic and multi-accented identities and allegiances.

This study has shown that it is a mistake to categorize individuals and groups in terms of one rigidly defined notion of identity and belonging. The experiences of the small number of musicians focused on here display the ability of individuals to maintain a coherent sense of self which is both stable and reflexive. The range and diversity of their understanding and articulation of elements of Asian identity show us that any attempt – no matter how well meaning – to assert an essential and 'authentic' sense of Asianness is both flawed and inappropriate. Any assertion of Asian culture or identity in a contemporary setting should not have to turn towards a mythic or idealized vision linked to some imagined past, but should instead celebrate the range and diversity of the multiple positions and increasingly syncretic subjectivities lived out by millions of Asian people. The transformative processes at work in the lives of young Asians (or other non-whites) is not merely characteristic of changes within ethnic 'minority communities' but has important implications for the whole of society. Our contemporary landscape is populated by new generations of Asian, black and white youth, whose sense of Britain and Britishness is one which matter-of-factly accepts and celebrates the experiences of intercultural exchange and syncretism. The need to recognize the dynamism and integrity of new identities that are borne out through the dynamic and shifting modes of Asianness and Britishness shown here is essential if we are to celebrate and make sense of our multi-ethnic pasts, present and futures. The lived experiences reflected by the musicians in this study are evidence of the changing character of multi-ethnic Britain, and as such this research represents a modest attempt to highlight how such transformative processes can be achieved and maintained.

Note

1. In the local council elections held during the spring of 2003 the success of the far-right British National Party in Burnley, Lancashire, resulted in the party becoming the second largest group on the council, with a total of eight seats. The success of the party in the north of England reflects a resurgence of the politics of race in the UK, which once again has focused on the issue of immigration, this time surrounding the issue of so-called 'bogus' asylum seekers.

Appendix 1: Interviews

Interviewees

Ben Ayres is one of the founder members of Cornershop, forming the nucleus of the band alongside chief songwriter Tjinder Singh (these two also make up the personnel of Cornershop's dance offshoot Clinton which has released a number of singles and an album in 1999), and plays a number of instruments including guitar, percussion and tanpura.

Anjali Bhatia was founder member of Voodoo Queens and the band's chief songwriter, singer and guitarist. She was also the driving force behind the band's short-lived Voodoo record label which released the 'Eat the germs' single in 1995. Following the band's demise in the same year, Anjali took time off from music before returning to pursue a solo career in 1996. She is now signed as a solo artist to Wiiija Records and released her debut album *Anjali* in 2000.

Paul Cox is co-owner of London-based independent record label Too Pure, which he formed in 1989 with Richard Roberts, and has since helped to launch the recording careers of a number of successful artists including Th' Faith Healers, Stereolab and PJ Harvey. Paul was responsible for signing Voodoo Queens in 1992 and his company also helped support the fledgling Voodoo label when the band left Too Pure in 1994.

Choque Hosein is a musician, producer and songwriter who, along with Chris Harrop and Tom Salmon, founded Leeds-based band Black Star Liner in 1994. All the band's releases – including the Mercury Music Award nominated album *Bengali bantam youth experience* (1999) – have been recorded and produced in Choque's home studio. Following the protracted breakdown in the relationship between Black Star Liner and their label Warner Music UK in 2000/1 Tom and Chris left the band, leaving Choque as the sole member.

Aki Nawaz is a musician with Fun^Da^Mental and also co-owner of Nation Records. He has been involved in the independent music scene for a number of years (he previously played drums in seminal Bradford post-punk band Southern Death Cult), the experience of which is embodied in the music of both his band and record label. Aki's outspoken political and religious views, particularly around issues of race and Islam, have ensured that he has gained a high media profile.

Tjinder Singh is founder member, vocalist and chief songwriter for Cornershop and, as such, has been the band's major driving force since the early 1990s. As well as being the creative centre of Cornershop's music, he also acts as spokesperson for the band; media interviews invariably focus on him and are rewarded with a number of assertive and often outspoken opinions.

David Stubbs was (until its demise in 2001) a staff writer at the national music weekly *Melody Maker* – one of only a handful of full-time workers at the magazine – contributing to weekly features, reviews and interviews.

Caroline Sullivan writes regularly for *The Guardian* and is one of the newspaper's chief rock and pop critics. She contributes to reviews of albums and live performances and also produces features and reports on contemporary bands and trends; she has written a number of pieces on Asian bands.

Clare Wadd was in 1987 the co-founder (with Matt Haynes) of Bristol independent record label Sarah Records, which was notorious for its ideological independence and refusal to conform to the tenets of profit and commercialism. The label was dissolved in 1994 with a farewell concert in Bristol and the declaration that its voluntary dissolution was 'the most gorgeous pop-art statement'.

Gary Walker is the founder of London-based independent label Wiiija, which he set up in 1990 initially at the premises of the Rough Trade record shop which had been at the heart of the 1980s independent boom period. In 1996 the label merged with the larger Beggars Banquet company, who aquired a 50 per cent stake in Wiiija, and in the autumn of 2000 Gary sold the remainder of his interest in the label and left the music business to return to full-time education.

Dave Watts is both a musician with Fun^Da^Mental and an employee of Nation Records in London. Dave joined the band in 1993, shortly before the original line-up split and has been a core member ever since, as co-writer of material with Aki Nawaz as well as occasional vocalist.

Interview schedule

Ben Ayres 6 June 1996.
Anjali Bhatia 14 July 1996 and 3 April 2003.
Paul Cox 1 May 1996.
Choque Hosein 6 August 1996 and 24 April 2003.
Aki Nawaz 28 February 1996 and 22 November 2002.
Tjinder Singh 12 March 1996 and 21 April 2003.
David Stubbs 24 November 1995.

Caroline Sullivan 23 January 1996 and 21 November 2002.
Clare Wadd 29 October 1995.
Gary Walker 30 April 1996.
Dave Watts 25 June 1996.

Appendix 2: Liner notes

Fun^Da^Mental, *With intent to pervert the cause of injustice* (1995)

GLOBAL TIMES

The disgusting and inexcusable sperm of your ancestors is ingrained on my forehead, whilst you teach your beautiful children to masturbate over the lies and deceit of your history books.
Denying the truth of your exploitative nature yesteryear, today and tomorrow.
Ruling by economics, maintaining your status with not a hint of morality.
Stories from Africa, Asia, Australia, Canada, South America, all in tune with one and another.
The same method
The same Excuse
The same Justification
The same song
No one is accountable
Who is accountable
Where do I make my claim?
Until there is a solution
I have every right to use whatever method is at my disposal
You cannot question my method as it is reactionary, not inherent
Resolving the past is your salvation, if not your destruction
I stand guilty of the charge
With intent to pervert the cause of injustice.

***… And still no hits – Nation Records – the story so far* (1997)**

Nation …

It all began there … just plain and simple music and the love of …
Actually it began with punk, 70s into 80s into 90s even … and it continues with punk. What's Nation got to do with punk?
Bhangra on a sunny afternoon in Leicester Square's Empire Ballroom … you should have seen it. 2,000 kids … 'we're going to study in the library, dad …'

Wall to wall dancing, non-stop dancing, from eleven in the morning to five in the evening. 'Sex Pistols' with glittery orange turbans onstage. Energy!! Punk!!
As punk, in energy, as in the seventies: replacing grunge guitars with sitar, tablas and dholaks … 'never mind the dholaks' … meet Holle Holle, Alaap, Apna Sangeet, Heera. John Peel was playing them, last night...! 'Habiba' shouted Bappi Lahiri, 'Yeke Yeke' replied Mory Kante whilst Ofra Haza helped Eric B get 'Paid in Full' via Coldcut. What shall we look for then? A bit of Eastern spice laced with the energy of the Pistols, with the rhythms of the Clash and the beats … oh, those glorious beats! Let's not forget the voices, though, real voices. Nusrat Fateh Ali Khan – bet there aren't many like that … and an Ofra … maybe we can find one. Really? Why not – never say never! Okay, so a bit of Public Enemy in attitude – no safety mechanisms – or more like Al Pacino? The voice of Karen Carpenter or Sinatra or Dean Martin … you can't admit that! What a task … what a buzz!
Show it can be done … nay, show it SHOULD be done. What's there to lose … only dole money? Whoops … Yup, let's fuse it.
It's where it all began … followed fairly quickly by the doorstep people (and so you let them in?) clutching copies of that initial 'Fuse' sampler.
'We can do that … in fact we've been doing it for some time … kop a listen to this.' Public Image Ltd … know them … wow! Jah Wobble, great bass player. Invaders of the Heart? Do you think they might want to do one …? Balearic beats …! Loca! … Natacha Atlas? Now there's a twist in the tale. Oh, and Talvin Singh – he came from nowhere, didn't he? Doubt that … try Mahatma T's 'Jihad' … What … with Nation? Bit of this, bit of that … see what they think. Weatherall? Yeh, sure you can have some … glad you like it. No, don't keep it to yourself, let them all know! Love that track, you know, the one that goes… 'Na, na, na … na, na, na …' Yeh, we love it too. TransGlobal Underground climbed aboard, jumped ship and rejoined. Long term soulmates. Our friends are doing something similar … meet Loop Guru. What about a rock band … a black rock band? A band fusing hardcore rhythms, into hardcore politics, fusing the classicals … Carnival 1991, Fun^Da^Mental emerged … power unleashed … um, not exactly what people expected of Asian musicians … and where are those glittery turbans!
Hustlers HC … just Asian musicians? Never just … You name them … we've had em! That's where it continues … Nation Records … almost ten years ago.
Take a trip through time and grab a hold of that vibe. Feel the energy as it was … as it is … Global Chaos … punk rock … all of this, AND STILL NO HITS!!

Discography

Abba 1979: I have a dream, Polydor.
Anjali 1997: Maharani, Wiiija.
Anjali 1999: *Sheer witchery*, Wiiija.
Anjali 2000: *Anjali*, Wiiija.
Anjali 2003: *The world of Lady A*, Wiiija.
Apache Indian 1995: Arranged marriage, Island.
Apache Indian 1995: *No reservations*, Island.
Apache Indian 1996: *Make way for the Indian*, Island.
Asian Dub Foundation 1995: *Facts and fictions*, Nation.
Asian Dub Foundation 1998: *Rafi's revenge*, London.
Asian Dub Foundation 2000: *Community music*, London.
Babylon Zoo 1996: *Boy with the X-ray eyes*, EMI.
Babylon Zoo 1996: Spaceman, EMI.
Bally Sagoo 1996: Dil cheez (my heart), Columbia.
Bally Sagoo 1996: *Bollywood flashback*, Columbia.
Beatles, The 1965: *Rubber soul*, Parlophone.
Beatles, The 1966: *Revolver*, Parlophone.
Beatles, The 1967: *Sgt. Pepper's lonely hearts club band*, Parlophone.
Black Star Liner 1994: *Smoke the prophets* (EP), Soundclash Sound.
Black Star Liner 1995: *High Turkish influence* (EP), Soundclash Sound.
Black Star Liner 1995: The jawz (promo), EXP.
Black Star Liner 1996: *Haláal rock* (EP), EXP.
Black Star Liner 1996: *Yemen Cutta connection*, EXP.
Black Star Liner 1997: *Rock freak* (EP), WEA.
Black Star Liner 1999: *Bengali bantam youth experience*, WEA.
Clinton 1995: Jam jar, Wiiija.
Clinton 1995: Superloose, Wiiija.
Clinton 1999: *Disco and halfway to discontent*, Meccico.
Cornershop 1992: *In the days of Ford Cortina* (EP), Wiiija.
Cornershop 1992: *Lock, stock and double barrel* (EP), Wiiija.
Cornershop 1993: *Hold on it hurts*, Wiiija.
Cornershop 1993: *Elvis sex change*, Wiiija.
Cornershop 1995: 6am Jullander Shere, Wiiija.
Cornershop 1995: *Woman's gotta have it*, Wiiija.
Cornershop 1996: *6am Jullander Shere-remixes*, Wiiija.
Cornershop 1996: *WOG-remixes*, Wiiija.
Cornershop 1997: *When I was born for the 7th time*, Wiiija.
Cornershop 1998: Brimful of Asha, Wiiija.
Cornershop 2002: *Handcream for a generation*, Wiiija.

DetRiMental 1995: *Xenophobia*, Debt.
Dreadzone 1995: Little England, Virgin.
Fun^Da^Mental 1992: Janaam: righteous preacher, Nation.
Fun^Da^Mental 1993: Sista India/Wrath of the blackman, Nation.
Fun^Da^Mental 1993: Countryman, Nation.
Fun^Da^Mental 1994: Dog tribe, Nation.
Fun^Da^Mental 1994: *Seize the time*, Nation.
Fun^Da^Mental 1995: *With intent to pervert the cause of injustice*, Nation.
Fun^Da^Mental 1996: God/devil, Nation.
Fun^Da^Mental 1997: Ja sha taan, Nation.
Fun^Da^Mental 1998: *Erotic terrorism*, Nation.
Fun^Da^Mental 1999: *Why America will go to hell*, Nation.
Fun^Da^Mental 2001: *The last gospel* (EP), Nation.
Fun^Da^Mental 2001: *There shall be love!*, Nation.
Fun^Da^Mental 2003: *Voices of mass destruction* (EP), Nation.
Gabriel, Peter 1989: *Passion: music for the Last Temptation of Christ*, Real World.
Jackson, Michael 1995: Earth song, Sony.
Kula Shaker 1996: *K*, Columbia.
Kula Shaker 1999: *Peasents, pigs and astronauts*, Columbia.
Madonna 1998: Ray of light, WEA.
Monsoon 1982: Ever so lonely, Indipop.
Morrissey 1988: *Viva hate*, Parlophone.
Morrissey 1992: *Your arsenal*, EMI.
Nusrat Fateh Ali Khan 1989: *Shahen-shah*, Realworld.
Nusrat Fateh Ali Khan 1990: *Mustt mustt*, Realworld.
Nusrat Fateh Ali Khan and Michael Brook 1997: *Remixed/Star rise*, Realworld.
Oasis 2002: The Hindu times, Big Brother.
Panjabi MC 2003: *Mundian to bach ke*, Instant Karma.
Rolling Stones, The 1966: Paint it black, Decca.
Saddar Bazaar 1995: *The conference of the birds*, Delerium.
Saddar Bazaar 1998: *Path of the rose*, Delerium.
Sawhney, Nitin 1995: *Migration*, Outcaste.
Sawhney, Nitin 1996: *Displacing the priest*, Outcaste.
Sawhney, Nitin 1999: *Beyond skin*, Outcaste.
Sawhney, Nitin 2001: *Prophesy*, V2.
Sex Pistols 1976: Anarchy in the UK, EMI.
Shankar, Ravi 1967: *Ravi Shankar at the Monterey International Pop Festival*, WPS.
Shankar, A 1970: *Ananda Shankar*, Reprise.
Simon, Paul 1983: *Graceland*, WEA.
Talvin Singh 1998: *OK*, Mango.
Talvin Singh 2001: *Ha*, Island.
TransGlobal Underground 1993: Templehead, Nation.
TransGlobal Underground 1993: *Dream of 100 nations*, Nation.
TransGlobal Underground 1994: *International times*, BMG/Nation.
TransGlobal Underground 1996: *Psychic karaoke*, Nation.
Various 1994: *Natural Born Killers soundtrack*, Nothing.
Various 1996: *Anokha: Soundz of the new Asian underground*, Mango.

Various 1997: *...And still no hits – Nation Records – the story so far*, Nation.
Various 1997: *Eastern uprising: dance music from the Asian underground*, Sony.
Various 1997: *Untouchable outcaste beats vol.1*, Outcaste.
Voodoo Queens 1993: Supermodel, superficial, Too Pure.
Voodoo Queens 1993: Kenuwee head, Too Pure.
Voodoo Queens 1994: *Chocolate revenge*, Too Pure.
Voodoo Queens 1994: *John Peel sessions*, Too Pure.
Voodoo Queens 1995: Eat the germs, Voodoo
Youssou N'Dour and Neneh Cherry 1995: 7 seconds, EMI.
White Town 1997: Your woman, Chrysalis.
White Town 1997: *Women in technology*, Chrysalis.
Who, The 1966: My generation, Polydor.

Bibliography

Adorno, T. (1991), *The Culture Industry*, London: Routledge.

Allen, S. (1971), *New Minorities Old Conflicts: Asian and West Indian Migrants in Britain*, New York: Random House.

Allinson, E. (1994), 'It's a black thing: hearing how whites can't', *Cultural Studies*, **8** (3), 438–56.

Anderson, M.L. (1993), 'Studying across difference', in J. Stanfield and R. Dennis (eds), *Race and Ethnicity in Research Methods*, London: Sage Publications.

Anwar, M. (1979), *The Myth of Return: Pakistanis in Britain*, London: Heinemann.

Appadurai, A. (1991), 'Global ethnoscapes: notes and queries for a transnational anthropology', in R.G. Fox, (ed.), *Recapturing Anthropology: Working in the Present*, Santa Fe, NM: School of American Research Press.

Awan, S. (1997), 'Full of Eastern promise: women in South Asian music', in S. Cooper (ed.), *Girls! Girls! Girls!: Essays on Women and Music*, London: Cassell.

Back, L. (1996), *New Ethnicities and Urban Culture: Racisms and Multiculture in Young Lives*, London: UCL Press.

Barker, M. (1981), *The New Racism: Conservatives and the Ideology of the Tribe*, London: Junction Books.

Banerji, S and Baumann, G. (1990), 'Bhangra 1984–8: fusion and professionalization in a genre of South Asian dance music', in P. Oliver (ed.), *Black Music in Britain: Essays on the Afro-Asian Contribution to Popular Music*, Milton Keynes: Open University Press.

Barrett, J. (1996), 'World music, nation and postcolonialism', *Cultural Studies*, **10** (2), 237–47.

Barth, F. (ed.) (1969), *Ethnic Groups and Boundaries: the Social Organization of Culture Difference*, Boston, MA: Little Brown, and Co.

Barthes, R. (1989), *Mythologies*, London: Paladin.

BBC (1997), 'India 5-O special', *The Ozone*, first broadcast 26 August 1997.

Becquer, M and Gatti, J. (1991), 'Elements of vogue', *Third Text*, **16–17**: 65–81.

Bennett, T., Frith, S., Grossberg, L., Sheperd, J. and Turner G. (eds) (1993), *Rock and Popular Music*, London: Routledge.

Bennun, D. (1995), 'Instru-mental!', *Melody Maker*, 15 July, 35.

Bennun, D. (1996), 'Supernova mob', *Melody Maker*, 12 September, 23.

Bhabha, H. (1988), 'The commitment to theory', *New Formations*, **5**, 5–23.

Bhabha, H. (1990), 'The third space', in J. Rutherford (ed.), *Identity, Community, Culture, Difference*, London: Lawrence and Wishart.

Bhabha, H. (1996), 'Culture's in-between', in S. Hall and P. DuGay (eds), *Questions of Cultural Identity*, London: Sage Publications.

Born, G. and Hesmondhalgh, D. (eds) (2000), *Western Music and its Others: Difference, Representation and Appropriation in Music*, London: University of California Press.

Boyne, R. and Rattansi, A. (eds) (1990), *Postmodernism and Society*, London: Macmillan.

Britten, N. (2002), 'Ethnic radio station to ban "Asian" description', *Daily Telegraph*, 23 January 2002.

Bulmer, M. (1981), *Sociological Research Methods*, London: Sage Publications.

Carlin, M. (1995), 'Letter of the week', *Melody Maker*, 22 July, 14.

Chambers, I. (1985), *Urban Rhythms: Pop Music and Popular Culture*, London: Macmillan.

Chambers, I. and Curti, L. (eds) (1996), *The Postcolonial Question: Common Skies, Divided Horizons*, London: Routledge.

Chrisman, L. (1997), 'Journeying to death: Gilroy's Black Atlantic', *Race and Class*, **39** (2), 51–64.

Cigarettes, J. (1993), 'National confront', *New Musical Express*, 1 May, 17.

Clark, G. (1981), 'Defending ski-jumpers: a critique of theories of youth subcultures', reprinted in S. Frith (ed.) (1990), *On Record: Rock, Pop, and the Written Word*, London: Routledge.

Cleaver, E. (1968), *Soul on Ice*, New York: McGraw-Hill.

Cohen, P. (1972), 'Subcultural conflict and the working class community', *Working Papers in Cultural Studies*, no. 2 (University of Birmingham, CCCS).

Cook, E. (1996), 'The best of both worlds', *Independent on Sunday*, 27 July, 32.

Cooper, S (ed.) (1997), *Girls! girls! girls!: Essays on Women and Music*, London: Cassell.

Cross, B. (1992), *It's Not About a Salary: Rap, Race and Resistance in Los Angeles*, London: Verso.

Dalton, S. (1993), 'No model army', *New Musical Express*, 24 July, 17.

Datar, R. (1997), 'Asia major', *The Guardian*, 25 July, 14.

Davies, C. L. (1993), 'Aboriginal rock music: space and place', in T. Bennett et al. (eds), *Rock and Popular Music*, London: Routledge.

Dent, G. (ed.) (1992), *Black Popular Culture*, San Francisco: Bay Press.

Eisen, J. (1978), 'The age of rock', in S. Frith (ed.), *The Sociology of Rock*, London: Constable.

Evans, L. (1995), *Women in Rock*, London: Virago.

Eshun, K. (1994), 'Rebels without a pause', *i-D*, 124, January, 24–7.

Facio, E. (1993), 'Ethnography as personal experience', in J. Stanfield and R. Dennis (eds), *Race and Ethnicity in Research Methods*, London: Sage Publications.

Fadele, D. (1994), 'Repeat defender', *New Musical Express*, 20 August, 10.

Fanon, F. (1986), *Black Skins, White Masks*, London: Pluto Press.

Farrell, G. (1988), 'Reflecting surfaces: the use of elements from Indian music in popular music and jazz', *Popular Music*, **7**, 189–205.

Farrell, G. (1997), *Indian Music and the West*, Oxford: Clarendon Press.

Feld, S. (1991), 'Voices of the rainforest', *Public Culture*, **4** (1), 134.

Feld, S. (2000), 'The poetics and politics of pygmy pop', in G. Born and D. Hesmondhalgh (eds), *Western Music and its Others: Difference, Representation and Appropriation in Music*, London: University of California Press.

Fielding, N.G. (1987), 'Qualitative interviewing', in G.N. Gilbert, *Researching Social Life*, London: Gower.

Fornäs, J. (1994), 'Listen to your voice: authenticity and reflexivity in rock, rap and techno', *New Formations*, **24**, 155–73.

Fornäs, J. Lindberg, U. and Sernhede, O. (1995), *In Garageland: Rock, Youth and Modernity*, London: Routledge.

Fox, R.G. (ed) (1991), *Recapturing Anthropology: Working in the Present*, Santa Fe, NM: School of American Research Press.

Freestone, P. and Evans, D. (2000), *Freddie Mercury: an Intimate Memoir by the Man Who Knew Him Best*, London: Omnibus Press.

Frith, S. (ed.) (1978), *The Sociology of Rock*, London: Constable.

Frith, S. (1983), *Sound Effects: Youth, Leisure and the Politics of Rock*, London: Constable.

Frith, S. (1987), 'The industrialisation of popular music', in J. Lull, (ed.), *Popular Music and Communication*, London: Sage Publications.

Frith, S. (ed.) (1990), *On Record: Rock, Pop, and the Written Word*, London: Routledge.

Frith, S. (1996a), 'Music and identity', in S. Hall and P. DuGay (eds), *Questions of Cultural Identity*, London: Sage Publications.

Frith, S. (1996b), *Performing Rites: Evaluating Popular Music*, Oxford: Oxford University Press.

Frith, S. (2000), 'The discourse of world music', in G. Born and D. Hesmondhalgh (eds), *Western Music and its Others: Difference, Representation and Appropriation in Music*, London: University of California Press.

Frith, S. and Street, J. (1992), 'Rock against racism and red wedge: from music to politics, from politics to music', in R. Garafalo, *Rockin' the Boat: Mass Music and Mass Movements*, New York: South End Press.

Fryer, P. (1984), *Staying Power: the History of Black People in Britain*, London: Pluto Press.

Garafalo, R. (1992), *Rockin' the Boat: Mass Music and Mass Movements*, New York: South End Press.

Gelner, K. and Thornton, S. (eds) (1997), *The Subcultures Reader*, London: Routledge.

George, I. (1994), 'Let sleeping dogs die', *New Musical Express*, 7 May, 16–18.

George, I. (1996), 'Yemen cutta connection', *Vox*, October, 65.

Gilbert, G.N. (1987), *Researching Social Life*, London: Gower.

Gilroy, P. (1988), 'Nothing but sweat inside my hand: diaspora aesthetics and black arts in Britain', in *Black Film/British Cinema,* London: ICA Document no. 7.

Gilroy, P. (1993a), *Small Acts*, London: Verso.

Gilroy, P. (1993b), *The Black Atlantic: Modernity and Double Consciousness*, London: Verso.

Glanvill, R. (1996), 'CD of the week: Babylon Zoo', *The Guardian*, 14 February, 14.

Gopinath, G. (1995), 'Bombay, UK, Yuba City: bhangra music and engendering of diaspora', *Diaspora*, **4** (3), 303–21.

Gottlieb, J. and Wald, G. (1994), 'Smells like teen spirit: riot grrrls, revolution and women in independent rock', in A. Ross and T. Rose (eds), *Microphone Fiends: Youth Music, Youth Culture*, London: Routledge.

Grenier, L. (1989), 'From diversity to difference: the case of socio-cultural studies of music', *New Formations*, **9**, 125–43.

Hall, S. (1988), 'New ethnicities', in *Black Film/British Cinema*, London: ICA Document no. 7.

Hall, S. (1991), 'Old and new identities, old and new ethnicities', in A. King (ed.), *Culture, Globalisation and the World-System*, London: Macmillan.

Hall, S. (1992a), 'What is this "black" in black popular culture?', in G. Dent (ed.), *Black Popular Culture*, San Francisco: Bay Press.

Hall, S. (1992b), *Modernity and its Futures*, London: Oxford University Press.
Hall, S. (1994), 'Culture, community, nation', *Cultural Studies*, **7** (3), 349–63.
Hall, S. (ed.) (1997), *Representation: Cultural Representations and Signifying Practices*, London, Sage Publications.
Hall, S. and DuGay, P. (eds) (1996), *Questions of Cultural Identity*, London: Sage.
Hall, S. and Jefferson, T. (eds) (1976), *Resistance Through Rituals*, London: Hutchinson.
Harker, D. (1980), *One For the Money: Politics and Popular Song*, London: Hutchinson.
Harvey, D. (1989), *The Condition of Postmodernity*, Oxford: Blackwell.
Hebdige, D. (1979), *Subculture: The Meaning of Style*, London: Routledge.
Heller, R. (1996), 'Shooting sitars!', *New Musical Express*, 4 May, 28.
Hesmondhalgh, D. (1995), 'Justified and ancient: primitivism and futurism in contemporary urban music', paper given at the British Sociological Association Contested Cities conference, Leicester, April.
Hesmondhalgh, D. (1998), 'Post-punk's attempt to democratise the music industry: the success and failure of Rough Trade', *Popular Music*, **16** (3), 255–74.
Hraba, J. and Grant, G. (1970), 'Black is beautiful: a re-examination of racial preference and identification', *Journal of Personality and Social Psychology*, **16**, 398–402.
Huq, R. (1996), 'Asian Kool? Bhangra and Beyond', in S. Sharma, J. Hutnyk and A. Sharma (eds), *Dis-orienting Rhythms: the Politics of the New Asian Dance Music*, London: Zed Books.
Hutnyk, J. (1996), 'Repetitive beatings or criminal justice?', in S. Sharma, J. Hutnyk and A. Sharma (eds), *Dis-orienting Rhythms: the Politics of the New Asian Dance Music*, London: Zed Books.
Hutnyk, J. (2000), *Critique of Exotica: Music Politics and the Culture Industry*, London: Pluto Press.
Ice-T (1994), *The Ice Opinion*, London: Pan.
Jackson, P. (1989), *Maps of Meaning*, London: Unwin Hyman.
Jones, L. (1998), *Freddie Mercury: the Definitive Biography*, London: Coronet.
Julien, I. and Mercer, K. (1996), 'De margin and de Centre', in D. Morley (ed.), *Stuart Hall: Critical Dialogues in Cultural Studies*, London: Routledge.
Kabbani, R. (1986), *Europe's Myths of Orient: Devise and Rule*, London: Macmillan.
Kalra, V.S, Hutnyk, J. and Sharma, S. (1996), 'Re-sounding (anti) racism, or concordant politics? revolutionary antecedents', in S. Sharma, J. Hutnyk and A. Sharma (eds), *Dis-orienting Rhythms: the Politics of the New Asian Dance Music*, London: Zed Books.
Kelly, D. (1987), 'From C86 to catch-22', *New Musical Express*, 11 April, 29–30.
Khan, V. S. (1977), 'The Pakistanis: Mirpuri villagers at home and in Bradford', in J. Watson (ed.), *Between Two Cultures*, Oxford: Oxford University Press.
King, A. (ed.) 1991), *Culture, Globalisation and the World-system*, London: Macmillan.
Kulkarni, N. (1995), '*Damaged Goods*', *Melody Maker*, 15 July, 25.
Kureishi, H. (1986), *My Beautiful Launderette and the Rainbow Sign*, London: Faber and Faber.
Lash, S. (1990), *The Sociology of Postmodernism*, London: Routledge.
Lazarus, N. (1994), 'Unsystematic fingers at the conditions of the times: "Afropop" and the paradoxes of imperialism', in J. White (ed.), *Recasting the World: Writing After Colonialism*, Baltimore and London: John Hopkins University Press.
Lipsitz, G. (1990), *Time Passages: Collective Memory and American Popular Culture*, Minneapolis: University of Minnesota Press.

Lipsitz, G. (1994), *Dangerous Crossroads: Popular Music, Postmodernism and the Poetics of Place*, London: Verso.
Lull, J. (ed.) (1987), *Popular Music and Communication*, London: Sage Publications.
Lury, C. (1996), *Consumer Culture*, London: Polity Press.
MacRobbie, A. (1991), *Feminism and Youth Culture*, London: Macmillan.
Mailer, N. (1959), *Advertisements for Myself*, Cambridge, MA: Harvard University Press.
Malcolm X (with Haley, A.) (1966), *The Autobiography of Malcolm X*, New York: Hutchinson/Collins.
Mann, P. (1986), *Methods of Social Investigation*, London: Allen and Unwin.
Melody Maker (1996), 'What did you do in 76?', 12 September, 14.
Mercer, K. (ed.) (1994), *Welcome to the Jungle*, London: Routledge.
Miles, R. (1989), *Racism*, London: Routledge.
Mir, S. (1998), 'Bollywood bites back at the Blue Note', *The Independent*, 13 February, 15.
Mishra, V. (1996), 'The diasporic imaginary: theorizing the Indian diaspora', *Textual Practice*, **10** (3), 421–47.
Mitchell, T. (1996), *Popular Music and Local Identity*, London: Leicester University Press.
Modood, T. (1988), ' "Black", racial equality and Asian identity', *New Community*, **14** (3), 297–304.
Modood, T. (1990), 'Catching up with Jesse Jackson: being oppressed and being somebody', *New Community*, **17** (1), 85–96.
Modood, T. (1994), 'Political blackness and British Asians', *Sociology*, **28** (4), 859–76.
Modood, T. (1997), ' "Difference", cultural racism and anti-racism', in P. Werbner and T. Modood (eds), *Debating Cultural Identity*, London: Zed Books.
Morley, D. (ed.) (1996), *Stuart Hall: Critical Dialogues in Cultural Studies*, London: Routledge.
Morton, D. (1994), 'Sikh and destroy', *Melody Maker*, 17 April, 11.
Morris, G. (1993), '... so what is this Asian kool?', *Select*, August, 46.
Mueller, A. (1997), 'Come again', *The Independent*, 29 August, 12.
Muggleton, D. (1995), 'From "subculture" to "neo-tribe": identity and postmodernism in alternative style', paper given at the Shouts From the Street conference, Manchester Metropolitan University, September.
Muggleton, D. (2000), *Inside Subculture: the Postmodern Meaning of Style*, Oxford: Berg.
Negus, K. (1992), *Producing Pop: Culture and Conflict in the Popular Music Industry*, London: Edward Arnold.
Odell, M. (1996), 'Playing the race chord', *The Guardian*, 5 April, 22.
Oliver, P. (ed.) (1990), *Black Music in Britain: Essays on the Afro-Asian Contribution to Popular Music*, Milton Keynes: Open University Press.
Parsons, T. (1993), 'What now mozzer?', *Vox*, April, 35.
Ragin, C.C. and Hein, J. (1993), 'The comparative study of ethnicity: methodological and conceptual issues', in J. Stanfield and R. Dennis (eds), *Race and Ethnicity in Research Methods*, London: Sage.
Reck, D. (1978), 'The neon electric saraswati', *Contributions to Asian Studies*, **12**, 3–19.
Reynolds, S. (1994), 'Out of the cornershop and into the charts', *The Observer*, 23 May, 7.
Rex, J. and Mason, D. (eds) (1986), *Theories of Race and Ethnic Relations*, Cambridge: Cambridge University Press.
Robinson, S. (1991), *Music at the Margins*, London: Sage Publications.

Rose, T. (1994), *Black Noise: Rap Music and Black Culture in Contemporary America*, London: Wesleyan University Press.

Ross, A. and Rose, T. (eds) 1994), *Microphone Fiends: Youth Music, Youth Culture*, London: Routledge.

Rowden, B. (1994), 'Art in "stall" ation – Doll Bathroom', *Fad* magazine, London.

Rowe, D. (1995), *Popular Cultures: Rock Music, Sport and the Politics of Pleasure*, London: Sage Publications.

Rutherford, J. (ed.) (1990), *Identity, Community, Culture, Difference*, London: Lawrence and Wishart.

Said, E. (1978), *Orientalism*, London: Routledge.

Said, E. (1993), *Culture and Imperialism*, London: Chatto and Windus.

Shankar, R. (1994), *My Music, My Life*, New York: Simon and Shuster.

Sharma, S., Hutnyk, J. and Sharma, A. (eds) (1996), *Dis-orienting Rhythms: the Politics of the New Asian Dance Music*, London: Zed Books.

Shuker, R. (1994), *Understanding Popular Music*, London: Routledge.

Siddiqui, I. (2000), *The Muslim Parliament of Great Britain, 1992–1998*, London: The Institute of Contemporary Islamic Thought.

Silverman, D. (1985), *Qualitative Methodology and Sociology*, London: Sage Publictions.

Silverman, D. (1993), *Interpreting Qualitative Data*, London: Gower.

Simpson, D. (1993), 'Fant-asia!', *Melody Maker*, 13 February, 42–3.

Simpson, D. (1996), 'Yemen Cutta connection', *Melody Maker*, 24 August, 43.

Simpson, D. (1997), 'Bombay mixers!', *Melody Maker*, 28 June, 22.

Solomos, J. (1988), *Black Youth, Racism and the State*, Cambridge: Cambridge University Press.

Stanfield, J. (1993), 'Epistemological considerations', in J. Stanfield and R. Dennis (eds), *Race and Ethnicity in Research Methods*, London: Sage Publications.

Stanfield, J. and Dennis, R. (eds) (1993), *Race and Ethnicity in Research Methods*, London: Sage Publications.

Stephens, G. (1992), 'Interracial dialogue in rap music: call and response in a multicultural style', *New Formations*, **23**, 62–79.

Stokes, M. (ed.) 1994), *Ethnicity, Identity and Music: the Musical Construction of Place*, Oxford: Berg Publishers.

Strinati, D. (1995), *An Introduction to Theories of Popular Culture*, London: Routledge.

Sullivan, C. (1994), 'Islam with attitude', *The Guardian*, 17 June, 2.

The Sun (1998), 'Hit band in hotel rampage', 3 March, 3.

Swedenburg, T. (1989), 'Homies in the hood: rap's commodification of insubordination', *New Formations*, **17**, 53–66.

Sweet, S. (1993), 'Fear and loathing in Pakistan', *Melody Maker*, 13 November, 8.

Theberge, P. (1989), 'The sound of music', *New Formations*, **8**, 91–113.

Thompson, B. (1997), 'Old values, new treats from Cornershop', *The Independent*, 26 September, 20.

Thornton, S. (1995), *Club Cultures: Music, Media and Subcultural Capital*, London: Blackwell.

Wallis, R. and Malm, K. (1987), 'The international music industry and transnational communication', J. Lull (ed.): *Popular Music and Communication*, London: Sage Publications.

Wallman, S. (ed.) (1981), *Ethnicity at Work*, London: Macmillan.

Wallman, S. (1986), 'Ethnicity and the boundary in context', in J. Rex and D. Mason (eds),

Theories of Race and Ethnic Relations, Cambridge: Cambridge University Press.
Watson, J. (ed.) (1977), *Between Two Cultures*, Oxford: Oxford University Press.
Werbner, P. and Modood, T. (eds) (1997), *Debating Cultural Identity*, London: Zed Books.
Wells, S. (1992), 'ANL carnival review', *New Musical Express*, 23 August, 6.
Wells, S. (1993), 'Ch-ch-ch-change!', *New Musical Express*, 13 February, 13.
Wells, S. (1995), 'Bummer holiday', *New Musical Express*, 8 July, 29–31.
Whitcomb, I. (1994), *Rock Odyssey: Chronicle of the Sixties*, London: Hutchinson.
Williams, S. (1997), 'Happy happy Jyoti Jyoti', *New Musical Express*, 1 March, 15.
Willis, P. (1977), *Profane Culture*, London: Routledge and Kegan Paul.
Willmott, B. (1997), 'It don't mean a thing if it ain't got that Singh!', *New Musical Express*, 22 February.

Index